JOURNAL FOR THE STUDY OF THE NEW TESTAMENT
SUPPLEMENT SERIES
208

Executive Editor
Stanley E. Porter

Sheffield Academic Press

The Coming Crisis

The Impact of Eschatology on
Theology in Edwardian England

Mark D. Chapman

Journal for the Study of the New Testament
Supplement Series 208

Copyright © 2001 Sheffield Academic Press

Published by
Sheffield Academic Press Ltd
Mansion House
19 Kingfield Road
Sheffield S11 9AS
England

www.SheffieldAcademicPress.com

Typeset by Sheffield Academic Press
and
Printed on acid-free paper in Great Britain
by MPG Books Ltd,
Bodmin, Cornwall

British Library Cataloguing-in-Publication Data

A catalogue record for this book is available
from the British Library

ISBN 1 84127 185 3

CONTENTS

PREFACE

This book is written in the hope that a neglected period of history might be better understood. What will be argued is that many of the themes which began to dominate theology in the 1920s were already present well before the First World War. Similarly, the criticism of liberalism which Barth refined into an art form after the First World War was paralleled many years earlier in perhaps unlikely places. The plot itself is complex and has many unexpected turns, especially in the matter of theological diplomacy between England and Germany. That in itself is interesting enough. Yet what I hope is more interesting are the relationships between theology, Bible, culture and society which emerge. I have sought to situate theological ideas in their broader context: eschatology was particularly suited as a theological counterpart to the cultural contradictions and inequalities of modernity which found expression in the years before 1914. Although its genesis lay outside England, the rediscovery of eschatology filled a vacuum left by the gradual breakdown of the liberal synthesis in the years of crisis. The theological modernism of Burkitt, Sanday, Figgis and Tyrrell, and the New Liberalism of pre-war politics, have family resemblances, and both to some extent prepared the ground for future developments in theology and politics.

This book was conceived during my time as Sir Henry Stephenson Fellow at Sheffield University from 1989 to 1991, and it has slowly matured (and contracted in scope) since then. A number of people have read or heard various chapters. Small sections of Chapter 3 were published in 'The Socratic Subversion of Tradition: William Sanday and Theology, 1900–1920' (in *JTS* 45 [1994], pp. 94-116). Chapter 6 was my contribution to a conference held in Cuddesdon on the legacy of J.N. Figgis in the summer of 1997. An earlier version of Chapters 4 and 5 was given as a paper to the Scripture, Theology and Society Group meeting in 1997. I would like to thank my fellow members of that group, especially John Rogerson, for their encouragement and stimulation over the years. I would also like to thank by name: Robert Morgan, John Riches, Ruth Edwards, Chris Rowland and especially Christopher Evans, a living biographical dictionary of twentieth-century theology and a marvellous neighbour, now in his ninety-second year. I am also grateful to my College for allowing me to inflict my passion for things Edwardian on about three hundred present and future clergy of the Church of England with as yet unknown results. Finally, I would like to thank my wife, Linda, for keeping me on the straight and narrow. It is to her that this book is affectionately dedicated.

ABBREVIATIONS

AAR	American Academy of Religion
AJT	*American Journal of Theology*
BOD	Bodleian Library, Oxford
CUL	Cambridge University Library
DNB	*Dictionary of National Biography*
ExpTim	*Expository Times*
HTR	*Harvard Theological Review*
JEH	*Journal of Ecclesiastical History*
JTS	*Journal of Theological Studies*
MC	*Modern Churchman*
RGG	*Religion in Geschichte und Gegenwart*
TRu	*Theologische Rundschau*
TLZ	*Theologische Literaturzeitung*
TRE	*Theologische Realencyclopädie*
ZTK	*Zeitschrift für Theologie und Kirche*

Chapter 1

INTRODUCTION: THE PROBLEM OF
ESCHATOLOGY AND THE EDWARDIAN CRISIS

After the First World War the doctrine of 'eschatology' had become such a commonplace in theology that Karl Barth could boldly proclaim in a well-known passage in his *Epistle to the Romans*: 'If Christianity be not altogether restless eschatology, there remains in it no relationship whatever with Christ'.[1] Similarly, in his history of twentieth-century German-language theology, Heinz Zahrnt saw the dominance of eschatology after the First World War as one of the great turning points in modern theology.[2] The importance of eschatology after the First World is undeniable, yet, perhaps because of histories of theology (of which Zahrnt's is a good example) which have regarded the First World War as a kind of caesura, few commentators have looked in detail at the emergence and the significance of eschatology in the years *before* 1914.[3] What is offered in this book is a case study of one distinctive theological theme—the eschatological interpretation of the historical Jesus in Edwardian England—as a modest attempt to add greater precision to the history of theology in a neglected period. It will become clear that the future course of theology, in which eschatology played such a crucial role, was, to some extent at least, already mapped some years before the deluge of the First World War. Indeed the War may have served merely to accelerate theological currents that were already well under way.

1. *The Epistle to the Romans* (trans. E.C. Hoskyns; London: Oxford University Press, 6th edn, 1933), p. 314. For a discussion of the general moves towards 'eschatology' in theology in the beginning of the twentieth century, see Elmar Fastenrath, *'In Vitam Aeternam'. Grundzüge christlicher Eschatologie in der ersten Hälfte des 20. Jahrhunderts* (Sankt Ottilien: Eos Verlag, 1982).

2. See *The Question of God* (London: Collins, 1969), p. 52.

3. Cf. Thomas A. Langford, *In Search of Foundations: English Theology, 1900–1920* (Nashville: Abingdon Press, 1960), p. 50.

The relative ease with which an eschatological interpretation of the historical Jesus, particularly as developed by Albert Schweitzer in his book *Von Reimarus zu Wrede*,[4] made inroads into England is far from self-explanatory, and it certainly baffled many contemporary commentators. For instance, Ernst von Dobschütz, who was one of more widely-read German theologians in England before the First World War (and who will be discussed in detail below), asked in his lectures on eschatology given at the Oxford Summer School in Theology in 1909:

> I wonder how it happened that [Schweitzer's] theory [i.e. thoroughgoing eschatology], put forth in the form of a history, or rather an historical review, of the research on the life of Christ in the last hundred years 'from Reimarus to Wrede' [1906], met with much more appreciation in England than in Germany.[5]

Similarly, looking back in 1951, J.K. Mozley remarked: 'As to Schweitzer's work, it is not too much to say that for a quarter of a century New Testament study in England has been continually concerned with the interpretation that he gave of the Kingdom of God in the preaching of Jesus'.[6] Indeed, as the Dean of Wells Cathedral remarked to F.C. Burkitt, one of the leading figures in the reception of Schweitzer in England, so important had eschatology become that it had grown into a 'blessed word'.[7] Although Schweitzer's book was not without some immediate (albeit slight) impact in his native Germany,[8] it is one of the quirks of the history of theology that the 'thoroughgoing eschatology' developed there should have exerted significantly more influence in England, at least in the years immediately after its publication.[9]

---

4.   Albert Schweitzer, *Von Reimarus zu Wrede. Eine Geschichte der Leben-Jesu-Forschung* (Tübingen: J.C.B. Mohr [Paul Siebeck], 1906). A second edition was published as *Geschichte der Leben-Jesu-Forschung* in 1913. References are to W. Montgomery's English Translation of the first edition, *The Quest of the Historical Jesus*.

5.   'The Eschatology of the Gospels', *The Expositor* 9 (1910), pp. 97-113 (105).

6.   J.K. Mozley, *Some Tendencies in British Theology* (London: SPCK, 1951), p. 36.

7.   Letter from J. Armitage Robinson (1858–1933) to F.C. Burkitt, 17 July 1911 (Cambridge University Library (CUL) MS Add. 7658 B. 844).

8.   Schweitzer had been born in Alsace shortly after its annexation by the Germans. On Schweitzer, see Chapter 3.

9.   Norman Perrin explains this fact by suggesting (probably implausibly, given the extraordinary impact of Harnack's *Das Wesen des Christentums* [Leipzig: J.C.

If my interpretation of the story of the reception of eschatology into English theology in the Edwardian period is plausible, this study should also assist in clarifying some of the difficulties of Edwardian social history. Although the twists and turns of the story are complex and sometimes surprising, what should become clear is that theological ideas, while not necessarily direct products of their social and historical context, gain academic and ecclesial currency in response to broader social, political and intellectual movements. As Gregory Baum remarked in relation to the use of a sociology of culture in theology: 'Theologians often tend to regard the variations of doctrine and theology simply as a development of ideas, without paying sufficient attention to the socio-political reality, of which this development is a reflection'.[10] It is surely implausible to suggest that it was simply accidental that an eschatological picture of Jesus, which viewed him primarily as an apocalyptic preacher, should have gained currency in a society in which the relatively harmonious social order of Victorian England had reached breaking point.

In summary, what will be argued is that under the impact first (and to a very limited extent) of Alfred Loisy, and then (far more decisively) of Johannes Weiss and Albert Schweitzer, the picture of the historical Jesus changed for many English theologians. No longer was he seen as the comfortable and relatively safe ethical teacher with a decidedly Johannine flavour who had dominated the preceding Victorian culture; instead he became the herald of an apocalyptic crisis, who simply could not be contained within the old liberalism. The fact that the 'real' apocalyptic Christ could no longer be tamed[11] by the theologians meant that the strange amalgam of eschatology and ethics included in the term

Hinrichs, 1901]) that '[in] the English-speaking world...theological issues are much more widely discussed [than in Germany]...Under these circumstances Schweitzer's work, in which the general interest is greater than the purely academic merit, was bound to arouse more interest in Britain and America than it would in Germany' (*The Kingdom of God in the Teaching of Jesus* [London: SCM Press, 1963], p. 35).

10. Gregory Baum, 'Sociology and Theology', *Concilium* NS 1 (1974), pp. 22-31, here p. 23. Baum's causality may be a little one-sided in that theological ideas can also contribute (in Weberian manner) to socio-political reality. On this, see David Nicholls, *Deity and Domination: Images of God and the State in the Nineteenth and Twentieth Century* (London: Routledge, 1989), p. 3.

11. This metaphor is used to effect by Robert P. Carroll in *Wolf in the Sheepfold* (London: SPCK, 1991), esp. ch. 5.

'Kingdom of God' was decisively re-ordered.[12] This served to disrupt the theological scene with a crisis at least as profound as the social and political crisis described by many contemporary critics. In short, my suggestion is that the revitalization of eschatological theology was an expression of a broader crisis which struck at the very foundations of religion, politics and society.

The Edwardian Crisis[13]

Like its theology, Edwardian society is hard to characterize. It contains so many contradictions and countercurrents that it is almost impossible to reach any definitive understanding. In the words of a recent historian, it was 'a ramshackle and amorphous society...capable of evolving contingently in many different ways. It was not (despite the fashionable jargon of the Edwardian era) a coherent "organism", still less a "corporation", a "system", or a "machine" '.[14] Despite the best of the efforts of the New Liberals and others to work towards some form of integrated social whole, it seems nevertheless true to say that many of the competing intellectual, social and political currents served, often invisibly, to undermine the sense of social harmony and stability which had marked an earlier generation. Far from being the final triumphant expression of Victorian self-satisfaction, the Edwardian period can be viewed as a period of transition, an 'interregnum',[15] which contained the germs of the future. Indeed a case study of Edwardian theology provides as clear an example as any of the breakdown of what might be described as the old liberal synthesis; at the same time it reveals emergent expressions of themes which were to dominate in the future.[16]

12. For some of the problems associated with the concept of the 'Kingdom of God' see my survey, 'The Kingdom of God and Ethics: From Ritschl to Liberation Theology', in Robin Barbour (ed.), *The Kingdom of God and Human Society* (Edinburgh: T. & T. Clark, 1993), pp. 140-63.

13. Cf. Langford, *In Search of Foundations*, ch. 2.

14. José Harris, *Private Lives, Public Spirit: Britain 1870–1914* (London: Penguin Books, 1994), p. 3. There are many accounts of the 'organismic' approach to society which dominated much New Liberal thinking. A particularly useful (and provocative) survey of special relevance to the present discussion can be found in Nicholls, *Deity and Domination*, ch. 2.

15. On this see Raymond Williams, *Culture and Society, 1780–1950* (Harmondsworth: Penguin Books, 1963), pp. 165-95.

16. On the notions of 'dominant', 'residual' and 'emergent' see Raymond

As Ensor put it in his classic history of the period:

> Most of the familiar post-war tendencies were already developing in [the pre-war years]. The war altered direction less than is often supposed. It accelerated changes—at least for the time being; but they were already germinating before it. It may have been that some would have been carried through more wisely but for the war's revolutionary atmosphere... What is not [a matter of speculation] is the seething and teeming of this pre-war period, its immense ferment and its restless fertility.[17]

Although the term 'crisis' might in hindsight be something of an overstatement when describing English society in the ten years or so before the outbreak of war in 1914,[18] there was undeniably a sense of unease, at least among those in positions of authority.[19] This was provoked by many factors, including the increasing number of strikes, the movement for women's suffrage, the militancy in Ireland, as well as the constitutional crises provoked by the conflict between the Liberals and 'Mr Balfour's poodle', the House of Lords.[20] In addition, there was (to some extent at least) an identifiable religious crisis.[21] Discussing

Williams, *Marxism and Literature* (Oxford: Oxford University Press, 1977), ch. 8. Such terminology, which will be followed only loosely in the present discussion, helps clarify the sense of movement, which seems so appropriate for the Edwardian period (p. 121).

17. R.C.K. Ensor, *England, 1870–1914* (Oxford: Clarendon Press, 1936), pp. 556-57.

18. See, for example, Martin Pugh, *State and Society: British Political and Social History 1870–1992* (London: Arnold, 1994), ch. 9; Alan O'Day, introduction to *The Edwardian Age: Conflict and Stability, 1900–1914* (Basingstoke: Macmillan, 1979).

19. See Paul Thompson, *The Edwardians* (London: Routledge, 2nd edn, 1992), p. 249.

20. On this period in general, see especially the survey by David Powell, *The Edwardian Crisis: Britain 1901–1914* (Basingstoke: Macmillan, 1996). For a useful account of the social history of the period see S. Nowell-Smith (ed.), *Edwardian England* (London: Oxford University Press, 1964). There is, perhaps rather surprisingly, no essay on religion in this volume.

21. On this, see the survey by Hugh McLeod, *Religion and Society in England, 1850–1914* (Basingstoke: Macmillan, 1996), esp. ch. 4. Cf. Harris, *Private Lives, Public Spirit*, ch. 6. For a useful overview of the religious response to the increasing pluralism and fragmentation if not secularization of society in late Victorian and Edwardian Britain, see Gerald Parsons, 'Social Control to Social Gospel: Victorian Christian Social Attitudes', in *idem* (ed.), *Religion in Victorian Britain*, II (5 vols.; Manchester: Manchester University Press, 1988), pp. 39-62. For a not always

this growing sense of crisis Asa Briggs remarked:

> Edwardian Society was picturesquely but perilously divided, and the greatest of the many contrasts of the age was not with that which had gone before but that between the divergent outlooks and fortunes of different groups within the same community. The implications of the clash of outlooks, fortunes, and tactics could seldom be completely evaded... More particularly during the four years after the king's death in 1910, there was open and violent internal conflict. Will transcended both law and conviction. The greater international violence of 1914 was a culmination as well as an historical divide.[22]

All these different symptoms seem to be manifestations of the tensions which accompanied the pluralization and fragmentation of culture in the often disturbing transition from *Gemeinschaft* to *Gesellschaft* which characterizes the movement towards an advanced industrial society: social bonds are weakened and the hitherto dominant model of a society held together by a semi-feudal network of duty and obligation collapses as a result of increasing mobility and the concomitant destruction of close-knit communities.[23] Yet alongside

sympathetic discussion of the response of the Church of England to social conditions in Edwardian England, see Edward Norman, *Church and Society in England, 1770–1970* (Oxford: Clarendon Press, 1976), ch. 6. More generally, see the account by Paul T. Phillips, *A Kingdom on Earth: Anglo-American Social Christianity 1880–1940* (University Park, PA: Penn State University Press, 1996).

22. Asa Briggs, 'The Political Scene', in Nowell-Smith, *Edwardian England*, pp. 43-101 (45-46).

23. Ferdinand Tönnies and many others recognized the social changes involved in this movement from community to society. In his *Division of Labour in Society* (New York: Macmillan, 1933), for instance, Emile Durkheim asks: 'If pre-industrial societies are held together by common ideas and sentiments, by shared norms and values, what holds an industrial society together?' (quoted in Stephen Lukes, *Emile Durkheim* [London: Penguin Books, 1975], p. 141). The breakdown of order which had dominated the 'mechanical solidarity' of traditional societies led to a sense of *anomie*. At least part of Durkheim's sociological project was normative as it sought to rebuild the sense of community in a modern society by means of a socialist egalitarianism based on the 'organic solidarity' of mutual dependence in the division of labour: 'What we must do to relieve this anomie is to discover the means for making the organs which are still wasting themselves in discordant movements harmoniously concur by introducing into their relations more justice by more and more extenuating the external qualities which are the source of the evil' (*Division of Labour*, p. 409). Tönnies himself called for a strong central authority built on contract and strong organization to rebuild a sense of community in industrial society.

increasing fragmentation and rootlessness, the movement towards a modern industrial economy was also marked, perhaps somewhat paradoxically, by increasing levels of social uniformity: the machine mentality of the age encouraged suppression of individuality.[24] Given these tensions it is hardly surprising that the transition to modernity in England was painful; and that it looked to many like a crisis.

To others, however, there was little cause for anxiety; Paul Thompson writes in his oral history of the period, of a London hatter who remarked: 'When my Lord comes in to have his hat ironed on those spring mornings in the spring-time of this century I firmly believed that kind of life was to continue forever. Catastrophes might and did happen elsewhere'.[25] Such an attitude is evocative of the sunny days of the more settled times to which people looked back after the catastrophe of the First World War. Among some Edwardians at least there was undoubtedly a complacency and an inflated sense of well-being: 'In contrast with the last decade of the nineteenth century in England, the first decade of the twentieth showed a mood of sunrise succeeding one of sunset'.[26] Yet to other observers storm clouds were gathering: on 19 January 1909, for instance, *The Times* emphasized that people had begun to 'place the golden age behind them, and assume that no generation ever had to deal with evils so great and perplexing as those of the present day'. By 1909 a sense of gloom had begun to permeate some sections of British politics and society.

The following year, however, things seemed far worse, as George

24. For Max Weber modern society was becoming ever more bureaucratized, as human beings were increasingly made into objects of calculation: 'The fully developed bureaucratic apparatus compares with other organisations exactly as does the machine with the non-mechanical modes of production. Precision, speed, unambiguity, knowledge of the files, continuity, discretion, unity, strict subordination, reduction of friction and of material and personal costs—these are raised to the optimum point in the strictly bureaucratic organisation' (*Economy and Society*, III [New York: Bedminster Press, 1968], p. 973). In *Division of Labour*, Durkheim recognizes that division of labour requires a spontaneity that can so easily be oppressed by anything that might 'shackle the free employment of the social force that each person carried within himself. This not only supposes that individuals are not relegated to particular functions by force, but also that no sort of obstacle whatever prevents them from occupying in the social framework the position which accords with their capacities' (p. 377).

25. Fred Willis, cited in Thompson, *The Edwardians*, p. 226.

26. Ensor, *England, 1870-1914*, p. 527.

Dangerfield argued in his forceful and vivid interpretation of the years 1910–1914, *The Strange Death of Liberal of England 1910–1914*. For him the year 1910, with the struggles in parliament, marked a watershed on the march towards chaos and war, symbolically indicated by the appearance of Halley's comet: 'true pre-war Liberalism—supported as it was in 1910 by Free Trade, a majority in Parliament, the ten commandments, and the illusion of Progress—can never return. It was killed or it killed itself in 1913'.[27] Similarly, David Thomson suggested that the picture of harmony was in reality an optical illusion: there were 'already present in Britain of the pre-war decade many of the seeds of later troubles which were attributed, wrongly, to the war'.[28] Even if other historians[29] have been rather more understated, preferring to see the period before 1914 as an age of innocence that was entering its painful period of adolescence which would become all the more distressing after the outbreak of war, what is clear is that society before the First World War, even if it was not yet experiencing a full-blown crisis, was at the very least riven with profound social tensions.

Of the contemporary social commentators it was perhaps Charles Masterman, the liberal minister and journalist, who, describing *The Condition of England*[30] in 1909, offered the most incisive analysis of the era: 'Of all illusions of the opening twentieth century', he wrote, 'perhaps the most remarkable is that of security...[H]e would be but a blind prophet, who looking to the future, would assert that all things will continue as until now'.[31] Indeed it was an open question as to

---

27. *The Strange Death of Liberal England 1910–1914* (London: Macgibbon and Kee, 1966 [1935]), p. 14. Cf. Virginia Woolf, 'Mr. Bennett and Mrs. Brown' (in *The Hogarth Essays* [London: Hogarth Press, 1924], pp. 4-5): 'On or about December 1910 human character changed... All human relations have shifted—those between masters and servants, husbands and wives, parents and children. And when human relations change there is at the same time a change in religion, conduct, politics and literature.'

28. *England in the Twentieth Century* (Harmondsworth: Penguin Books, 1965), p. 16.

29. Cf. Donald Read, *Edwardian England* (London: Harrap, 1972); and 'Crisis Age or Golden Age?', in Donald Read (ed.), *Edwardian England* (London: Croom Helm, 1982), pp. 14-39.

30. C.F.G. Masterman, *The Condition of England* (London: Methuen, 1909. On Masterman, see Edward David, 'The New Liberalism of C.F.G. Masterman', in K.D. Brown (ed.), *Essays in Anti-Labour History* (London: Macmillan, 1974), pp. 17-41.

31. Masterman, *The Condition of England*, pp. 288-89.

whether 'civilisation [was] about to blossom into flower, or wither in tangle of dead leaves and faded gold'. As a politician caught in the struggles between the Commons and Lords, he saw England as a divided nation where the old social harmony which prevailed in the Victorian period had finally broken down. For Masterman, the gap between rich and poor seemed unbridgeable: 'even national distinctions seem less estranging than the fissure between the summit and the base of society'.[32] Indeed so divided did things seem that the most likely outcome might be war:

> That with the vertical division between nation and nation armed to the teeth, and the horizontal division between rich and poor which has become a cosmopolitan fissure, the future of progress is still doubtful and precarious. Humanity-at-best appears but as a shipwrecked crew which has taken refuge on a narrow ledge of rock, beaten by wind and wave; which cannot tell how many, if any at all, will survive when the long night gives place to morning. The wise man will still go softly all his days; working for greater economic equality on the one hand, for understanding between estranged peoples on the other; apprehending how slight an effort of stupidity or violence could strike a death-blow to twentieth-century civilisation, and elevate the forces of destruction triumphant over the ruins of a world.[33]

Unless drastic measures were taken, according to Masterman, the twentieth century would be in danger of visible collapse: indeed, the scent of the final battle was in the air.

The sense of continual and evolutionary progress, which had been so important in defining the dominant world-view of the high Victorian years, seemed to ring hollow in the divisions of the Edwardian period.[34] Instead of a gradual movement towards the promised land, it appeared to Winston Churchill, who at the time was a Liberal Cabinet Minister, that

> [w]e are at the cross-ways. If we stand on in the old-happy-go-lucky way, the richer classes growing in wealth and in number, and ever declining in responsibility, the very poor remaining plunged and plunging even deeper into hopeless, hopeless misery, then I think there is nothing before us but savage strife between class and class.[35]

32. Masterman, *The Condition of England*, pp. viii-ix, 249, 288.
33. Masterman, *The Condition of England*, p. 303.
34. Cf. J.B. Bury, *The Idea of Progress* (London: Macmillan, 1920).
35. Winston S. Churchill, *Liberalism and the Social Problem* (London: Hodder & Stoughton, 1909), pp. 361-62.

Others too, including, for example, the socialists George Bernard Shaw and H.G. Wells, pointed to defects in English society, and offered their own distinctive solutions.

Gradually colourful, even apocalyptic, language began to permeate the political debate as the old stable system began to shake.[36] The parallels between theology and politics here are quite clear: during the Edwardian period there were a number of powerful theological critiques of contemporary 'civilization'. The most important examples were probably George Tyrrell's *Christianity at the Cross-Roads*,[37] which will be discussed in detail in Chapter 7, and J.N. Figgis's Harvard lectures, *Civilisation at the Cross Roads*,[38] which form the subject of Chapter 6. It looked to Figgis that the world was visibly collapsing. Indeed, in a sermon preached shortly before the First World War at a fashionable London church, he remarked that the forces of civilization were

> visibly dissolving. Its tall towers are shaking, and the splendid spires of the edifice of the western world are crumbling. Catastrophe is threatening. We can almost hear the thunders of the avalanche of war— war on a scale unknown. Hardly does the world even look stable any longer. It is not like the forties of Victorian complacency, but looks all tottering—tottering.[39]

A new age had dawned and the old Victorian settlement was collapsing, however much one might long for 'the halcyon days when the Old Testament was the main trouble and *Lux Mundi* was thought a dangerous book'.[40] In short, Figgis claimed, the ' "Alexandrian" age of Westcott was gone'.[41]

This apocalyptic mood was shared by Neville Talbot, who, writing in 1912 on 'The Modern Situation' in *Foundations*, remarked that

36. Cf. G.K. Chesterton's deeply ironic poem on Welsh disestablishment, 'Antichrist, or the Reunion of Christendom: An Ode', in *The Works of G.K. Chesterton* (London: Wordsworth, 1995), p. 115. On Chesterton's social and political context, see esp. John D. Coates, *Chesterton and the Edwardian Cultural Crisis* (Hull: Hull University Press, 1984).

37. George Tyrrell, *Christianity at the Cross-Roads* (London: Longmans, 1910) was published posthumously by Maude Petre.

38. J.N. Figgis, *Civilisation at the Cross Roads* (London: Longmans, 1912).

39. J.N. Figgis, *Antichrist and Other Sermons* (London: Longmans, 1913), p. 31.

40. J.N. Figgis, *Religion and English Society* (London: Longmans, 1910), p. 15.

41. J.N. Figgis, *Hopes for English Religion* (London: Longmans, 1919), p. 24.

[t]his generation is modern in the sense that it never knew the world 'before the [Darwinian] flood'. While it has been growing up the assumptions of Mid-Victorian liberalism have been going bankrupt. Their capital has been running out. Even their last survivor, Progress, has been at grips with a doubt deeper than itself to man's place in the universe. For the infection of a kind of cosmic nervousness has become widespread. Somehow the world is now felt to be less domestic than it was. The skies have darkened and men's minds have become more sombre.[42]

The optimism of the Victorian period, which had placed such weight upon 'education as the way of all salvation', was over.[43]

This generation in Great Britain is modern in the sense that it is not Victorian... In fact, the change from genuinely Victorian times to to-day is a change from the reliance upon, to the criticism of, assumptions.[44]

In a memorable phrase, he continued, '[s]omehow or other the rose colour has faded out of Victorian spectacles'.[45] Yet, if the world of Westcott and T.H. Green was visibly dying, it had not been replaced by any new sense of harmony and order: the modern human being was being 'swept by violent tides out of old anchorages, both religious and moral'.[46] In this way, modern times even began to resemble the crisis of New Testament times:

The times of the impotence of Christ are passing... Once men were darkness and once they became light in the Lord. Since then the light has been diffused into twilight, and in half-Christianized Europe generations have had no knowledge either of the light or of the darkness. But to-day all changes... The darkness of the universe in its incomprehensible age and vastness overcasts the vision of post-Darwinian science. The darkness of human hearts emancipated, and void of all allegiance but to themselves, creeps ever on.

Therefore to-day the light begins to shine anew, as men begin again to know the need of it.[47]

42. Neville S. Talbot, 'The Modern Situation', in B.H. Streeter (ed.), *Foundations: A Statement of Christian Belief in Terms of Modern Thought: by Seven Oxford Men* (London: Macmillan, 1912), pp. 1-24 (7).
43. Talbot, 'The Modern Situation', p. 5.
44. Talbot, 'The Modern Situation', p. 4.
45. Talbot, 'The Modern Situation', p. 9.
46. Talbot, 'The Modern Situation', p. 11.
47. Talbot, 'The Modern Situation', p. 24.

But 'they know the need of it', Talbot claimed, in a world whose very foundations have changed beyond all recognition.

The Old and New Liberalism

Though perhaps with less vigour than these religious writers, some secular social commentators explicitly linked the collapse of old liberalism with the breakdown of the perceived religious consensus of Victorian England. This is probably clearest in the work of another New Liberal, the economist J.A. Hobson, who commented in his book, *The Crisis of Liberalism: New Issues in Democracy*,[48] that the old fixed faith which had dominated the Victorian world had had its foundations 'undermined by the new thought. The engines of criticism were battering each of them'.[49] The two most obvious examples of this change he identified as the old political parties and the churches, both of which were being subjected to a criticism which had begun 'corroding the old cast-iron dogmas, eating away the old theology, the old social conventions'.[50] The old comfortable conservatism of the British was beginning to collapse under the challenge of what he called 'realism'.[51] There were, at least in the mind of Hobson, parallels between the New Liberalism in politics and the modernist movement in the churches. 'In a word, just as the theologians are beginning to seek a re-statement of religion that is "real", comprehensive, vital, so it is with the more enlightened politicians.'[52]

A new realism was shaking theology just as it was shaking politics: 'Twenty years ago', Hobson remarked, 'it would have been impossible for such a publication as the *Hibbert Journal* to have obtained the influence it wields today. The whole modernist movement in Catholic and Protestant countries', he went on, 'is a striking confession of the

---

48. J.A. Hobson, *The Crisis of Liberalism: New Issues in Democracy* (London: P.S. King and Son, 1909). Cf. Nicholls, *Deity and Domination*, p. 67. On Hobson, see John Allett, *New Liberalism: The Political Economy of J.A. Hobson* (Toronto: University of Toronto Press, 1981). See, more generally, Peter Weiler, *The New Liberalism: Liberal Social Theory in Great Britain, 1889–1914* (New York: Garland, 1982).

49. Hobson, *The Crisis of Liberalism*, p. 269.

50. Hobson, *The Crisis of Liberalism*, p. 270.

51. Hobson, *The Crisis of Liberalism*, p. 267.

52. Hobson, *The Crisis of Liberalism*, p. 271.

failure of the silent protest to keep the new wine out of the old bottles. In every church the new bottling industry is going on with more or less success'. The shock of the real was beginning to reveal signs of

> great intellectual and spiritual revival. At the very moment when blind critics are deploring the decline of genius and the barrenness of the age, an abundance of fresh inspiration is beginning to breathe through new forms of realism in poetry, the drama, prose, fiction and art.[53]

For Hobson, there were close parallels between all branches of life and thought as they sought to express in

> a 'practical philosophy' of life what is common to mankind... Those who accept the view that experiments in collective self-consciousness, as a means of accelerating and directing the 'urge of the world' towards human enlightenment and well-being, are likely to yield great results, will recognise that a rendering of realism in many fields of thought and art is the most profitable task of our age.[54]

Hobson recognizes, in words that are redolent of theological critics like Figgis,[55] that '[t]here are three adjectives commonly recognised by foreigners as peculiarly representative of English valuations, the terms 'respectable', 'comfortable', and 'shocking'. They denote the inward fortress of conservatism, primarily in conduct, but secondarily in thought'.[56] Against such a conservatism there was a need for risk, and for an injection of the challenge of realism. And this emphasis on realism provides a striking parallel with the rediscovery of mystery which lay at the heart of Modernism—perhaps the theological equivalent of the New Liberalism—which made such an impact on the English theological scene in the Edwardian years.

Despite the continued predominance of ideas of progress which coloured the general perception of the 'old-liberal' theology character-ized in, say, the thought of Hastings Rashdall (which will be discussed in detail below), other theologians from a variety of theological back-grounds, saw the contemporary value of other more apocalyptic currents, which led to some disturbing pictures of dismemberment, disintegration and crisis. Thus, although it may no doubt have been accidental that

---

53. Hobson, *The Crisis of Liberalism*, p. 270.
54. Hobson, *The Crisis of Liberalism*, pp. 275-76.
55. See, for example, J.N. Figgis, *Some Defects of English Religion and Other Sermons* (London: Robert Scott, 1917).
56. Hobson, *The Crisis of Liberalism*, p. 267.

apocalyptic re-emerged as a vital theme in biblical studies and theology in the Edwardian period, it seems that, unlike Halley's comet, the timing was more than a happy (or indeed unhappy) coincidence. Apocalyptic or eschatology[57] provided a radical language capable of critique, which helped re-orientate theology away from the prevailing theological-philosophical consensus of the old liberalism towards a renewed emphasis on mystery and the supernatural characteristic of modernism.

The impact of eschatology, or more strictly an eschatological interpretation of the historical Jesus, on Edwardian theology thus provides an illuminating case study of the more general breakdown of the liberal consensus. The tidiness of contemporary interpretative systems was shattered by the figure of a Jesus who was radically strange and disturbing. What I will argue through the course of this book is that as a consequence some varieties of theological liberalism began to die a slow lingering death well before the First World War. Thus what Dangerfield claimed in the field of politics was equally true for theology. Where liberalism in its Victorian plenitude had been easy to bear, in Edwardian England 'it began to give out a dismal rattling sound'[58] as it tried in vain to withstand the twin threats of fragmentation and social uniformity. Within this broader social perspective the rediscovery of eschatology can perhaps best be understood as theology's plea for transcendence, mystery and individuality in a society bent on taming difference through the hedonism of the few or through its social engineering of the human machine. It comes as no surprise that when society was finally shattered by the First World War, especially in Germany, eschatology rapidly began to dominate theological discourse.

Eschatology and Theology:
Some Problems in Theological Diplomacy[59]

Before looking in detail at the course of the reception of eschatology in England, however, there are some significant points that need to be

57. Despite their different connotations today these two words were used virtually interchangeably throughout the Edwardian period, at least in relation to the historical Jesus.

58. Dangerfield, *The Strange Death*, p. 20.

59. On this, see Stephen W. Sykes (ed.), *England and Germany: Studies in Theological Diplomacy* (Studien zur interkulturellen Geschichte des Christentums, 25; Frankfurt: Peter Lang, 1982), esp. the essay by Robert Morgan, 'Historical Criticism and Christology: England and Germany', pp. 80-112.

borne in mind throughout this discussion: since eschatological interpretations of the historical Jesus originated in Germany this book is inevitably at once a history of 'theological diplomacy' between England and Germany. This obviously raises problems of nationalism and insularity which complicate any historical study of theological ideas still further; again the broader context of anglo-German rivalry cannot be ignored. It is perhaps because of traditional English theological insularity, that, whereas the move in Germany towards an eschatological interpretation of the Synoptic Gospels at the end of the nineteenth and at the beginning of the twentieth centuries has been fairly well documented,[60] the history of the English reception of this German scholarship has only been sketched.[61]

Again the distorting lens of two world wars may be a decisive factor in this neglect. A survey of the years before 1914 reveals, however, that English theology was nowhere near as isolated as it had been in the nineteenth century or as it was to become after the First World War (with a few notable exceptions): despite the arms build-up and the naval race, German scholars continued to be highly valued and widely read among English theologians, and many formed close personal

---

60. See esp. W.G. Kümmel, 'Die "konsequente Eschatologie" Albert Schweitzers im Urteil der Zeitgenossen', in *idem*, *Heilsgeschehen und Geschichte. Gesammelte Aufsätze* (Marburger Theologische Studien, 3; Marburg: N.G. Elwert, 1965), pp. 328-39; W.G. Kümmel and C.H. Ratschow, *Albert Schweitzer als Theologe* (Marburg: N.G. Elwert, 1966); Berthold Lannert, *Die Wiederentdeckung der neutestamentlichen Eschatologie durch Johannes Weiss* (Tübingen: Francke Verlag, 1989). See also Klaus Koch, *The Rediscovery of Apocalyptic* (London: SCM Press, 1972); W.G. Kümmel, *The New Testament: The History of the Investigation of its Problems* (London: SCM Press, 1973), pp. 226-44; Robert Morgan, 'From Reimarus to Sanders', in R.S. Barbour (ed.), *The Kingdom of God and Human Society* (Edinburgh: T. & T. Clark, 1993), pp. 80-139; and Walter P. Weaver, *The Historical Jesus in the Twentieth Century 1900–1950* (Harrisburg: Trinity Press International, 1999). For a general survey of the recent discussion with a comprehensive bibliography, see D.E. Aune, 'Eschatology (Early Christian)', in D.N. Freedman (ed.), *Anchor Bible Dictionary*, II (6 vols.; New York: Doubleday, 1992), pp. 594-609; and Bruce Chilton, *Pure Kingdom: Jesus' Vision of God* (London: SPCK, 1996), esp. ch. 1.

61. See esp. Langford, *In Search of Foundations*; A. Michael Ramsey, *From Gore to Temple* (London: Longmans, 1960), pp. 171-74. Mozley, *Some Tendencies in British Theology*, pp. 36-39; Perrin, *The Kingdom of God*, pp. 37-45; Morgan, 'From Reimarus to Sanders', p. 82; John Riches, *A Century of New Testament Study* (Cambridge: Lutterworth Press, 1993), pp. 24-28; Chilton, *Pure Kingdom*, ch. 1.

friendships with their English counterparts. Scholarship was perhaps at its most international: before the First World War, German theologians were frequent contributors to British and American journals and there were successful collaborations which produced international journals, most importantly the *Constructive Quarterly*. Far from being understood as apologists for the Wagnerian excesses of German culture or for Prussian militarism, most German theologians were perceived as in some degree hostile to German foreign policy. Thus even Adolf von Harnack (who later made a significant contribution to or possibly even wrote the manifesto in support of Germany's war aims in 1914) was actively engaged in pre-war international reconciliation, giving the keynote address to the first meeting of the Associated Councils of the Churches of the British and German Empires for the Fostering of Friendly Relations between the Two Peoples in 1911. The perception of German scholarship, at least by the more enlightened scholars, was well summed-up by H. Latimer Jackson[62] in his lengthy discussion of eschatology based on his Hulsean lectures. Jackson, who was a close friend of von Dobschütz, could write in the preface: 'Such as it is my book tells its own tale of continued indebtedness to German scholarship on the part of one who can never be unmindful of those highly-prized friendships which bind him to the "Fatherland" as to a second home'.[63] As will become clear, however, other theologians were more suspicious of German scholarship at least in its liberal protestant guises: overcoming some varieties of liberalism involved a more or less manifest anti-Germanism.

As I have already suggested in the opening section, at least one of the reasons for the relative success of an eschatological interpretation in England was the social and political crisis, which made apocalyptic language such an appropriate medium of expression. However, a further preliminary point needs to be made: it would be foolish to ignore the power of the personalities involved in the story. In particular

---

62. Henry Latimer Jackson (1851–1926) was Rector of Little Canfield near Great Dunmow in Essex from 1911. After education at Highgate and in Germany he studied at Christ's College, Cambridge, becoming a Fellow of St Paul's College, Sydney in 1885. In 1895 he became incumbent of St Mary's, Huntingdon. He was also Lecturer at Cambridge in Modern and Medieval Dutch literature from 1918.

63. H. Latimer Jackson, *The Eschatology of Jesus* (London: Macmillan, 1913), p. xi.

William Sanday and F.C. Burkitt, who are the two most important protagonists in this book, were held in high esteem by their peers and were extraordinarily influential as teachers and mentors. Between them, as will become clear, these two highly respected scholars ensured that eschatology was given a special prominence in English theological thought before the First World War, and it is to this story, described by Kümmel as 'astonishing',[64] that Chapters 2–5 are dedicated.

The neglect of the Edwardian period in general, and the theme of eschatology in particular, is surprising, since in many ways it offers an arresting story which displays the connections between theological language and social context in perhaps an unparalleled way. Several theologians were captivated by a language which seemed to offer an escape route from the impasse reached by so many of their pre-decessors who appeared to have trivialized Jesus' message or to have universalized it beyond any historical particularity. Although an eschatological interpretation of the historical Jesus was admittedly occasionally used as a conservative weapon to wield against certain varieties of liberalism, it was used more often by some who were far from straightforward defenders of conservative orthodoxy. Sanday hovers between these two poles, whereas Burkitt is far more of a Modernist in his theological style. The other characters who feature below, most importantly J.N. Figgis and George Tyrrell, drew more far reaching consequences and might best be described as radicals, as they paved the way for the next generation of scholars exemplified most obviously before the First World War by B.H. Streeter and afterwards by Sir Edwyn Hoskyns, whose eschatological theology will be discussed briefly in the concluding Chapter.

What will become clear is that it was precisely the radical strange-ness of the historical Jesus that some saw as giving new impetus to the mission of the Church in the pessimism of the late Edwardian era: the supernatural otherness of Jesus' message, and by extension the other-ness of the proclamation of the contemporary church, led some to resist the old liberal synthesis through cultural critique and to develop a theology of Modernism, which in some varieties defined itself against the old liberalism.[65] Consequently a somewhat more domesticated

---

64. 'Die "konsequente Eschatologie" ', p. 334.

65. On this, see Henry Major, *English Modernism: Its Origin, Methods, Aims* (Cambridge, MA: Harvard University Press, 1927), p. 36.

version of the radical otherness of God, and a general dissatisfaction with some forms of liberal theology can be found in English theology several years before the outbreak of war. One might even suggest that Barth's *Epistle to the Romans* is thus not without (admittedly more modest) earlier parallels.

Chapter 2

HARNACK, LOISY AND THE BEGINNINGS OF ESCHATOLOGY

Harnack and the Historical Jesus in 1900

In 1900 it was certainly not usual to see the historical Jesus solely as a preacher of the coming catastrophe. At least among more liberal scholars, particularly in Germany, the essence of Jesus' preaching was understood as a straightforward ethic of love for neighbour under the Fatherhood of God. Dominant among such German theologians at the time was Adolf von Harnack (1851–1930), a figure who had an immense international reputation.[1] Harnack, who was Professor at Berlin University from 1889–1921, had helped to revitalize interest in theology beyond the academy in his famous extempore lectures delivered before six hundred students drawn from across the different faculties in the Winter Semester of 1899–1900. Consciously recalling Schleiermacher's great *Speeches* of a hundred years earlier, Harnack met with great success and by the end of 1900 the published version of the lectures, *Das Wesen des Christentums* prepared from Walter Becker's transcription had already been through three editions. By 1927 the book had reached its eleventh edition, had been translated into fourteen languages, and had sold over 71,000 copies.[2]

Many from outside the confines of academic theology were captivated by the book's apologetics. The economist Gustav Schmoller, for instance, found the lectures a confirmation of all he had hoped for.

1. On Harnack, see Agnes von Zahn-Harnack, *Adolf von Harnack* (Berlin: W. de Gruyter, 1951). For a contemporary comprehensive reappraisal see Kurt Nowak, 'Bürgerliche Bildungsreligion? Zur Stellung Adolf von Harnacks in der protestantischen Frömmigkeitsgeschichte der Moderne', *Zeitschrift für Kirchengeschichte* 99 (1988), pp. 326-53.

2. On the publication history of these lectures see Friedrich Smend, *Adolf von Harnack. Verzeichnis seiner Schriften* (Leipzig: J.C. Hinrichs, 1927), and the supplement published in 1931.

They marked a 'dissolution of doubt—I might even go as far as saying a revelation—the revelation of the historical Christ as he is possible for the educated and intelligentsia of today'.[3] Against the complexities of the age, as the church historian, Friedrich Loofs, noted, the Gospel of simplicity had returned.[4] In *Das Wesen des Christentums*, Harnack had attempted to reduce Christianity to its simplest essence, thereby trying to return to the piety of Jesus and, at the same time, removing the church's corruption of the original gospel. For Harnack, what was important about the Gospel was that it should touch the heart: it was there that absoluteness made contact with human reality, thereby overcoming the vagaries of the relativities of historical knowledge, and it was there too, rather than in historical miracle, that the supernatural content of the Gospel was felt.[5] The essence of the Gospel, according to Harnack, was straightforward:

> Firstly the kingdom of God and its coming. Secondly God the Father and the infinite value of the human soul. Thirdly the higher righteousness and the commandment of love. That Jesus' message is so great and so powerful lies in the fact that it is so simple and on the other hand so rich; so simple as to be exhausted in each of the original thoughts that he uttered; so rich that every one of those thoughts seems to be inexhaustible and the full meaning of the sayings and parables beyond our reach.[6]

The kernel of this message was embodied in the Kingdom of God which comes 'to the individual, by entering into his soul and laying hold of it'.[7] Indeed it contained nothing other-worldly: everything supernatural was an accretion which had to be removed from the original kernel like the husk from a nut. This meant that in essence

---

3.   Letter from Schmoller to Harnack, 1 July 1900, cited in von Zahn-Harnack, *Adolf von Harnack*, p. 186.

4.   Letter to Harnack, 3 Nov 1901, in Zahn-Harnack, *Adolf von Harnack*, p. 186.

5.   Cf. Harnack, *What is Christianity?* (trans. T.B. Saunders; London: Williams and Norgate, 1904), p. 187. English translation of *Das Wesen des Christentums*.

6.   Harnack, *What is Christianity?*, pp. 52-53.

7.   Harnack, *What is Christianity?*, p. 57. J.C. O'Neill's rather harsh verdict on Harnack is not far from the mark. Harnack suggests that Goethe's phrase, 'From the necessity that binds all human beings, the man who overcomes himself is the man who frees himself' is really at the heart of the matter. O'Neill comments: 'Harnack talks endlessly of God and history, but he is really only concerned with himself and his own unremitting task of talking about himself' (*The Bible's Authority* [Edinburgh: T. & T. Clark], 1991, p. 229). There is indeed little doubting that Harnack's theology is a typical 'pectoral' theology in the pietist mould.

Jesus himself possessed no supernatural powers; instead the urgency and greatness of his message consisted in the individual's call

> to listen to the glad message of mercy and the Fatherhood of God, and to make up his mind whether he will be on God's side and the Eternal's, or on the side of the world and time. The Gospel, as Jesus proclaimed it, has to do with the Father and not with the Son.[8]

Through the passage of time, however, this simple message had gradually been distorted by the accretions of Catholicism with its hierarchy and its claim to divine foundation. For Harnack, however, the Catholic Church could claim no basis in the Gospel. Protestantism had admittedly been a major advance in calling for a return to a simpler Gospel, but even this had not been able to clear away the baggage of scholasticism: thus what was required in the present day was a new reformation to return to the purity of Jesus' message. In response to this need, Harnack developed his simple message of 'eternal life in the midst of time',[9] which sought to overcome the perceived distortions introduced by the church through the course of its history. It was primarily for this reason that Harnack's work provoked almost immediate criticism from the more ecclesiastically-minded theologians at work in England.

William Sanday

One of the first important responses to Harnack was made by William Sanday, perhaps the most influential figure in Edwardian theology, who features as a major player throughout this book. After education at Repton, Sanday became an undergraduate at Balliol and Corpus Christi Colleges, Oxford, before being elected to a Fellowship of Trinity in 1866. After ordination he held various College livings before becoming Principal of Hatfield Hall, Durham from 1876–1882. He became Dean Ireland Professor of Exegesis in Oxford from 1882 before being elected in 1895 to the significantly better endowed Lady Margaret Professorship, which carried a canon's stall at Christ Church. He retired, a year before his death, in 1919.[10] After his wife's death in 1904, an '*annus funestus*', he withdrew from society to concentrate on his work: 'I

---

8.   Harnack, *What is Christianity?*, p. 147.

9.   Harnack, *What is Christianity?*, p. 8.

10. Sanday was offered, but declined, the Regius Chair in 1910. (Asquith to Sanday, 22 Nov 1910. BOD MS misc. d. 122 (I) no. 71.)

cannot suppress the surmise that...the year 1904 was sent to me specially in order that I might be less unfit to write what I have undertaken to write'.[11]

Sanday had a reputation as a man of extreme caution, who, although extraordinarily fair to all sides, would normally opt for the traditional solution. Following in the English conservative tradition of Westcott, Lightfoot and Hort, Sanday was highly regarded as a textual critic.[12] Similarly his reviews, although often providing brilliant analysis, were hardly characterized by radical conclusions.[13] If anything he was given to understatement, writing in 1907, in *The Life of Christ in Recent Research*: 'When I came to Oxford, the doctrine I ventured to preach was: Don't let us be too ambitious; let us plan our work on a large scale, and be content to take the humbler departments first'.[14] Even from his own account, given to an audience gathered to mark the presentation of his portrait to Christ Church in 1907, Sanday is modest almost to a fault:

> What is there in anything of mine that should enjoy more than a very ephemeral life?... I am not a scholar, where a scholar comes. I am not an able man, where an able man comes. I am certainly not a good writer where a good writer comes.

His primary failing was, he remarked, 'just plain shortness of brains... Most hats go down over my ears'.[15]

---

11. Autobiographical fragment, *Effigies Mea* (BOD MS Eng. misc. d. 128 no. 380) included with Sanday's Correspondence in the Bodleian Library, Oxford, MS Eng. misc. d. 122-128; d. 140. Obituaries by Walter Lock in *JTS* 22 (1921), pp. 97-104; by C.H. Turner in *DNB* (1912–1921), pp. 482-85; *MC* 10 (1920), pp. 407-13; *The Times* (17 Sept 1920), p. 11; fairly complete bibliography by A. Souter in *JTS* 22 (1921), pp. 193-205.

12. For a conservative and typically English treatment of this tradition, see Stephen Neill, *The Interpretation of the New Testament, 1861–1961* (Oxford: Oxford University Press, 2nd rev. edn., 1988 [1964]), pp. 35-64; and Kümmel, *The New Testament*, ch. 4.

13. See, for example, his review of *Contentio Veritas*, *JTS* 4 (1902), pp. 1-16; 'Theological Reconstruction at Cambridge', *JTS* 7 (1906), pp. 161-85; and 'The Cambridge Biblical Essays', *JTS* 11 (1910), pp. 161-79.

14. *The Life of Christ in Recent Research* (Oxford: Oxford University Press, 1907), p. 38. After his conversion to modernism, Sanday gave up this project, recognizing the impossibility of ever reaching definitive conclusions about Jesus.

15. *Effigies Mea* (BOD MS Eng. misc. d. 128 no. 380).

Even an admirer like Hensley Henson, the future bishop of Durham, commented on his modesty, regarding him as

> a scrupulously fair man, and, in order to make sure he was doing full justice to his opponents, he read everything that he could lay his hands on… Thus he dissipated his energies on the work of inferior men, and subordinated his own incomparably superior intelligence to theirs.[16]

His reputation for humility meant that he was highly regarded as a teacher, who was prepared to listen to even the most lowly student.[17] This situation could, however, sometimes work as something of a two-edged sword, as the Anglo-Catholic controversialist, T.A. Lacey, (whose work will be discussed in detail below), commented:

> Dr. Sanday is Socratic: he spends his time in thinking aloud, or in conversing with those whom he likes to think his equals. He mounts his Chair, and proceeds to elicit information from his hearers… Dr. Sanday puts out from his Chair questions which he has not been able to answer, gently desiring the help of the more fortunate. The effect is usually to make the interrogated feel small.[18]

As will become clear in Chapter 5, however, it was precisely his caution and his Socratic manner of working that eventually led him to a position far more radical than even the most liberal scholars. Sanday secretly announced his conversion to the 'Modernist cause' in 1912,[19] which created something of a scandal in Oxford. As Sanday confessed to his German friend, Friedrich Loofs on 3 May 1913, 'I got into some little trouble with friends who are not prepared to go along with me'.[20]

---

16. *Retrospect of an Unimportant Life*, II (2 vols.; London: Oxford University Press, 1942), p. 50.

17. Sanday was one of the first Professors in England to organize a seminar, in which B.H. Streeter was a prominent member, and which led to influential collaborative efforts, most importantly B.H. Streeter (ed.), *Studies in the Synoptic Problem* (Oxford: Clarendon Press, 1911). Cf. A.C. Headlam, *The Life and Teaching of Jesus Christ* (London: John Murray, 1923), pp. 5-6.

18. Cited in G.L. Prestige, *The Life of Charles Gore* (London: Heinemann, 1935), p. 347.

19. Sanday announced his conversion at a meeting of the Theological Dinner in 1912. Cf. G.L. Prestige, *The Life of Charles Gore*, p. 347. His opinions circulated in printed form in the 'private and confidential' *Theses on the Biblical Miracles* of 1913. I have discussed Sanday's modernism in 'The Socratic Subversion of Tradition: William Sanday and Theology, 1900–1920', *JTS* 45 (1994), pp. 94-116.

20. BOD MS Eng. misc. d. 128 no. 110. Friedrich Loofs (1858–1928) was from

Perhaps Sanday's major contribution to English scholarship was in digesting the massive output of New Testament as well as much other theological work from Germany (even though like most English theologians of his day he distrusted most of its findings). Throughout his life he maintained close personal links with German theologians, especially Ernst von Dobschütz[21] and Friedrich Loofs, two figures who like himself stood between the theological camps of traditionalism and 'modernism'. Paul Wernle, professor in Basel, spoke of Sanday's 'astonishing knowledge' of German literature[22] and C.H. Turner, in his obituary, remarked that Sanday read practically everything published in Germany and was 'wont to lament that Englishmen produced so much less that was conceived on an encyclopaedic scale as did the Germans'. His bound pamphlets, which he presented to Queen's College, Oxford, number 900 volumes, and as well as these, there are numerous other German texts from Sanday's collection scattered in other Oxford Libraries including Trinity College, and Pusey House.[23] During the First World War Sanday assumed the rather unlikely[24] role of mediator between English and German academics and managed to maintain personal relations with his friends in Germany.[25]

Sanday's method is well exemplified in his work on the life of Christ which seems to have originated in the commission from James Hastings

---

1888 Ordinary Professor of Church History in Halle and co-founded *Die Christliche Welt*, the Ritschlian Church newspaper (1886). He stood very much between the opposing camps, always claiming an allegiance to Ritschlianism, not having been grasped by the 'new metaphysical and mystical wave' (*RGG*, IV, col. 448). There are letters dating from 1899–1920 in Sanday's correspondence.

21. Sanday's correspondence with von Dobschütz dates from 1907. Most of von Dobschütz's letters are written in (an often contorted) English.

22. Review of Sanday, *Life of Christ*, *TLZ* 34 (1909), cols. 98-101 (98).

23. For a brief discussion of Sanday and German scholarship see Morgan, 'Historical Criticism and Christology', pp. 88-94.

24. Sanday was an 'ardent student of military history, and a member of the Oxford Krieg Spiel Club, where his military combinations often overpowered his more professional opponents, and when the war came his interest in it was great' (*The Times*, 17 Sept. 1920, p. 11).

25. On this see Mark D. Chapman, 'The Sanday, Sherrington and Troeltsch Affair: Theological Relations between England and Germany after the First World War', *Mitteilungen der Ernst Troeltsch Gesellschaft* 6 (1991), pp. 40-71; and 'Anglo-German Theological Relations during the First World War', *Zeitschrift für neuere Theologiegeschichte* 7 (2000), pp. 109-26.

to write articles on 'God (in New Testament)' and 'Jesus Christ' for his *Dictionary of the Bible* (T. & T. Clark, 1898). For these Sanday turned to the vast literature from Germany, which he weighed from his distinctively Anglican viewpoint, placing great emphasis on the Church tradition (such as the historical reliability of the Fourth Gospel).[26] In the appendix to the reprint of the article on Jesus, where he discusses the state of historical Jesus research in 1903, Sanday suggested that

> the critics of whom I have been speaking seem to me to be in too great haste to rationalize the Gospel history... I have always considered the ideal temper to be one that renders to Caesar the things that are Caesar's and to God the things that are God's; in other words, that gives to criticism all that properly belongs to it, and yet leaves room for the full impression of that which is Divine.[27]

It was from such a cautious background that Sanday approached Harnack's *Das Wesen des Christentums*.

Sanday and Harnack

He discussed the book at length in a paper he read to the Oxford Tutors Association on 24 October 1901 which shows a knowledge of the whole range of the German debate.[28] He claims to have written his paper

> in the hope that it may contribute a little to the settlement of opinion at a time when it is exposed to some disturbing influences. Harnack's book is but a sample—perhaps the best, in any case a brilliant sample—of a particular form of the critical movement that is most conspicuous in Germany, but by no means unrepresented among ourselves. In it the questions at issue stand out with great distinctness; and the opportunity seems a good one for taking our bearings in regard to them as well as we can.[29]

Though Sanday recognized that Harnack was trying to reach the 'living realities of religion'[30] typical of the Ritschlian school, he had nevertheless been far too willing to leave the New Testament as a whole out of account, unduly restricting his discussion to the synoptic Gospels. Thus

26. Cf. Sanday, *Criticism of the Fourth Gospel* (Oxford: Clarendon Press, 1905).
27. Sanday, *Outlines of the Life of Christ* (Edinburgh: T. & T. Clark, 2nd rev edn, 1905 [1906]), pp. 248-49.
28. Sanday, *An Examination of Harnack's 'What is Christianity?'* (London: Longmans, 1901).
29. Sanday, *An Examination*, p. 1.
30. Sanday, *An Examination*, p. 3.

'[w]hat he offered was a "reduced" Christianity—I think myself unduly reduced'.[31] Although Sanday agreed with Harnack that the most important question to be addressed by New Testament scholars was, 'What think ye of Christ?', he did not consider it possible to answer this 'by considering only His teaching, and stopping short of the interpretation which is given to His teaching by His followers'.[32] Indeed, according to Sanday, it was impossible to have a 'Christian life without a Christology'.[33] Paul and John were thus essential elements in any account of the New Testament.

Neglect of the remainder of the New Testament led Harnack to underestimate what Sanday calls Jesus' 'force', something which had no parallel in other religions, and which could only be grasped from a study of the whole New Testament. This meant that the apostolic age simply had to be taken into account in the study of Christian origins, since its roots 'stuck deep down into the original soil' of the period of Christ.[34] Arguing from a typically conservative Anglican standpoint, Sanday claimed that Harnack had underestimated the antiquity of his sources, which meant that his success depended far more on 'his command of the materials, his extraordinary energy and power of production' rather than 'the correctness of his results'.[35] Thus what was wrong with German scholarship, Sanday claimed, was its extreme one-sidedness which was all too willing to cast off long cherished traditions as well as any proper ecclesiology:

> It would ill become me to speak in any but terms of deep respect of the Protestantism of Germany. It is without doubt the most learned of all the confessions, and there is probably no confession that is marked by finer spirit of intellectual sincerity. And yet in my heart of hearts I have no doubt that on the whole side of corporate and external religion the conception that prevails in those circles with which I am most acquainted (the literary and professorial) is defective.[36]

Sanday is thus highly critical of Harnack's individualization of the Gospel.[37] To reduce the Gospel purely to a matter of the individual was

---

31. Sanday, *An Examination*, p. 6.
32. Sanday, *An Examination*, p. 7.
33. Sanday, *An Examination*, p. 13. Cf. pp. 16-17.
34. Sanday, *An Examination*, p. 23.
35. Sanday, *An Examination*, p. 25.
36. Sanday, *An Examination*, p. 26.
37. Sanday, *An Examination*, pp. 25-26.

to remove something essential. Simply because the ecclesiological dimension of religion had been so easily open to abuse, Sanday maintained, this did not necessarily mean that it was redundant.[38] Indeed Harnack had been all too ready to throw out the baby with the bathwater, when the real task of theology was to try to make the church worthier of its calling.[39] Similarly, for Sanday, dogmas, the church and worship were not simply to be considered as constraints on the true religion, but rather had the potential to become instruments of liberation. For Sanday, then, the role of the church was paramount: 'Without church, no organisation; without organisation, no consciousness of unity, no enterprise and powerful action'.[40] He concludes with a statement that bears more than a passing resemblance to his later position (and which betrays a position of extreme relativism):

> All doctrine is relative—relative in the first instance to the age in which it was drawn up, and relative at all times to the limitations of our human faculties at that which is infinite and divine. All doctrine is relative.[41]

At this stage, however, Sanday, representing typical English conservatism, was nevertheless willing to claim that, even though doctrine might be relative, 'we have the faith that the church has been guided aright. A really patient and sympathetic study of the process by which doctrine has been formed will, I think, give us sufficient warrant for believing that it has been so guided'.[42] In short, what Harnack, who, according to Sanday, was 'not a bigoted writer', needed to do, was to 'cross-examine rather severely the assumptions' made on the three subjects of church, doctrine and worship.[43]

At this point in his career, Sanday's main problem with liberal theology lay in its failure to pay due attention both to the church, and to the supernatural element of religion. Indeed criticism, Sanday wrote in a discussion of the life of Jesus, was not to intrude on the 'things of God'—on 'Church, Doctrine and Worship', 'three things of which Harnack rarely speaks'.[44] Thus, against the sort of German criticism which resulted in a 'professorial religion which exists rather in the air,

---

38. Sanday, *An Examination*, p. 27.
39. Sanday, *An Examination*, p. 27.
40. Sanday, *An Examination*, p. 27.
41. Sanday, *An Examination*, p. 27.
42. Sanday, *An Examination*, p. 28.
43. Sanday, *An Examination*, p. 29.
44. Sanday, *Outlines of the Life of Christ*, p. 250.

in a religious Cloud-Cuckoo-Town',[45] Sanday was convinced that
'[the] true solution…is to be sought more on Church lines, *i.e.*, with
more regard for historical continuity, with a firmer faith that the Divine
guidance of the Church all these centuries has not been really, and even
fundamentally, wrong'.[46]

Sanday's critique of Harnack was mirrored by others. For instance
the Lady Margaret Reader in Divinity at Cambridge, A.J. Mason,
delivered a set of lectures in St Giles' Church, Cambridge, in October
1901, which, although praising Harnack for his 'intense moral earnest-
ness',[47] nevertheless considered his book to be littered with very great
defects. In the same vein as Sanday, Mason felt that neither St Paul nor
St John could simply be left out of the picture. Jesus' sayings in the
Synoptic Gospels were insufficient for a full picture of Christ, and it
consequently became clear, according to Mason, that 'you cannot help
feeling that they justify, that they require for their interpretation, all the
Johannine, the Pauline theology'.[48] For Mason, as for Sanday, it was
mystery that was of the essence in Christianity, and which was required
in all proper dogmatic theology. In turn, the church, which bore this
mystery in its sacramental life, proved necessary for the progress of
Christianity. It simply could not be left out of account:

> No-one who has a true idea of history will attempt to arrest the process in
> mid-development, and give a portrait of Christianity, which professes to
> depict the full-grown thing, derived exclusively from what we know of
> its immature condition. What would be thought of a historian who
> professed to give a critical account—let us say—of Sir Thomas More,
> but who refused to take into his reckoning anything which he wrote or
> did after the publication of the *Utopia*.[49]

Thus what was crucial for Christianity was the survival of the spirit of
Christ in the church and the sacraments, which simply could not be
divorced from any historical study. In short, Christianity was

> a life—a life of worship, a life of service, a life of obedience, a life of
> sanctity—because it is the life of Christ working itself out in the willing

45. Sanday, *Outlines of the Life of Christ*, p. 250.
46. Sanday, *Outlines of the Life of Christ*, p. 251. Cf. Sanday, *An Examination*,
p. 29.
47. A.J. Mason, *Christianity—What is it? Five Lectures on Dr Harnack's
'Wesen des Christentums'* (London: SPCK, 1902), pp. 10-11.
48. Mason, *Christianity*, p. 76.
49. Mason, *Christianity*, p. 107.

and active self-devotion of the believer—or in the converse but equally true form, it is the life of man endeavouring to put itself wholly under the influence and guidance of the Spirit of God and Christ.[50]

Although Sanday's and Mason's critiques of Harnack follow along somewhat predictable lines, both retaining, for instance, high regard for the historicity of the Fourth Gospel, there is nevertheless an element of continuity with Sanday's later work produced after he had begun to accept an eschatological understanding of the historical Jesus. From his discussion of Harnack it is clear that Sanday was convinced that neither the cultic, nor the mysterious, nor the supernatural could be separated from the essence of Christianity. Yet the problem remained as to how this element could be incorporated in a historical understanding of Jesus. In the years that followed it became increasingly clear that eschatological language provided an escape route from the failings of Harnack's system. In 1901, however, Sanday had no means of locating such mystery in the figure of Jesus, except perhaps by resorting to conservative and somewhat unconvincing interpretations of the New Testament. As will become clear, eschatology allowed mystery to be relocated in the very figure of Jesus himself, which meant that Jesus and the Church were once again to be united in a sincerely held historical position.

The Abbé Loisy[51]

Perhaps the most influential criticism of Harnack, however, came not from England or Germany, but from the French Roman Catholic Modernist, A.F. Loisy, whose influence, like Harnack's, quickly spread

---

50. Mason, *Christianity*, p. 127.

51. Alfred Firmin Loisy (1857–1940) was Professor of Sacred Scripture at the Institut Catholique from 1880 but was dismissed for his controversial views in 1883. His *L'evangile et L'eglise* (Bellevue: Chez L'Auteur, 1902) was perhaps the most notorious work in the development of Modernism, and it was denounced by the Archbishop of Paris soon after publication. Modernism was eventually condemned in 1907 as the 'synthesis of all heresies'. Loisy was finally excommunicated in 1908. From 1909 until 1930 he was Professor at the Collège de France. For discussions in English see Alec Vidler, *The Modernist Movement in the Roman Catholic Church: Its Origins and Outcome* (Cambridge: Cambridge University Press, 1934), part II; and Gabriel Daly, O.S.A., *Transcendence and Immanence: A Study of Catholic Modernism and Integralism* (Oxford: Clarendon Press, 1980), chs. 3 and 4.

beyond his native country. Indeed, Hastings Rashdall,[52] one of the leading representatives of the more liberal protestant strand of Anglican theology, remarked in 1904, that '[t]here are probably two, and two only, continental theologians [Loisy and Harnack] whose names at least are known to the average educated man who reads the newspapers and sometimes glances at a magazine'.[53] Loisy offered a similar (though rather more searching) criticism of Harnack to Sanday, but with an important difference: instead of accepting the broad picture of the Jesus of the Synoptics presented by Harnack (which had not been disputed by Sanday) and then going on to call for the need for the Pauline and Johannine corpus to be taken into account, Loisy, although emphasizing the need for the church to supplement Jesus' witness, painted a very different picture of Jesus. Influenced to some extent by Johannes Weiss[54] (who will be discussed in detail in the next chapter),

52. Hastings Rashdall (1858–1924) was born in Worthing, Sussex, and after schooling at Harrow, studied at New College, Oxford. He was elected to a Fellowship there in 1895, staying until 1910 when he became a Canon of Hereford, dividing his time between there and Oxford. In 1917 until his death he was Dean of Carlisle. As the 'Socrates of Cornmarket' Rashdall, an extraordinary polymath, was one of the leading liberal theologians of his time. See P.E. Matheson, *The Life of Hastings Rashdall D.D.* (London: Oxford University Press, 1928); and Jane Garnett, 'Hastings Rashdall and the Renewal of Christian Social Ethics, c. 1890–1920', in Jane Garnett and H.C.G. Matthew (eds.), *Revival and Religion Since 1700: Essays for John Walsh* (London: Hambledon Press, 1993), pp. 297-316. There are fairly comprehensive bibliographies compiled by Margaret Marsh, *Hastings Rashdall: Bibliography of the Published Writings* (Leysters: Modern Churchpeople's Union, 1993); and Mark D. Chapman, 'Rashdall, Hastings', in F.W. Bautz and T. Bautz (eds.), *Biographisch-Bibliographisches Kirchenlexikon*, VI (Herzberg: Bautz, 1994), cols. 1368-1373.

53. 'Harnack and Loisy', in *Principles and Precepts* [Oxford: Basil Blackwell, 1927], pp. 228-36, here p. 228.

54. There is little doubting that Loisy was influenced by the picture of Jesus drawn by Johannes Weiss, even if, as Daly maintains, he had 'played down his basic debt to, and agreement with, Weiss's consistent eschatology' (*Transcendence and Immanence*, p. 56). The review of Loisy by the French Protestant Gabriel Monod (in A.F. Loisy, *Autour d'un petit livre* [Paris: Alphonse Picard, 1903], pp. 287-90), emphasizes the importance of an eschatological interpretation of the historical Jesus in Loisy's work. On the relationship between Weiss and Loisy, see esp. F. Heiler, *Der Vater des katholischen Modernismus, A. Loisy* (Munich: Erasmus, 1947), pp. 44-45; D. Hoffmann-Axtheim, 'Loisys L'évangile et l'église: Besichtigung eines zeitgenössischen Schlachtfeldes', *ZTK* 65 (1968), pp. 291-328, esp. p. 297. Unlike most of his Anglican contemporaries Loisy was highly sceptical

Loisy maintained, in *L'évangile et l'église*,[55] that the message of the Kingdom of God preached by the Jesus of the synoptics was thoroughly eschatological in tone and was dominated by apocalyptic:

> [I]t cannot be too often repeated that Jesus only announced [the moral revolution] in the kingdom about to come, and He did not represent it as a work of slow progress... The message of Jesus is contained in the announcement of the approaching kingdom, and the exhortation to penitence as a means of sharing therein. All else, though it is the common preoccupation of humanity, is as though non-existent.[56]

Loisy's book was an immediate bestseller, selling 1500 copies in the month after its publication on 10 November 1902.[57]

Attacking Harnack, Loisy claimed that the essence of the Gospel was not to be located in the ethical teaching of Christ embodied in the universal 'brotherhood' but was instead to be seen in the hope incarnate in the proclamation: the Kingdom was 'nothing but a great hope, and it is in this hope or nowhere that the historian should set the essence of the Gospel, as no other idea holds so prominent and so large a place in the teaching of Jesus'.[58] This great hope could simply not be reduced to the individualistic pietism of Harnack's Gospel.[59] Instead

of John's Gospel, which led in part to his final excommunication (see *Le quatrième évangile* [Paris: E. Nourry, 1903]).

55. Loisy, *L'évangile et l'église* (Bellevue: Chez L'Auteur, 1902). References are to the English translation, *The Gospel and the Church* (London: Isbister, 1903).

56. Loisy, *The Gospel and the Church*, pp. 85-86. On Loisy's understanding of early Christianity, see esp., Alan H. Jones, *Independence and Exegesis: The Study of Early Christianity in the Work of Alfred Loisy (1857–1940), Charles Guignebert (1857–1939) and Maurice Goguel (1880–1955)* (Beiträge zur Geschichte der biblischen Exegese, 26; Tübingen: J.C.B. Mohr, 1983).

57. See Francesco Turrani, *The Condemnation of Alfred Loisy and the Historical Method* (Uomini e Dottrine, 24; Rome: Edizioni di Storia e Letteratura, 1979).

58. Loisy, *The Gospel and the Church*, p. 59.

59. Cf. Loisy, *The Gospel and the Church*, p. 109. For a comparison of Loisy and Harnack, see Jan Hulshof, *Wahrheit und Geschichte* (Essen: Ludgerus Verlag, 1973), pp. 85-87. Harnack's own review of Loisy, *L'évangile et l'église*, was published in *TLZ* 30 (1904), cols. 59-60. Although recognizing that Loisy had a 'distinguished mind' he felt that he placed too much emphasis on the church and because of this it was 'less necessary for him than for us to arrive as a definitive judgement on the primitive form of the Christian religion and its nature. He is, in this respect, more resigned to scepticism than a Protestant could be. Unconsciously, to make up the deficit which could result from historical investigation he counts on

the future formed the kernel of the message and simply could not be discarded as part of the husk. And, for Loisy, it was this future that was preserved through the centuries in the teaching of the church as it proclaimed the message of the coming Kingdom. Indeed

> to reproach the Catholic Church for the development of the constitution is to reproach her for having chosen to live, and that, moreover, when her life was indispensable for the preservation of the Gospel itself. There is nowhere in her history any gap of continuity, or the absolute creation of a new system.[60]

Yet as the church changed through the centuries, so naturally her teachings developed in their own way in that process of keeping alive the message of the coming Kingdom. The religion of Jesus was a distant memory:

> To be identical with the religion of Jesus, it has no more need to reproduce exactly the forms of the Galilean gospel, than a man has need to preserve at fifty the proportions, features, and manner of life of the day of his birth, in order to be the same individual. The identity of a man is not ensured by making him return to his cradle.[61]

In turn, dogmas were ways of keeping alive the message, rather than truths 'fallen from heaven'.[62] They were flexible, adaptable and open to increased perfectibility.[63] Similarly, it was quite impossible to suppose that ritual was a dispensable part of Christianity since 'history knows no instance of a religion without a ritual',[64] yet ritual too was something dynamic: 'Jesus no more decided the form of Christian worship beforehand than He laid down the constitution of the Church'.[65] The great task of the present, then, was to adapt dogma and ritual to the modern world, even if, as Loisy admits, his book had not sought to achieve this.[66]

Although Loisy had little interest in defending the official curial catholicism with its revitalized mediaevalism, he did not deliberately

---

the church, that has been, that is and that is to come'. Loisy replied in *Revue Critique* 7 (1906), p. 66.

60. Loisy, *The Gospel and the Church*, p. 165.
61. Loisy, *The Gospel and the Church*, p. 170.
62. Loisy, *The Gospel and the Church*, p. 210.
63. Loisy, *The Gospel and the Church*, p. 166.
64. Loisy, *The Gospel and the Church*, p. 226.
65. Loisy, *The Gospel and the Church*, p. 230.
66. Loisy, *The Gospel and the Church*, p. 277.

set out to criticize his own church. Instead he saw his task as

> tactfully to instruct the Catholic clergy about the real situation of Christian origins, while at the same time demonstrating against Protestant criticism that this situation was far from making a defence of Catholicism impossible—, that, on the contrary, the Church could now be seen as a necessary and legitimate development of the Gospel and that what was rationally untenable was a position of Liberal Protestantism with its supposed essence of Christianity.[67]

What proved controversial for the hierarchy, however, rested not primarily with Loisy's defence of the church, but with his separation of the message of the church from the original message preached by Jesus, which he understood as completely rooted in its Jewish milieu. Thus, fighting Harnack on his own ground, he insisted:

> The historian must resist the temptation to modernize the conception of the kingdom. If the theologian feels bound to supply an interpretation for the needs of the present day, no one will contest his right, provided he does not confuse his commentary with the primitive meanings of the gospel texts; and while this is true for the conception of the kingdom, it is also true for the appreciation of the relations of the gospel to the different aspects of human life.[68]

This meant that to see the essence of Christianity solely in the Synoptic witness was unnecessarily to restrict Christianity. As Loisy claims with rhetorical flourish:

> It is a pitiful philosophy that attempts to fix the absolute in any scrap of human activity, intellectual or moral. The full life of the gospel is not in a solitary element of the doctrine of Jesus, but in the totality of its manifestation which starts from the personal ministry of Christ, and its development in the history of Christianity. All that has entered into the gospel of Jesus has entered into Christian tradition. The truly evangelical part of Christianity to-day, is not that which has never changed, for, in a

---

67. Introduction to the fifth French edition (*L'évangile et l'église*, Paris: Nourry, 1929) cited in Alec Vidler, *Twentieth Century Defenders of the Faith* (London: SCM Press, 1965), p. 40. In his *Autour d'un petit livre* which he wrote to defend *L'évangile et l'église*, Loisy claims that it was a very catholic book (p. 208). For an interesting account of his own thoughts on the circumstances surrounding publication, see his *Choses passées* (Paris: Emile Nourry, 1913), pp. 247-56 and *Mémoires pour servir à l'histoire religieuse de notre temps*. II. *1900–1908* (Paris: Emile Nourry, 1931). By 16 December 1903, five of Loisy's books including *L'évangile et l'église* and *Auteur d'un petit Livre* were on the Index.

68. Loisy, *The Gospel and the Church*, p. 73.

sense, all has changed and has never ceased to change, but that which in spite of all external changes proceeds from the impulse given by Christ, and is inspired by His Spirit, serves the same ideal and the same hope.[69]

Loisy thus discerned (in the language of the next generation) a significant breach between Jesus and the Kerygma, and it is in this sense that *L'évangile et L'église* 'can be said to mark the disappearance of the "liberal" conception of Jesus'.[70]

Loisy and English Interpretation

Among English scholars, Loisy's critique of liberal pictures of Christ made some impact both among those who had little sympathy with German liberal Protestantism, as well as those who aligned themselves closely to Harnack.[71] Although it would be far from true to say that Loisy exerted any profound influence on the development of English theology, there is nevertheless a case to be made for suggesting that his particular interpretation prepared the ground for the eschatological bombshell that was cast in Schweitzer's *Von Reimarus zu Wrede* (which will be discussed in the next Chapter). Some hints which suggest the future course of theology can be glimpsed in Loisy's English critics.

Hastings Rashdall, in his expository sermon on Harnack and Loisy, links Loisy's theology to his Roman Catholicism, seeing its vital connection with the 'heart and conscience and life' in stark contrast to the Lutheran churches of Germany.[72] Offering his own responses to Harnack and Loisy, Rashdall suggests that there is much to be learnt from them both:

> You will find Harnack, as well as some of the more constructive members of that school, I think, both in regard to matters of pure criticism and in point of spiritual insight, better guides than Loisy as to what Jesus actually taught and did, and was—and to what he ought to be to us now.[73]

69. Loisy, *The Gospel and the Church*, p. 117

70. L. Salvatorelli, 'From Locke to Reitzenstein: The Historical Investigation of the Origins of Christianity', *HTR* 22 (1929), pp. 263-367, here p. 340.

71. On the English responses to Loisy, see Alec Vidler, *A Variety of Catholic Modernists* (Cambridge: Cambridge University Press, 1970), pp. 153-90. As well as the reviews discussed below there was a review by Algernon Cecil which appeared in *The Oxford Magazine: Literary Supplement*, 25 May 1904.

72. Rashdall, 'Harnack and Loisy', p. 231.

73. Rashdall, 'Harnack and Loisy', p. 232.

Nevertheless Harnack's reduction of the Gospel to the Synoptic tradition could not be understood as the whole of Christianity. Any full account of Christianity required, if not the historical church, then at least some form of metaphysics. Loisy was here to be preferred since 'his view of Christianity is far more philosophical'.[74] In turn, the principle of development—and for Rashdall that meant correction of false doctrine—was necessary in any historical expression of Christianity. Consequently he suggests that '[t]he words which are due to the working of Christ's spirit in the hearts of His first followers are hardly second in importance to those he uttered himself'.[75] In short, he concluded:

> The Christian Creed has two aspects. Every version of Christianity is imperfect and one-sided which fails to recognise both of them—the unique importance and supremacy of the historic Christ, the ever-present progressive work of the Spirit in the Church and in the world.[76]

Though highly critical of 'Catholicism' (which at the time conjured up for him a picture of 'Gore and the persecutionists'),[77] Rashdall nevertheless pointed to the need for a living spirit in the church. The anti-metaphysical thrust which dominated the Ritschlian school (which was upheld with ever greater vigour by Harnack and Wilhelm Herrmann), could not adequately contain the strongly idealist strain of Rashdall's thought. It is, however, not clear that Rashdall's 'philosophical' reading of Loisy is adequate. Loisy does not seem to have been as sympathetic to metaphysics as Rashdall: indeed a philosophy of life, which was shared by most of the Modernists, is a deliberate attack on systems of metaphysics.

From the more conservative strand of Oxford theology, William Sanday wrote an article on Loisy in *The Pilot*[78] which, though sympathetic, was typically judicious in tone:

---

74. Rashdall, 'Harnack and Loisy', p. 233.
75. Rashdall, 'Harnack and Loisy', p. 235.
76. Rashdall, 'Harnack and Loisy', p. 236.
77. Rashdall to Lilley, 18 June 1905, cited in Vidler, *A Variety of Catholic Modernists*, p. 182.
78. William Sanday, 'An Anglican View of M. Loisy', *The Pilot* (23 Jan. 1904), pp. 84-85. Although Sanday is typically cautious in his estimate of Loisy, he again unwittingly betrays his later position: 'Every presentation of truth in human forms and in human language is of necessity relative' (p. 85).

Many of us in the Church of England have been following with deep
interest and sympathy the fortunes of M. Loisy.[79] Neither the interest nor
the sympathy have been wholly personal. Of course, I need not say that
the Abbé Loisy himself is an attractive and even more than attractive
figure.[80]

Indeed, according to Sanday, Loisy had managed to precipitate a crisis,
which had not yet affected the Church of England to anything like the
same degree:

79.   Loisy remained in close contact with English theologians throughout his life,
and his name was frequently brought up in conversation. For instance, von Hügel
had written to Sanday on 1 Aug. 1896 asking him to defend and to publish Loisy
(BOD MS Eng. misc. d. 123 (2) no. 612). Loisy's *Mémoires* are full of references to
English supporters—at one point he refers to Burkitt as 'Le brave Burkitt' (II, p.
413). He was suggested as a possible speaker at the Oxford 1908 Summer School
for Theology, although eventually he was not invited (Webb Diaries, 13 Dec. 1908,
BOD MS Eng. misc. e. 1154). On 14 Dec. 1908 another entry records a letter from
von Hügel who 'wishes his part in inviting Loisy [be] kept confidential—owing to
his passionate desire not, without necessity, to be deprived of the sacraments of his
church' (von Hügel's letter is printed in Michael de la Bedoyère, *The Life of Baron
von Hügel* [London: J.M. Dent, 1951], p. 214). Webb spoke with S.R. Driver and
Sanday about Loisy, communicating von Hügel's wish that the invitation should
come from them. On 20 Dec. he wrote to von Hügel (St Andrew's University
Library, MS 3179):

> The executive committee of the theological lecture scheme met on Friday. I did not
> show your letter to any one, but informed them of the points it contained and told them
> that you wished your part in it considered confidential. This they quite understood to be
> natural. I spoke in a similar way to Sanday and Driver, whom I met independently.
>   It was thought best, in view of what you said, to postpone inviting Loisy until the
> result of his candidature for Jean Revell's chair should be announced. But in case he
> should be eventually invited, I should like to ask you how far you could accept
> Rashdall, [R.H.] Charles or A.J. Carlyle as Anglicans whose share in the invitation
> would carry off the participation of Carpenter and the Hibbert trustees? There may be
> difficulty otherwise in raising *four* names. The number of people actually co-operating
> in the scheme here is not large. Sanday has promised me that he would sign an
> invitation. Driver, though favourable to it being sent, would not, on the ground that L.
> has passed from O.T. to N.T. and that D. would perhaps be thought to be trespassing
> outside his own province in inviting him. It seems to me an odd point of view in some
> ways but that is his decision. I have no doubt that Rashdall and Carlyle [Rector of the
> City Church at Oxford and joint author of the political theories of the Middles Ages]
> would sign and probably also Charles, whom you know: but I do not know whether a
> quartette of Anglican clerics could otherwise be made up.

80.   Sanday, 'An Anglican View of M. Loisy', p. 84.

> In this one decade, and largely through the work of this one man, the
> Church of Rome seems to have caught and even in some ways passed us.
> For I look upon it that in his main object M. Loisy has practically
> succeeded. The cause of freedom within limits, is substantially won. It is
> not likely that the shadow on the dial will ever go seriously backward.[81]

Sanday agreed with most of Loisy's points, although at the time he still
retained a high view of the historicity of the Fourth Gospel. Such a conservative position prompted A.L. Lilley, vicar of St Mary's, Paddington
Green, London and a friend of several Catholic Modernist writers, to
write a letter in defence of Loisy's method, which was published in the
next edition of *The Pilot*:

> M. Loisy is a radical historical critic, but he can afford to be one because
> of the wide sweep and the boldness of his theological outlook, because
> of the freedom of his faith from dependence on past habits of thought.[82]

On receiving a copy of this letter, Loisy wrote to Lilley: 'Your reply to
the Rev. Sanday's article is excellent. I do not see how these half-
critical conservatives can maintain their position. It seems to me that
they adopt a lofty tone, which does not remedy the fragility of their
arguments'.[83] Within a few years Sanday had come to agree with this
diagnosis.

Probably the most important discussion of Loisy, however, came
from the perhaps unlikely source of T.A. Lacey,[84] whose chief contribution to theology hitherto had been in the Anglican orders controversy
which had occupied Anglo-Catholics in the 1890s. However, the year
after penning the solidly Anglo-Catholic hymn, 'O Faith of England
taught of Old',[85] he published in 1904 an essay on *Harnack and Loisy*,

---

81. Sanday, 'An Anglican View of M. Loisy', p. 84.

82. A.L. Lilley, letter, in *The Pilot* (30 Jan 1904), p. 117.

83. Loisy to Lilley, 14 Feb 1904, cited in Vidler, *A Variety of Catholic Modernists*, p. 184.

84. Thomas Alexander Lacey (1853–1931) was educated at Balliol College, Oxford becoming one of the most accomplished Latinists of his time. In the 1890s he wrote extensively (and usually in Latin) on Anglican orders, visiting Rome in 1896. He was on the editorial staff of the *Church Times*, and wrote many leading articles during his time (1903–18) as chaplain and later warden of the London Diocesan Penitentiary at Highgate. He was appointed to a canonry at Worcester in 1918.

85. *English Hymnal*, no. 544. Lacey was on the editorial board of the English Hymnal translating twelve Latin hymns for the collection.

with an Introductory Letter by the Right Honourable Viscount Halifax, which had originally been read 'before certain members of the University of Oxford on Friday, November 27, 1903'.[86] George Tyrrell, the leading Modernist working in England at the time, wrote to A.L. Lilley, expressing his surprise, given its authorship, at the stance of the pamphlet: 'Lacey's "Harnack and Loisy" looks, at first glance, more liberal and sympathetic than I had expected from one whom I associated with dreary controversies about "orders" '.[87]

In his introductory letter, Lord Halifax, the leading Anglo-Catholic layman of the time, remarked that although '[w]e may distrust his methods, we may reject on critical grounds his conclusions,...the Abbé Loisy denies no article of faith'. Harnack, on the other hand, '...denies the central doctrine of Christianity. The criticism of the Abbé Loisy is, no doubt, destructive of Protestantism, but is that a reason why he should be condemned by the church?'[88] Indeed, to condemn Loisy was to repeat the error of Galileo, which would be little short of a 'blunder' that would 'injure religion at large'.[89] After this provocative introduction from an influential figure, Lacey's paper itself is more guarded. He defends Loisy not chiefly for his views on the character of the historical Jesus, but for his attacks on liberal protestantism, a theological position which, like Loisy, Lacey saw as excessively reductionist, and which placed undue weight on such a small number of events. Thus, while

---

86. T.A. Lacey, *Harnack and Loisy, with an Introductory Letter by the Right Honourable Viscount Halifax* (London: Longmans, 1904). In a leader of 15 Jan. 1904, 'On the Case of the Abbé Loisy', written by Lacey, the *Church Times* had called for unbridled biblical criticism. This was published in *Wayfarer's Essays* (London: Oxford University Press, 1934), pp. 141-45. On the reception of Loisy's Modernism in Anglo-Catholic theology, see Vidler, *The Modernist Movement*, pp. 234-69. Because of his work on Anglican orders, Lacey was known in Rome. Lord Halifax had sent his writings to Genocchi (Turrani, *The Condemnation of Alfred Loisy*, p. 129).

87. Tyrrell to Lilley, 15 Jan. 1904, cited in Vidler, *A Variety of Catholic Modernists*, p. 178.

88. Halifax, introductory letter in T.A. Lacey, *Harnack and Loisy*, p. 4.

89. Halifax, introductory letter in T.A. Lacey, *Harnack and Loisy*, p. 7. There were many other defenders active in the English churches in 1904. For instance, in *The Guardian* of 2 March 1904, a 'Roman Catholic layman' wrote: 'The fight of "Loisy and Co." in the Roman Catholic Church is primarily a fight for faith against those who seek to make it impossible, except under those scholastic categories which are rationalistic without being reasonable' (p. 383).

admitting that Harnack had produced an apologetics 'of the noblest type',[90] he nevertheless regarded him as hopelessly restrictive.

What impressed Lacey about Loisy, on the other hand, was his emphasis on the totality of the picture of Christ:

> He sees him proclaiming the kingdom of righteousness and love, to be established on the near coming of the Christ, not by any means at first proclaiming himself as the Christ... after his death he is openly declared by his disciples to be himself the Christ.[91]

In this way Christianity proves to be 'une grande espérance', 'the perfect ideal subsisting always in hope. This attempted realisation, more or less approximating to the ideal, is the Catholic Church'.[92] A move away from a narrow fixation on the Jesus of the synoptics (who on Harnack's account had been 'promulgating one great thought forever unchanged'[93]), allowed Jesus to be viewed far more as one capable of gathering up ideas and developing them, and in turn 'leaving them to be fruitful of immense developments'.[94]

The role of the Church as it developed this dynamic message, according to Lacey, was thus included in the heart of Christianity:

> if [Jesus] be accepted as the Christ he is to be understood in relation to the future; his particular environment is of secondary importance; his persistent influence, the assemblage of forces gathered up in him, and the impulse which he transmitted—it is with these that we are concerned.[95]

Thus Lacey separates the 'static' picture of Christ in his pre-resurrection form from the 'dynamic' Christ who existed afterwards: the synoptics, he suggests, point to the 'physionomie historique' whereas the Pauline and Johannine witnesses express the dynamic truth.

At this point, however, Lacey acknowledges that Loisy had gone too far in separating these two different aspects of the New Testament. His

90. Lacey, *Harnack and Loisy*, p. 9.

91. Lacey, *Harnack and Loisy*, p. 10. In a devotional article, 'The Parousia and the Passion', published on 16 April 1908 in the *Church Times*, Lacey remarked that Jesus could not have foreseen his own moment of death. He suffered a 'truly human bewilderment... We must not imagine death robbed of any of its terrors for Him; and the greatest terror of death is the uncertainty in which the passing of the soul is wrapped' (p. 531).

92. Lacey, *Harnack and Loisy*, p. 10.

93. Lacey, *Harnack and Loisy*, p. 11.

94. Lacey, *Harnack and Loisy*, p. 11.

95. Lacey, *Harnack and Loisy*, p. 12.

refusal to accept the historicity of at least parts of John, and his dismissal of any mysticism in Jesus' original message were, according to Lacey, as much a product of his own religious sentiment as of serious historical scholarship:

> In his conscientious endeavour to abstract everything that savours of the French ecclesiastic, [Loisy] approximates perhaps rather too closely to the French layman of the pious unlettered sort: even as Harnack by means of a corresponding abstraction arrives at something very like a pietist of Halle.[96]

With a perhaps surprising awareness of the eisegesis present in even the most outwardly neutral presentations of Jesus, Lacey asks 'whether any modern European mind can be trusted to depict those lineaments' except possibly a Jew.[97]

Despite this criticism, however, Lacey still regards Loisy as significant in showing the importance of the dynamic presentation of Christ, which is capable of seeing the germ of the future development of Catholicism, the 'Christ of Chalcedon, the Christ of our altars',[98] as present in the Jesus of the New Testament. Indeed, for Lacey, this is the 'historic Christ' of our faith. Although he admits that it requires a connection with Jesus of Nazareth, he nevertheless regards this only as a starting point 'from which faith soars high'.[99] '[T]heology', he claims, 'goes far afield, but begins with Jesus of Nazareth and the historic Christ'.[100] Thus 'history and theology cannot be kept so rigorously apart as M. Loisy desires... [I]t is impossible to shut out entirely the consideration that he whose lineaments are being traced is the king of Glory'.[101] Nevertheless, Lacey goes on, this 'should not be allowed to colour the glasses through which the historical records are examined'.[102] In short, he suggests, 'I must not try to show those features of the record by accommodations drawn from theological sources'.[103]

This pamphlet provoked a lively debate, which, although limited in scope, is clearly reminiscent of the debates over eschatology which will

96. Lacey, *Harnack and Loisy*, p. 15.
97. Lacey, *Harnack and Loisy*, p. 15.
98. Lacey, *Harnack and Loisy*, p. 15.
99. Lacey, *Harnack and Loisy*, p. 16.
100. Lacey, *Harnack and Loisy*, p. 18.
101. Lacey, *Harnack and Loisy*, p. 16.
102. Lacey, *Harnack and Loisy*, p. 16.
103. Lacey, *Harnack and Loisy*, p. 17.

be described in detail in Chapter 5. In a somewhat surprising move, W.R. Inge,[104] at the time Fellow of Hertford College, Oxford, responded to Lacey (and Loisy) in a University Sermon preached at St Mary's, Oxford on the second Sunday in Lent, 1904.[105] This sermon, as Inge pointed out in the preface to the reprint, 'led to some correspondence in the *Guardian* and *Church Times*, in consequence of the allusion to a pamphlet by Mr. Lacey and Lord Halifax,... Mr. Lacey maintaining that the quotations in the sermon did not fairly represent his position'.[106] The main reason for dealing with Loisy in the sermon, Inge claimed, was on account of Halifax's sturdy attack on Loisy's condemnation. Coming from such an influential churchman, this bore witness to Loisy's growing influence in England, which Inge regarded as remarkably dangerous for liberal theology.

With the rhetorical grace that was already beginning to mark him out as one of the great preachers of his generation, Inge suggested that the real purpose of Loisy's book was to defend a doctrine of development which claimed that 'the genius of the Church is identified with the Holy Spirit of God, and Catholic tradition becomes Christ Himself, reincarnated in each generation within the historic church'.[107] For Inge, to make this spirit alive in the church the decisive factor at the heart of the Gospel, while at the same time separating it from the historical Jesus, was a gross abuse of the intellect: 'The plea of necessity neither justifies nor condemns a change of character. A Church must prove its moral and spiritual descent from the life and teaching of its Founder'.[108] However, Inge claimed, this was not the main thrust of the sermon. 'I do not wish to delay over Loisy's anti-German polemic, since the English Church is far from being content either with the individualism or with the truncated creed of professorial Protestantism.'[109]

A far more important problem in Loisy's theology, however, was,

104. William Ralph Inge (1860–1954). Fellow of Hertford College, Oxford (1889–1905); Lady Margaret Professor at Cambridge (1907–11); Dean of St Paul's, London (1911–34).

105. Published as 'Mr. Inge on Liberal Roman Catholicism', *The Guardian*, 9 March 1904, p. 424. Reprinted under the title of 'Liberal Catholicism', in *idem*, *Faith and Knowledge* (Edinburgh: T. & T. Clark, 1904), pp. 279-92. The sermon was also printed in the *Church Times* on 15 April 1904.

106. Inge, *Faith and Knowledge*, p. vi.

107. Inge, *Faith and Knowledge*, p. 283.

108. Inge, *Faith and Knowledge*, p. 285.

109. Inge, *Faith and Knowledge*, p. 285.

according to Inge, the total separation of faith from historical knowledge. Somewhat caricaturing Loisy's position, he questioned (with more than a hint of irony) the plausibility of a method which called for ' "[u]nhesitating assent" to the full divinity of this person of limited intelligence, this victim of Jewish patriotic dreams'.[110] Indeed, he went on, 'the writer almost revels in the clash of science and faith... The Liberal Catholic School acknowledges two Christs—the Christ of the Synoptic Gospels and the Christ of faith'. And given that the historical Jesus was to be confined by his age, this meant that the Christ of faith is the Christ in the Church, 'the Gnostic *Aeon Ecclesia* invested with Divine attributes'.[111]

Misquoting Lacey's pamphlet, Inge then asks what is left of the historical Jesus. 'He is, we are told, dynamically the Christ of Chalcedon and (I suppose) the Christ of Trent'.[112] Listing the horrors of historical Christianity, Inge questions how this can possibly be the flowering of the germ planted by Jesus. Loisy's method was thus hopelessly flawed, and consequently, for Inge, any account of Christ had to retain a link with the historical Jesus as portrayed in the Gospels. Without this connection, all that can be demanded of the Christian is a 'loyal submission' which stultifies his 'intellectual faculties'.[113] In short, he went on, 'We do not believe in two Christs—one of them a Galilean prophet of "limited intelligence", and the other a half-religious, half-political organisation with a very checkered record'.[114]

> The fact that such a method of apologetics as that which we have been discussing should be advocated by learned and thoroughly loyal Churchmen proves that a grave state of tension exists between faith and reason. But Liberal Catholicism, as represented by the Abbé Loisy, surrenders far too much... It saves the Creeds, but loses the Gospels; it emancipates the will, but loses the intellect. It will be an evil day when the troubled faith of English Churchmen seeks refuge by this road.[115]

Lacey was justifiably deeply offended by this sermon and wrote in protest to *The Guardian*. Although he was tempted to criticize the sermon as a whole, he claimed that while he was unable to answer for

---

110. Inge, *Faith and Knowledge*, p. 286.
111. Inge, *Faith and Knowledge*, p. 286.
112. Inge, *Faith and Knowledge*, p. 287.
113. Inge, *Faith and Knowledge*, p. 290.
114. Inge, *Faith and Knowledge*, p. 290.
115. Inge, *Faith and Knowledge*, p. 292.

Loisy as to his position on the 'two Christs' accusation, 'I can say for myself that no such grotesque image ever presented itself to my mind'.[116] Criticizing Inge for quoting Loisy out of context and for misunderstanding the relationship between faith and history, Lacey offers several quotations from Loisy's work in support of his position. Lacey misfired his criticism, however, and in the next edition of *The Guardian* Inge replied, observing (correctly) that the passages cited by Lacey did indeed suggest two Christs, 'and in order to convict me of an "absurd misconception", Mr. Lacey naïvely quotes a sentence of his own, in which he invites us to "distinguish Jesus of Nazareth in His habit as he lived from all that He was to become" '.[117] Inge goes on to ask: 'What process of "becoming" has taken place in the Person of our Lord since He left the world?' Thus, according to Inge, Loisy's (and Lacey's) position is quite untenable: if, on the one hand, the church becomes the outward expression of Christ, then this would amount to a deification of the church which is little short of idolatry. If, on the other hand, Jesus had become something he was not when alive, this would be little more than a surrender of the historical Jesus: in this case Jesus would become a 'semi-mythical founder of the Christian religion, the European counterpart of Buddha'.[118]

Inge's claim was that although he felt it unlikely, given his reputation for orthodoxy, that Lacey held either view, he had nevertheless defended Loisy who held both. Indeed, Inge adds, as for the 'schoolgirl' expression, so for Loisy: 'Faith is believing what you know to be untrue'. He concludes his letter with something of a broadside:

> I have seldom read a pamphlet which, in my humble judgment, is likely to do more mischief than that which appeared under the respected names of Lord Halifax and Mr. Lacey. Whatever changes (and they may be great) may be imposed upon us by the discredit into which supernaturalistic dualism has fallen; whatever reserves may be imposed upon

---

116. *The Guardian*, 6 April 1904, p. 589.

117. *The Guardian*, 13 April 1904, p. 625.

118. In a somewhat ephemeral essay, *Christianised Rationalism and the Higher Criticism* (London: John F. Shaw, 1903), Robert Anderson criticized the German protestants for their lack of mystery or what he called their 'splendid type of neo-Buddhism'. Mill or Renan could be called Christians on this account, 'their position differs from that of Harnack only in this, that they have the honesty to wear their true colours' (p. 77).

us in the communication of religious truth to simple folk, the very worst policy must be to embrace what Plato calls the 'lie in the soul', and to force ourselves to 'accept' what we cannot believe.

Hardly surprisingly, Lacey responded in the next edition of *The Guardian* complaining about Inge's reply which said 'in effect that if I did not mean what he said that I meant it was my own fault. I ought to have meant that and nothing else'.[119] After defending himself against the charge of having misunderstood Loisy (and himself), Lacey then protests 'vehemently against Mr. Inge's interpretation',[120] before suggesting that all he had meant in saying that the Jesus of history was different 'in his habit', was that he was not yet glorified. He then went on the attack:

> Does Mr. Inge really mean that our Lord is now for him exactly what he was for his contemporaries at Nazareth? If so, I hasten his disagreement with me, and I am glad that he thinks my pamphlet 'likely to do mischief'. That is at all events the precise position which I have assailed. It is the position which M. Loisy, I think, has rendered untenable. That is possibly Mr. Inge's grievance.[121]

In the following year, Lacey published a collection of Lent lectures given at St Philip's and St James' Church in Oxford, and St Mark's in Marylebone, in which he returned to his argument with Inge.[122] In the preface he refers to Inge's University sermon, remarking that he felt 'constrained to ask Mr. Inge whether he made no distinction between "Jesus of Nazareth in His habit as He lived", and the Christ of history.' 'To this question', he goes on, 'I have heard no answer'.[123] Lacey was astonished to find himself accused of basing his orthodoxy on 'scepticism'. All that he was trying to do, he insisted, was to distinguish between the two methods of theology and science, since,

119. *The Guardian*, 20 April 1904, p. 670.

120. *The Guardian*, 20 April 1904, p. 671.

121. *The Guardian*, 20 April 1904, p. 671. Loisy himself was aware of the English debate between Lacey (and Robert Dell) in the *Church Times* and Inge. He expressed some surprise at Inge's sermon preached 'ex professo contre moi' and at the subsequent debate. He was even more astonished at the accusation that he did not believe in the Creed. Commenting, with more than a hint of irony, he remarked: 'It was a little exaggerated since I admitted and continue to admit the crucifixion under Pontius Pilate' (*Mémoires*, II, p. 399; cf. III, p. 270).

122. T.A. Lacey, *The Historic Christ* (London: Longmans, 1905).

123. Lacey, *The Historic Christ*, p. ix.

otherwise the Christian faith will either be reduced to an acquaintance, more or less intimate, with certain events that happened some centuries ago—a sort of historical knowledge tinged with emotion—or shrivel into an acceptance of formal propositions defiant of reality.[124]

Religion, for Lacey, was concerned with the moral and spiritual interpretations of the historical facts; indeed, 'faith deals in the first place with the interpretation of facts, and those facts must be real, or faith is void'.[125] Dealing with St Paul, Lacey suggests that his purpose in writing was to explain the significance of facts that were already familiar; indeed it was from the seeds sown in Paul that the church grew:

[T]he Christ of conciliar definition is less the Christ of the synoptics than the Christ who was preached before the synoptics were written. The faith of Chalcedon is the Gospel of St Paul. The Christ of Chalcedon is the historic Christ.[126]

Similarly in the historic event of the resurrection alone there was nothing of any religious value; instead 'the religious value of the Resurrection lies, not in the mere event, but in the significance of the event'.[127]

In the two Chapters which Lacey wrote in response to Inge, he continues his vigorous defence of the method of faith which seeks to enlarge on the past event as it interprets its significance: 'Our faith is concerned with what [Jesus] was and is, with what he did and is doing'.[128] In turn, in relation to the resurrection, Lacey writes:

It is a historical fact. I can prove it by historical evidence. Well and good; I welcome the proof. It is more important that I receive the fact as an integral part of that body of doctrine which with the heart I believe unto righteousness.[129]

This means that Christianity is not a simple record of facts, 'nor is Christian faith identical with historical certainty'.[130] Nevertheless, Lacey claimed, there is some connection with the facts themselves as observed and recorded.

---

124. Lacey, *The Historic Christ*, p. x.
125. Lacey, *The Historic Christ*, p. 5.
126. Lacey, *The Historic Christ*, p. 96.
127. Lacey, *The Historic Christ*, p. 97.
128. Lacey, *The Historic Christ*, p. 119.
129. Lacey, *The Historic Christ*, pp. 129-30.
130. Lacey, *The Historic Christ*, p. 132.

Many years later Lacey returned to similar themes, and was able to survey his own progress: the 'impression' Christ made on the believer was still important, and it was that impression which had shaken him out of 'the external habit of religion' he had known in his boyhood.[131] 'What think ye of Christ?' was still the crucial question. Lacey goes on to discuss some current popular pictures of Jesus: the Galilean teacher, the Carpenter from Nazareth and the deluded apocalyptic fanatic, seeing none of them as containing the whole truth (although each a part). What was important about all of them, however, was that they always pointed to something beyond—that is, to Him, 'who was and is what St Paul declared him to be—Christ, the power of God and the wisdom of God'. And, according to Lacey, this offered the congregation enough to go on, and it was this that led to the adventure of the Catholic Church. Lacey concluded: 'I commend to you the same adventure'.[132] The power of Christ alive in the Church thus overcame the vagaries of history, helping to prepare the ground for the triumphalistic Anglo-Catholicism of the 1920s.[133]

Though it hardly amounts to a very satisfactory solution to the problem of faith and history, the importance of Lacey's contribution to the theological debate, particularly in relation to the reception of Loisy, is that it paved the way for conservative scholars to use what amounted to radical New Testament criticism for their own conservative ends: the church could survive the assaults of history as Inge (though himself hardly maintaining a credible position) was able to point out, despite Lacey's protestations. Although he does not develop anything other than a typically conservative view of the historical Jesus which places much weight on the Fourth Gospel, Lacey at least sees the importance of connecting the proclamation of the Church with that of the historical Jesus.

As will become clear in the next Chapter, however, a different reading of the historical Jesus (which Loisy had defended as a scholar but rejected as a theologian—even if he did see something of Jesus'

131. T.A. Lacey, *Shaken Beliefs: Three Lectures heard at All Saints, Margaret Street* (Oxford: Mowbray, 1922), p. 11.

132. Lacey, *Shaken Beliefs*, p. 22.

133. Lacey's colleague at the *Church Times*, C.G. Rawlinson, was also highly sympathetic to Loisy. Writing to von Hügel shortly before his death in 1922, he remarked: 'What Loisy originally intended and in part executed was right. It is still what we require' (9 Feb. 1922, cited in Vidler, *The Modernist Movement*, p. 252).

original spirit surviving in the Church) could prove extraordinarily potent in offering a contemporary Christology which was vitally connected with the historical Jesus. Loisy's two Christs gradually became one, but in the process, this disrupted both the conservative Christ of the Church as well as the 'thin figure' of the Christ of the German protestants.[134] Eschatology, as will become clear, offered a picture of Jesus which allowed the supernatural heart of the Gospel, patently alive in the Church, to find its home in the Jesus of history. There are consequently parallels to be drawn between Lacey's use of Loisy and some of the English responses—particularly Sanday's—to the thought of Weiss and Schweitzer.

134. Harnack's thought continued to exert some influence in England, at least as mediated by some later New Testament critics. C.H. Dodd, who spent a term in Berlin, and who was later influential in English New Testament scholarship from the 1930s onwards, viewed Jesus' eschatology as 'realised' (*The Parables of the Kingdom* [London: Nisbet, 1935], e.g. pp. 44-45). His biographer, F.W. Dillistone wrote: 'it is doubtful if Dodd ever deviated to any substantial degree from the attitude to history embodied in Harnack's work...he admired Harnack's methods, he shared his deep religious concern. Statements made by Harnack could have been made later on by Dodd; statements made about Harnack could equally well have been made later on about Dodd' (*C.H. Dodd: Interpreter of the New Testament* [London: Hodder & Stoughton, 1977], p. 54). In realized eschatology, the eternal makes contact with human history: 'the absolute, the "wholly other", has entered time and space', 'judgement and blessedness have come into human existence' (*The Parables of the Kingdom*, pp. 107-108).

Chapter 3

WILLIAM SANDAY, JOHANNES WEISS AND ALBERT SCHWEITZER

In his account of *The Modernist Movement in the Roman Catholic Church*, Alec Vidler remarked that '[i]n Germany and for German Protestants, it was no doubt J. Weiss and Schweitzer rather than Loisy who most effectively shattered the thesis of *Das Wesen des Christenthums* as to the nature of the original Gospel'. This, he claimed, was hardly surprising given that Loisy was a French Roman Catholic.[1] However, he went on to say that '[i]n England too, Loisy's part in establishing the eschatological interpretation of the original gospel is sometimes overlooked'.[2] In a footnote, Vidler cites Sir Edwyn Hoskyns's essay in *Essays Catholic and Critical* first published in 1926, as evidence.[3] This footnote provoked some correspondence from Hoskyns to Vidler, who remarked that Loisy had certainly been influential, but that, 'as a catholic', he sat 'lightly to the results' of

> liberal-radical N.T. criticism...because the Church was an altogether bigger thing than the particular beliefs and practices of primitive Christianity. No doubt... Loisy still held the Jesus of history to be important, but in such manner as to relieve us of the sense of his ultimate authority.[4]

Hoskyns thus felt Vidler's rebuke to be 'unnecessarily hard' since he

1. Vidler, *The Modernist Movement*, p. 122.
2. Vidler, *The Modernist Movement*, p. 124.
3. 'Recently...since the publication of Johannes Weiss' monograph,...and of the works of Albert Schweitzer..., most New Testament scholars have been compelled to treat the eschatological element in the teaching of Jesus far more seriously' 'The Christ of the Synoptic Gospels', in E.G. Selwyn (ed.), *Essays Catholic and Critical* (London: SPCK, 3rd edn, 1954 [1926]), pp. 151-78 (p. 155 n. 1).
4. Letter from Hoskyns to Vidler, cited in *A Variety of Catholic Modernists*, p. 189.

was not concerned with the history of the recognition of eschatology in
the Gospels, or with giving 'credit'; but simply with the fact that it was
Weiss and Schweitzer who introduced the tension of eschatology into
technical N.T. work for most of us. We ought perhaps to have got it from
Loisy, but we did not.[5]

Hoskyns's assessment of the period is probably an accurate record of
the influence of Loisy: as was shown in the previous Chapter his
impact in England was felt not so much because of his understanding
of the historical Jesus, but in his defence of the role of the Church, at
least in its preservation of Christ's message. His eschatological
interpretation of the historical Jesus itself was something of an aside to
the English critics. Thus, however much he might have prepared the
ground for some of the later responses to eschatological interpretations
of the historical Jesus, Loisy's influence was marginal compared with
that of Johannes Weiss and Albert Schweitzer.[6]

William Sanday

As the leading mediator of German-language New Testament scholarship in England, it was once again William Sanday who played the
most important role in making known the eschatological interpretations
of the historical Jesus which had been developed by Weiss and
Schweitzer. Sanday gradually moved from the conservative position
discussed in the previous chapter. Thus, in the Appendix added for the
second edition of the reprint of his *Outlines of the Life of Christ*, on the
position of Gospel scholarship in 1905, his approach to German
historical criticism had subtly changed, and had grown more sympathetic. Indeed he claimed that '[the] wholesale scepticism of the times
of Strauss and Baur has come to an end... The broad basis, so to speak,
of early Christian history is being more securely laid; extravagances are

---

5.   Letter from Hoskyns to Vidler, cited in *A Variety of Catholic Modernists*,
p. 188. See also Richard E. Parsons, *Sir Edwyn Hoskyns as Biblical Theologian*
(London: Hurst, 1985), pp. 33-34.
6.   Paul Elmer More's understanding of the situation, written in 1932, although
not without substance, is perhaps rather too tidy: 'I had supposed that the
"liberalische Theologie" had received its death-wound from Loisy and its *coup de
grâce* from Schweitzer' (A.H. Dakin, *Paul Elmer More* [Princeton: Princeton
University Press, 1960], p. 322).

being pruned away, and erratic experiments dropped'.[7] He went as far as recognizing that the movement towards a secure foundation of history was being laid especially in Germany and this 'factor is the most important' since '[what] Germany is saying today, many circles in Europe and America will be saying tomorrow'.[8]

With such new found sympathy and optimism Sanday regarded the most recent criticism of von Soden, Johannes Weiss and Wilhelm Bousset as 'sane'. It 'left the common matter of the Synoptic Gospels ...substantially unscathed',[9] and reached at the end of the critical process 'an irreducible minimum' of certain facts.[10] In principle at least, an unbiased study of the Gospels would yield secure information about Jesus, without the Christian having to resort to the more dubious and unscientific method of ecclesiastical supernaturalism. According to Sanday, von Soden in particular had provided the agenda for an Anglican theology which would no longer have to rely on the complacent 'docetism' of Bishop Gore, but which instead required a human picture of a Jesus capable of reconciling differences within his person, conferring unity on increasingly 'compartmentalized' lives,[11] which would serve to overcome tensions in a 'transcendent unity'. This search for a higher unity which would balance the findings of critical research with 'our own fundamental beliefs' determined the course of Sanday's future theology.

The Life of Christ in Recent Research

This more sympathetic approach to German scholarship led Sanday to publish in 1907 what he called the 'rather composite book', *The Life of*

---

7. *Outlines of the Life of Christ*, pp. 259-60. Sanday placed great emphasis (like most other English scholars of conservative persuasion) on the success of the 'searching examination' of the dating of the Ignatian epistles by Lightfoot and Zahn which he believed had put to an end some of the wilder speculations of Baur. For an excellent critique of the virtual wholesale English rejection of Baur, which survives unscathed in Neill, *The Interpretation of the New Testament* (esp. p. 55), see Robert Morgan, 'Non Angli sed Angeli: Some Anglican Reactions to German Gospel Criticism', in Stephen Sykes and Derek Holmes (eds.), *New Studies in Theology*, I (London: Gerald Duckworth, 1980), pp. 1-30, esp. pp. 13-17.

8. Sanday, *Outlines of the Life of Christ*, p. 261.
9. Sanday, *Outlines of the Life of Christ*, p. 266.
10. Sanday, *Outlines of the Life of Christ*, p. 268.
11. Sanday, *Outlines of the Life of Christ*, p. 272.

Christ in Recent Research, which was based on a series of four lectures he had given at Cambridge, and which, as F.C. Burkitt later recalled, excited those who heard them.[12] Although Sanday regarded this book as 'only a stage—and a temporary stage—on the road'[13] to his aim of writing a fully-fledged life of Christ (a project which he had originally announced in the preface to *The Sacred Sites of the Gospels* in 1903),[14] it nevertheless reveals the tensions in his method most clearly, even if at first sight it offers little more than an impressive but straightforward account of the development of New Testament scholarship in the previous twenty years, documenting virtually all the notable contributions.

As with his earlier work, most of Sanday's *The Life of Christ in Recent Research* is characterized by a sense of fairness, even to the most heterodox views of continental theologians:

> Those of us who make much use of German tools and who try to acknowledge adequately the debt they incur in doing so run the risk of becoming tedious to their own countrymen. The world is apt to grow weary of hearing Aristides called the Just. And yet, if one is constantly consulting Aristides, that is the least that is his due. On great problems, and from the point of view of research, it is a secondary merit in a book to be right.[15]

Though couched in heavy irony, Sanday points to the importance of German scholarship in developing his own position: 'while I agree more often with my own countrymen, I learn more from the Germans'.[16] The reason for this was clear. Rather than contenting itself with the 'neutral or defensive' attitude of English scholarship, the

> strong point of Teutonic science is its persistent spirit of forward movement. With us, if a good piece of work is done, it lasts for a generation; whereas in Germany, no sooner does a definite result appear to be gained, than new questions begin to be asked, and new combinations attempted.[17]

---

12. Cf. F.C. Burkitt, 'Twenty-five Years of Theological Study: A Lecture delivered at the University of Manchester on the occasion of the Twenty-fifth anniversary of the Faculty of Theology', *Bulletin of the John Rylands Library* 14 (1930), pp. 37-52 (11).

13. Sanday, *Effigies Mea* (BOD MS Eng. misc. d. 128 no. 380).

14. Sanday, *The Sacred Sites of the Gospels* (Oxford: Clarendon Press, 1903), p. v.

15. Sanday, *Life of Christ in Recent Research*, p. 37.

16. Sanday, *Life of Christ in Recent Research*, p. 38.

17. Sanday, *Life of Christ in Recent Research*, p. 41.

'With us', he went on, 'dashing but desultory raids are apt to take the place of what is in Germany the steady disciplined advance of a regularly mobilized army.'[18] Sanday's willingness to examine all opinions prompted much praise from his German friends. Von Dobschütz, for instance, remarked that for 'German theologians it is always of great value to see how our researches are reflected in the eyes of other nations. And you are in a high degree just even to our weaknesses.'[19]

Sanday's remarkable impartiality is exhibited throughout the book: even Wrede, the arch-sceptic, who 'never minces matters', is given a fair hearing[20] (even if his style is compared to that of a 'Prussian official'[21]). Similarly, Jülicher is regarded by Sanday as an 'honest writer' but 'at the same time a party man'.[22] By surveying the broad range of often conflicting opinions, the purpose of the book was to show, according to Sanday, that scholarship did not necessarily reach a logical and definitive conclusion: a balanced opinion simply could not be achieved through the 'either/or' method of the more rationalistic scholarship, but only through a 'both/and'. 'I should have thought', Sanday wrote to von Dobschütz on 30 October 1907, 'there were many things on which one was obliged to say at once Yes and No'.[23]

For this very reason Sanday refuses in *The Life of Christ in Recent Research* to dismiss any theological school before making a thorough assessment of its writings, and is able to find something of value even in the 'Modern-Positive' school of Reinhold Seeberg and Theodor Kaftan.[24] Although recognising that Christian truth had to be restated in every age, they nevertheless held that the 'marching route' was determined beforehand. In this, Sanday, again displaying his conservative Anglicanism, was 'entirely at one'.[25] He wrote to von Dobschütz:

18. Sanday, *Life of Christ in Recent Research*, p. 42.

19. Von Dobschütz to Sanday, 21 Oct 1907 (BOD MS Eng. misc. d. 123 nos. 83-92).

20. Sanday, *Life of Christ in Recent Research*, pp. 69-77.

21. Sanday, *Life of Christ in Recent Research*, p. 70.

22. Sanday, *Life of Christ in Recent Research*, p. 167. Sanday had earlier expressed this view in a review of Jülicher's book on parables ('A New Work on the Parables', *JTS* 1 (1900), pp. 161-80, here p. 133).

23. BOD MS Eng. misc. d. 128 no. 46.

24. He is, however, extremely critical of what he calls their Marcionism. Cf. Sanday to Birkitt, 16 Oct 1907 (BOD MS Eng. Misc. d. 122 (I) no. 259).

25. Sanday, *Life of Christ in Recent Research*, p. 178.

Where the new idea really contains the essence of the old, it seems to me
to be more important to emphasise the continuity with the past than the
discontinuity. I would venture to emphasise again, that we lay a good
deal more stress on the continuity of history than you do. We are anxious
to bring out that the Church of to-day is still the same living Church as in
the days of the Apostles.

   A consequence of this point of view is that we are very often engaged
in pointing out resemblances between the present and the past where you
are insisting on the differences. It may be true that neither method, taken
by itself alone, is ideal; but, at least from the religious point of view,
there is surely something to be said for ours.[26]

The creeds, Sanday held, could not be rewritten for every generation,
but rather, '[we] should aim at keeping up the continuity of Christendom... Although it is right that our marching route should leave us a
certain amount of latitude, we don't always want to be going off at a
tangent; we don't want to be a perpetual zigzag. Liberty should not
become licence'.[27] The opinion of the Church through the ages had to
be brought into the picture: *continuity* was as important as criticism.
Sanday thus likened his position to that of '*Vermittelungstheologie*, or
"mediating theology" '.[28] The main problem with the liberals, Sanday
felt, was that they were all too ready to apply 'the guillotine, as I
believe it is called in parliamentary language' and stop 'all further
debate, imposing some conclusion which is not what the facts appear to
point to',[29] a 'pure modernism of the most gratuitous kind'.[30] He
contrasts this with the greater common sense of the English Church
which had 'not yet ceased to think much of the Christian tradition' and
which repeated 'the language of the Ancient Faith' even though it
made 'some allowance for the difference of times'.[31] In a letter to
Sanday after the publication of *The Life of Christ in Recent Research* in
1907, F.C. Burkitt remarked that in his attitudes he displayed
remarkable continuity with the Catholic Modernists who had recently
been condemned by the Pope:

26. 30 Oct. 1907 (BOD MS Eng. misc. d. 128 no. 46).
27. Sanday, *Life of Christ in Recent Research*, pp. 178-79.
28. Sanday, *Life of Christ in Recent Research*, pp. 182-83.
29. Sanday, *Life of Christ in Recent Research*, p. 186.
30. Sanday, *Life of Christ in Recent Research*, p. 192.
31. Sanday, *Life of Christ in Recent Research*, pp. 186-87.

> I meant and do mean to congratulate you most sincerely on your book
> and to say how helpful I find it that one so truly loyal as you are for the
> Old Paths can walk so far with the Modernists—I borrow the word from
> the Encyclical[32] —Perhaps both ends do meet somewhere.[33]

Writing in response to the publication of Sanday's book, von Dobschütz remarked, however, that such a theology as Sanday's was fundamentally insincere in that it kept 'the words, the old terminology, to express something that is new'.[34] This prompted Sanday to admit that even in England the 'Ancient Faith' had undergone much 'simplification' which in Germany, with its greater degree of 'intellectual sincerity', would have been called rejection.[35] In the end, however, the two paths would converge: Anglicans adopted a 'minimum language' where the Germans adopted a 'maximum'. Von Dobschütz agreed:

> We want to show that we theologians are just as purely scientific as the
> philologists… We are—thanks particularly to Harnack—highly respec-
> table among other faculties… Besides this, we are—most of us—anxious
> to be as strictly honest as we can. Even one who is not altogether in
> sympathy with the liberals or modernizers would rather call himself so
> than give the appearance of being more ecclesiastically minded than
> he is.[36]

Paul Wernle of Basel, who had reviewed *The Life of Christ in Recent Research* for the *Theologische Literaturzeitung*, could well understand the English position, as he wrote to Sanday on 21 February 1909:

> We in Germany and in Switzerland have to carry the bad consequences
> of our radicalism alongside the good and I can well understand your wish
> to spare yourself and your Church from these.[37]

Because of the lack of a sense of continuity with the tradition, however, Sanday felt that German attempts to modernize, although worthy efforts to restate the Christian Faith 'in terms in which they can

---

32. Burkitt is here referring to the Papal condemnation of Modernism in the encyclical, *Pascendi*, of 8 Sept. 1907 which followed the decree, *Lamentabili*, of 3 July. See below, Chapter 7.

33. Burkitt to Sanday, 16 Oct. 1907 (BOD MS Eng. misc. d. 122 (I) no. 259.

34. Von Dobschütz to Sanday, 21 Oct. 1907 (BOD MS Eng. misc. d. 123 nos. 83-92.

35. Sanday, *Life of Christ in Recent Research*, pp. 187-88.

36. Von Dobschütz to Sanday, 21 Oct. 1907 (BOD MS Eng. misc. d. 123 nos. 83-92.

37. Wernle to Sanday, 21 Feb. 1909 (BOD MS Eng. misc. d. 140 no. 339.)

be best understood and best appropriated by modern men',[38] were often guilty of judging the past not in its own terms but in terms of the present. Sanday thus replied to von Dobschütz emphasizing the 'extraordinarily high standard of intellectual sincerity characteristic of your theologians', but pointing to a fundamental difference in the English people, who although 'honest at the core', were apt to display their honesty in a rather different form:

> What we lack is the widely diffused scientific interest and instinct in the sense of which you think and speak of science. The average Englishman is not much given to philosophising, or to study with the thoroughness which you devote to it. His canons of judgement are rather those of taste and feeling than of intellectual completeness, coherence and symmetry. Both our peoples are loyal in their way; but with us the loyalty is rather a loyalty of the affections towards inherited institutions and moral ideals than towards abstract speculative or scientific truth... On the side of intellectual sincerity I am very conscious that you set an example to the world. And yet I cannot help thinking that, in the way in which you state the matter, sincerity is carried almost to an extreme, and an extreme of a kind that is exposed to rather considerable danger.

In short, he goes on, to leave religion out of science was 'like performing the play of Hamlet with the part of Hamlet left out'.[39]

In this way, according to Sanday, too much sincerity led the Germans to attempt to impose present-day criteria for truth onto the past:

> I cannot but think that, in asking the question, What is true? we are very many of us not in the least aware what a tremendous thing it is we are asking. If we were aware of it, I believe that we should many of us refrain our lips; and although that would not be by any means the same thing as suppressing or abandoning the question altogether, I believe that it might often involve putting it by for a later season when we were more ripe to attempt the answer.[40]

Instead of the elusive quest for truth, Sanday suggests a more limited task: the question was not whether something was true but

> what did God mean by it, for the Church, for the world, for me. The page of history lies open before us, and we can read its meaning with comparative ease. In doing so, we do not attempt to transcend the limits

---

38. Sanday, *Life of Christ in Recent Research*, p. 197.
39. Sanday to von Dobschütz, 30 Oct. 1907 (BOD MS Eng. misc. d. 128 no. 46).
40. Sanday, *Life of Christ in Recent Research*, p. 199.

of the Relative, which is the real point at which the difficulties come in; and at the same time we fit our thought into that teleological contemplation of the universe which is an endless source of adoration.[41]

Sanday's view of history had thus changed significantly from the optimism of the view of the 'irreducible minimum' of 1905 and although he concludes *The Life of Christ in Recent Research* by re-affirming the *'verifiable minimum*—a minimum verifiable by the severest methods', he nevertheless affirms that 'we are glad to think that their admissions show that…they are really looking out beyond this minimum, as we look beyond it ourselves'.[42] *The Life of Christ in Recent Research* thus ends with a tension between the theology of mediation with its faith in a stable tradition and the realization of the historical relativity of truth. It would seem that German liberals had overstepped the limits of relativity: to apply contemporary criteria of truth to the past was to modernize the unmodernizable. It was for this reason that Sanday was so amenable to eschatological interpretations of the historical Jesus, as will be discussed below. His sympathy for Schweitzer displays his own unease with liberal pictures of Christ, which seemed to him to be reading a modern conception of truth back into the ancient world. Indeed Schweitzer's distrust of the constructions of liberal history was perhaps most decisive in Sanday's gradual recognition of the relativity of the criteria for truth.[43]

41. Sanday, *Life of Christ in Recent Research*, p. 200.

42. Sanday, *Life of Christ in Recent Research*, p. 200.

43. Others, for reasons that will become clear, were far less willing to concede anything to Schweitzer. See, for instance, Cyril W. Emmet, *The Eschatological Element in the Gospels* (Edinburgh: T. & T. Clark, 1911); and *idem*, 'Is the Teaching of Jesus an Interimsethik', *The Interpreter* 8.4 (1912), pp. 423-34. There were also contributions to eschatology by the Canadian, E.F. Scott, *The Kingdom and the Messiah* (Edinburgh: T. & T. Clark, 1910); E.C. Dewick (a Tutor at St Aidan's Theological College, Birkenhead), *Primitive Christian Eschatology* (Hulsean Prize Essay, 1908; Cambridge: Cambridge University Press, 1912), esp. pp. 229-231, 390-91. There were Scottish contributions from J. Moffatt, *The Theology of the Gospels* (London: Gerald Duckworth, 1912); J.H. Leckie, *The World to Come and Final Destiny* (United Free Church College, Glasgow, Kerr Lectures; Edinburgh: T. & T. Clark, 1918), esp. pp. 39-42; William Manson, *Christ's View of the Kingdom of God* (United Free Church College, Glasgow, Bruce Lectures; London: James Clarke, 1918).

Johannes Weiss, Albert Schweitzer and the
So-called 'Eschatological School'[44]

a. *Johannes Weiss*

The so-called 'rediscovery of apocalyptic' (Koch) had been making slow but steady progress in Germany, at least in relation to the Gospels. The decisive statement, however, in the application of thoroughgoing eschatology to Jesus' message of the Kingdom of God was made in 1892 when Johannes Weiss (1863–1914), son of the Old Testament scholar, Bernhard Weiss, who later became Professor in Marburg (1895) and Heidelberg (1908), published his short book *Die Predigt Jesu vom Reiche Gottes*, in which he interpreted Jesus' preaching from an 'eschatological' standpoint.[45] Weiss was in many ways reacting to the fatal weakness of the theology of his own father-in-law, Albrecht Ritschl, which lay in its reliance on untenable historical premises to establish a vocational ethic in the life and teachings of Jesus.[46] The

---

44. Schweitzer's own account of the rediscovery of apocalyptic is still important. See *The Quest of the Historical Jesus: A Critical Study of its Progress from Reimarus to Wrede* (trans. W. Montgomery; London: A. & C. Black, 1910), ch. 15, and *My Life and Thought* (London: Allen and Unwin, 1933), pp. 45-75. Cf. Gösta Lundström, *The Kingdom of God* (Edinburgh: Oliver and Boyd, 1963), pp. 27-95. For a modern re-assessment of Weiss, see esp. Richard Hiers, introduction in Johannes Weiss, *Jesus' Proclamation of the Kingdom of God* (trans. by Richard H. Hiers and D.L. Holland; intro. Richard H. Hiers, Philadelphia: Fortress Press, 1971); and *The Historical Jesus and the Kingdom of God* (Gainesville: University of Florida Press, 1973).

45. Johannes Weiss, *Die Predigt Jesu vom Reiche Gottes* (Göttingen: Vandenhoeck & Ruprecht, 1892). This book was not translated into English until 1971: *Jesus' Proclamation of the Kingdom of God*. A second edition, in which he modified some of his opinions and in which he answered many critics, was published in 1900. This edition has never been translated. Schweitzer (in *My Life and Thought*, p. 48), commented that 'the book was too short for establishing such a radical thesis'. At the time of writing his dissertation Weiss was a *Privatdozent* in Göttingen associated with the group known as the 'History of Religion School'. On this see my essay, 'Religion, Ethics and the History of Religion School', *Scottish Journal of Theology* 46 (1993), pp. 43-78. The most useful recent work on Weiss is Berthold Lannert, *Die Wiederentdeckung*.

46. Although rather overstated, Schultenover's judgment on Weiss contains an element of truth: 'Coincidentally or not, Weiss's book represented a double father-murder. On the one hand it ended the liberal dominance of the school of his father-in-law Albrecht Ritschl. On the other hand it repudiated the conservative orthodox

Kingdom of God, Ritschl had contended in his *magnum opus*, *Justifica-tion and Reconciliation*, had been initiated by Jesus, who conceived of himself as Messiah and lived in utter obedience to the Father, and in his person revealed the highest human capacity for obedience to a divine vocation.[47]

Weiss recognized the impossibility of this picture of the historical Jesus, and consequently addressed the questions: 'In what sense did Jesus speak of the *Basileia tou Theou*, and is this the sense in which the concept is normally used today?'[48] For Weiss's Jesus, unlike Ritschl's, the Kingdom of God was wholly future, and something which only God could realize. There could 'be no talk of an inner-worldly development of the Kingdom of God in the understanding of Jesus'.[49] In the future reign of God, Jesus believed he would be the messianic ruler of the twelve tribes of Israel,[50] a consciousness that he adopted at his baptism. This view, Weiss admitted, had 'something strange about it for our modern way of thinking, but also for the religious imagination',[51] and seemed to present an insurmountable gulf between Jesus' ideas and the concepts of dogmatics:

> Every dogmatics which employs Biblical concepts is always in the more or less clearly perceived danger of stripping these concepts of their original historical character by reinterpreting or converting them to new purposes in accordance with new viewpoints.[52]

This was particularly true with regard to the concept of the Kingdom of God:

> Though in retrospect *we* certainly can say as a judgement of faith that Jesus established the Kingdom of God within his Church, it is just as

position of his own father, Bernhard Weiss' (David G. Schultenover, S.J., *George Tyrrell: In Search of Catholicism* [Shepherdstown: Patmos Press, 1981], p. 263).

47. *Rechtfertigung und Versöhnung*, II (Bonn: A. Marcus, 4th edn, 1900), p. 37. This second volume was never translated. For a useful account of Ritschl's understanding of the historical Jesus, see Clive Marsh, *Albrecht Ritschl and the Problem of the Historical Jesus* (San Francisco: Mellen Research University Press, 1992).

48. Weiss, *Jesus' Proclamation*, p. 68.

49. Weiss, *Jesus' Proclamation*, p. 114.

50. In the second edition Weiss had come to the view that Jesus felt another would be ruler in the coming Kingdom.

51. Weiss, *Jesus' Proclamation*, p. 128.

52. Weiss, *Jesus' Proclamation*, p. 59.

certain that such a conception or expression is far-removed from the sphere of Jesus' ideas.[53]

Weiss thus addressed the question of whether theology could still employ the concept of the Kingdom of God. Could it, he asked, 'issue the old coinage at a new rate of exchange?'[54] According to Weiss, the idea of the actualization of the rule of God which dominated Ritschl's dogmatic concept seemed completely contrary to the transcendentalism of Jesus' original idea.[55] He expressed this dilemma most poignantly in the much revised and lengthened second edition of his essay:

> In the school of Albrecht Ritschl I convinced myself of the incomparable importance of the systematic concept of the Kingdom of God which was the central organising theme of his theology. I am today still of the opinion that his system and just this central concept represent that form of Christian doctrine which is most likely to bring our race closer to the Christian religion and which, when it is correctly understood and correctly evaluated, is most likely to inspire and encourage the wholesome and robust life which we stand in need of today. But from the outset I was disturbed by the clear discovery that Ritschl's concept of the Kingdom of God and the idea of the same name in the proclamation of Jesus are two very different things... The modern theological concept has a completely different form and resonance from the concept in the faith of the early Church. Further studies have convinced me that the actual roots of Ritschl's idea were in Kant and the theology of the Enlightenment.[56]

Weiss nevertheless drew back from regarding Jesus' message as so radically strange that it was without contemporary relevance. The Kingdom of God may have been utterly transcendent in the teaching of Jesus, but that was not the sum of his teaching. Indeed Weiss sought a way out of the impasse by unpacking the modern concept of the Kingdom of God and connecting it with ideas present under a different name in the preaching of Jesus. 'That which is universally valid in Jesus' preaching, which should form the kernel of our systematic theology', he wrote, 'is not the idea of the Kingdom of God but that of the religious and ethical fellowship of the children of God'.[57] It was

---

53. Weiss, *Jesus' Proclamation*, p. 79.
54. Weiss, *Jesus' Proclamation*, p. 60.
55. Weiss, *Jesus' Proclamation*, p. 135.
56. Foreword to Weiss, *Die Predigt Jesu*, 2nd edn, p. v.
57. Weiss, *Jesus' Proclamation*, p. 135. As Lannert (*Die Wiederentdeckung*, p. 263) makes clear, Weiss retained the practical emphasis of his father-in-law, even

thus quite possible, he concluded:

> to approximate to Jesus' attitude, if only in a different sense...We do not
> await a Kingdom of God which is to come down from heaven to earth
> and abolish this world, but we do hope to be gathered with the church of
> Jesus Christ into the heavenly *Basileia*. In this sense we, too, can feel
> and say, as did Christians of old, 'Thy Kingdom Come'.[58]

In a later essay, *Die Idee des Reiches Gottes*,[59] written chiefly to
counter R. Wegener's charge that Ritschl had completely ethicized the
concept of the Kingdom of God,[60] Weiss traced the historical course of
redefinitions of the concept of the Kingdom of God, which he saw as
culminating in the final edition of Ritschl's *Justification and Reconciliation*. This, he believed, had achieved a balanced theology where
the ethical (or 'teleological') conception of the Kingdom of God was
firmly grounded in faith.[61] According to Weiss, such a conception, although it was quite different from Jesus' historical proclamation of the
Kingdom of God, could still be of use for contemporary theology:

> However modernising and dogmatising Ritschl's biblical-theological
> basis might be, the concept of the Kingdom of God as he formulated it is
> still not without its uses. For history shows that apart from in the very
> earliest times the idea of Jesus has never been unchanged and unaltered,
> but has always been redefined and altered. It was not possible to give it a
> value in any other way. And if it is otherwise useful and constructive
> then it seems to me that a difference from the biblical use is absolutely
> necessary.[62]

The chief problem for Weiss (which bears similarities to the problem
of the 'two Christs' recognized by Inge in criticism of Loisy) was that
the universal world plan of God seemed to bear no relation to the
specific foundation in Jesus Christ: the act of reconciliation in the past

---

if this was often shrouded by his rediscovery of eschatology. In a letter to Martin
Rade (12 May 1905, cited in Lannert, *Die Wiederentdeckung*, p. 264), Weiss
believed the widespread misunderstanding of Ritschl as a Christocentric rather than
practical theologian was at the heart of 'many of the calamities of the present'.

58. Weiss, *Jesus' Proclamation*, p. 136.

59. Johannes Weiss, *Die Idee des Reiches Gottes in der Theologie* (Giessen: J.
Ricker'sche Buchhandlung, 1901).

60. R. Wegener, *Albrecht Ritschls Idee des Reiches Gottes* (Leipzig: Deichert,
1897).

61. Weiss, *Die Idee des Reiches Gottes*, p. 112.

62. Weiss, *Die Idee des Reiches Gottes*, p. 113.

appeared completely disconnected from the goal of the future.[63] Weiss's attempt to bridge this gap between historical and dogmatic theology led him to remove the historical sphere altogether in favour of a concentration on the future perfection of humanity on earth, something which was ultimately to be achieved only by God himself. The meaning of history could thus only be understood in the future, in the final consummation, and in no act of the past. Weiss finishes his book with some mystical musings:

> The final results of history are as follows: God surrounds himself with a highly diverse horde of perfected spirits, who represent the human ideal in the most different forms, and who are all similarly perfected because they have become the most perfect they could be to the best of their capacities and strengths. It appears to us to be a fitting conclusion to history and also for God, whose highest and most beautiful creation is the human personality, because it is not merely the last generation of humanity which has climbed onto the shoulders of the previous generation which finds its joy, but all achieve the goal of their development, each in their own way, from the rich abundance of individuals from all times. It is within this context that the biblical idea of the perfected Kingdom of God has its place.[64]

Although Weiss saw the importance of Ritschl's combination of faith and ethics, of biblical and dogmatic theology, he was forced by his dislocation of the dogmatic concept of the Kingdom of God from its rootedness in history into a one-sided concentration on the future, a future which appeared to lack any connection with the past and, perhaps more importantly, with the present. The study of history could provide no answers and appeared almost irrelevant for the dogmatic task. Consequently, if Christianity was to survive the onslaught of historical research, it had to be torn from its basis in history and in the teaching of Jesus himself. All that was left for Weiss was what Ernst Troeltsch called an 'ecclesiastically "impotent"'[65] Christ-mysticism (which Weiss shared with many of the other members of the History of Religion School).[66]

63. Weiss, *Die Idee des Reiches Gottes*, p. 125.

64. Weiss, *Die Idee des Reiches Gottes*, p. 155.

65. Ernst Troeltsch, *The Social Teaching of the Christian Churches* (London: Unwin, 1931), p. 985 n. 504a.

66. See Chapman, 'Religion, Ethics and the History of Religion School', esp. pp. 61-69.

b. *Albert Schweitzer*

The subtleties of Weiss's thought were usually overlooked at the time, and more often than not, Weiss has been understood in the light of Albert Schweitzer's somewhat derivative study of eschatology which made its lasting impact in his monumental discussion of nineteenth-century lives of Christ, *Von Reimarus zu Wrede*[67] which was published in 1906. In this book Schweitzer uses Johannes Weiss as the leading exponent of 'consistent eschatology',[68] a position which he sets against 'consistent scepticism', whose leading exponent was Weiss's colleague in the History of Religion School, William Wrede. This somewhat dialectical use of Weiss and Wrede has served to create a rather simplistic impression of the scholarship of the period, which has done much to distort both the theology of Weiss himself, as well as that of many other figures who have similarly been straitjacketed by Schweitzer's either/or.

Weiss had different motives from Schweitzer, and like many of the other members of the History of Religion School, he directed much of his theological polemic against the attempt to read the New Testament with dogmatic presuppositions and thus against the possibility of a biblical theology in the traditional sense.[69] Including Weiss with

---

67. Weiss is discussed directly in *The Quest of the Historical Jesus*, pp. 237-40. Albert Schweitzer (1875–1965) was from 1899 pastor, and later Professor in Strassburg. He wrote standard works on Kant's philosophy of religion, J.S. Bach as well as New Testament. In 1913 he set up a medical mission in Lambaréné. On Schweitzer see E. Grässer, *Albert Schweitzer als Theologe* (Tübingen: J.C.B. Mohr, 1979); J. Brabazon, *Albert Schweitzer* (New York: Putnam, 1975); J.L. Ice, *Schweitzer: Prophet of Radical Theology* (Philadelphia: Westminster Press, 1971); G.N. Marshall and D. Poling, *Schweitzer* (New York: Doubleday, 1971); and most recently Henning Pleitner, *Das Ende der liberalen Hermeneutik am Beispiel Albert Schweitzers* (Tübingen: Francke Verlag, 1992). For a clear account of Schweitzer's understanding of Jesus and his impact on New Testament studies, see Weaver, *The Historical Jesus*, ch. 1.

68. The phrase 'konsequente Eschatologie' is sometimes rendered 'consistent' or 'consequent' eschatology. Its first use in English was by Sanday in *The Life of Christ in Recent Research* where he rendered it 'thoroughgoing eschatology' (p. 77). Sanday recognized that 'eschatology' was an 'ugly and cumbrous word'. Schweitzer was not without his criticisms of Weiss, asserting that he 'comes to a stop halfway. He makes Jesus think and talk eschatologically without proceeding to the natural inference that His actions also must have been determined by eschatological ideas' (*My Life and Thought*, p. 48).

69. On this see F.W. Graf, 'Der >Systematiker< der >kleinen Göttinger

Schweitzer means that the Ritschlian context of Weiss's theology has been generally disregarded;[70] furthermore, it is impossible to find anything of Schweitzer's strange metaphysics of will in Weiss's theology.[71] Lannert has plausibly argued that Weiss's *Die Predigt* was regarded by his contemporaries (and many of his friends) as out on a limb; it is therefore misleading to speak of an 'eschatological school' as Schweitzer does. Indeed, according to Lannert, 'the term "eschatological school" which was used by Schweitzer masks the singularity of the *Predigt Jesu vom Reiche Gottes*, above all, its position against the "assertions of the systematic theologians" '.[72]

However, it is probably fair to say that the impact of Schweitzer's book was all the greater precisely because of his straitjacketing of contemporary opinion. Similarly, his pungent and provocative style displayed a prophetic challenge to the prevailing theological norms, which created its own momentum in a climate distrustful of liberal synthesis. This might indeed go some way towards explaining his success in England, even if it remains surprising, given the radical and sometimes iconoclastic nature of Schweitzer's most important conclusions. Historical criticism, he asserted,

> loosened the bands by which [Jesus] had been riveted for centuries to the stony rocks of ecclesiastical doctrine, and rejoiced to see life and movement coming into the figure once more, and the historical Jesus, as it seemed to meet it. But he does not stay; He passes by our own time and returns to his own. What surprised and dismayed the theology of the last forty years was that, despite all forced and arbitrary interpretations, it

Fakultät<. Ernst Troeltschs Promotionsthesen und ihr Göttinger Kontext', in H. Renz and F.W. Graf (eds.), *Troeltsch-Studien*, I (Gütersloh: Gerd Mohn, 1982), pp. 235-290, esp. pp. 259-65.

70. Cf. Lannert, *Die Wiederentdeckung*, p. 258. See also, Chilton, *Pure Kingdom*, p. 4.

71. Weiss did, however, develop a coherent metaphysics of his own, and, unlike Schweitzer, regarded Ritschl's ideas of community as of paramount importance. For Weiss's own rather visionary systematic theology, see Chapman, 'The Kingdom of God', p. 152.

72. Lannert, *Die Wiederentdeckung*, pp. 254-55. In his massive account of the development of eschatology, Fastenrath links Weiss and Schweitzer, and thinks it significant that 'in the epoch of an extreme *Lebensphilosophie* a radical eschatologism arose' (Fastenrath, *In Vitam Aeternam*, p. 35). Though this may be true for Schweitzer it seems a long way from Weiss. See also Perrin, *The Kingdom of God*, pp. 16-23.

could not keep him in our time, but had to let Him go. He returned to his own time, not owing to the application of any historical ingenuity, but by the same inevitable necessity by which the liberated pendulum returns to its original position.[73]

Theology was thus forced, Schweitzer claimed, 'by genuine history to begin to doubt the artificial history with which it had thought to give new life to our Christianity, and to yield to the facts which, as Wrede strikingly said, are sometimes the most radical critics of all'.[74]

Although Schweitzer's method is easy to fault by today's standards,[75] his findings helped call into question the liberal picture of Jesus as an ethical personality who founded the Kingdom of God. Schweitzer may have seemed to many an iconoclast, yet he did not believe that at the end of the day one was left with a picture of Jesus as merely a deluded apocalyptic fanatic. Instead, he felt: 'History will force [theology] to find a way to transcend history, and to fight for the lordship and rule of Jesus over this world with weapons tempered in a different forge'.[76] What was left after historical research proved to be of the utmost importance: Jesus was revealed quite simply as the 'man of eschatology', the man whose whole world-view was governed by his will, and a will to be discovered in a completely this-worldly spirituality. Thus Schweitzer wrote:

> The Baptist and Jesus...set the times in motion by acting, by creating eschatological facts. It is this mighty creative force which constitutes the difficulty in grasping historically the eschatology of Jesus and the Baptist. Instead of literary artifice speaking out of a distant imaginary past, there now enter into the field of eschatology men, living, acting men. It was the only time when that ever happened in Jewish eschatology.[77]

73. Schweitzer, *The Quest of the Historical Jesus*, p. 397.

74. Schweitzer, *The Quest of the Historical Jesus*, p. 399.

75. See esp. Morgan, 'From Reimarus to Sanders'; Riches, *A Century of New Testament Study*, pp. 24-28; Perrin, *The Kingdom of God*, esp. pp. 34-36. A bold defence is offered by Dennis Nineham in 'Schweitzer Revisited', in *idem*, *Explorations in Theology*, I (London: SCM Press, 1977), pp. 112-33 (129): 'There may well be mistakes in Schweitzer's (or anyone else's) analysis of the precise traits which make "the historical Jesus a stranger and an enigma to our time" as to all future times; but about that fact itself there can be no dispute.'

76. Schweitzer, *The Quest of the Historical Jesus*, p. 170.

77. Schweitzer, *The Quest of the Historical Jesus*, p. 368.

Thus for Schweitzer, as Grässer observes, what is important about Jesus is his utter strangeness: 'The strangeness of Jesus's world view was so sharply delineated by Schweitzer that it could finally be left behind, in order to obtain what was of ultimate significance in the person of Jesus'.[78] Jesus' ethics were consequently regarded by Schweitzer as an *Interimsethik*. There could be no direct application of the social teaching of, for instance, the Sermon on the Mount, in the different circumstances of today:

> [T]hat which is eternal in the words of Jesus is due to the fact that they are based on an eschatological world-view, and contain the expression of a mind for which the contemporary world with its historical and social circumstances no longer had any existence. They are appropriate, therefore, to any world, for in every world they raise the man who dares to meet their challenge, and does not turn and twist them into meaninglessness, above his world and his time, making him inwardly free, so that he is fitted to be, in his own world and in his own time, a simple channel of the power of Jesus.[79]

The chasm between Jesus' times and our own was thus to be bridged in the increasing awareness of the strangeness of his world-view, which revealed the 'überirdische Persönlichkeit' (supernatural personality) of Jesus, whose 'spirit could break out from its crystallisation in a time conditioned world-view, and which could permeate every world-view'.[80] For Schweitzer, then, Jesus is retained as a kind of good-willed Nietzschean *Übermensch*,[81] who could never be known through

---

78. Grässer, *Albert Schweitzer als Theologe*, p. 79. Nineham similarly emphasizes the importance of Schweitzer's understanding of the 'strangeness' of Jesus: 'What Schweitzer has done is to show that when the historical method is applied to the New Testament, the result is not just to necessitate minor modifications in the picture it gives of Jesus, but to confront the timeless Christ of orthodoxy with a historical Jesus who, as such, inevitably belongs to a particular cultural and religious context and cannot belong to any other in the same immediate way that he belonged to his own' ('Schweitzer Revisited', p. 129).

79. Schweitzer, *The Quest of the Historical Jesus*, p. 400.

80. Grasser, *Albert Schweitzer als Theologe*, p. 79.

81. The eschatological understanding of Jesus' personality was discussed at greater length in the second edition of Schweitzer's *Von Reimarus zu Wrede*. See esp. pp. 574-576. This edition has recently been translated into English: *The Quest of the Historical Jesus* (trans. J. Bowden; London: SCM Press, 2000). Heinrich Kahlert (in *Der Held und seine Gemeinde: Untersuchungen zum Verhältnis von Stifterpersönlichkeit und Verehrergemeinschaft in der Theologie des freien*

history,[82] but whose words were

> appropriate...to any world, for in every world they raise up the man who
> dares to meet their challenge, and does not turn and twist them into
> meaninglessness, above his world and time, making him inwardly free,
> so that he is fitted to be, in his own world and in his own time, a simple
> channel for the power of Jesus.[83]

The autobiographical resonances of this passage are strong: in 1913,
Schweitzer moved to Lambaréné as a medical missionary. The ethical
will of Christ persisted through time and could enthral the believer in
intensity of desire for the Kingdom. Thus, even though Jesus may have
been deluded in his plot to bring about God's Kingdom, his will for
transformation could still captivate the individual and inspire ethical
service. It will become clear, however, that very different theological
conclusions were drawn by Schweitzer's English interpreters.

The Reception of Weiss and Schweitzer in England

Whatever its shortcomings, in the mediation of an eschatological
interpretation of the Gospels to England, Albert Schweitzer's *Von
Reimarus zu Wrede* was of vital importance and Weiss was known, if
he was known at all, only second-hand. There appears to have been
very little contemporary discussion of either of the editions of Weiss's

Protestantismus [Frankfurt: Peter Lang, 1984], pp. 137-38) interprets this in terms
of the influence of Carlyle and the cult of the heroic on Schweitzer. This was
dominant in many other strands of (liberal) theology at the time. See, for example,
Wilhelm Bousset, *What is Religion?* (trans. F.B. Law; London: Unwin, 1907), p.
298. B.H. Streeter recognized the Nietzschean strand in Schweitzer, commenting in
1912 that 'he himself cannot quite escape the charge of modernising, and that his
own boldly-outlined portrait is a little like the Superman of Nietzsche dressed in
Galilean robes' ('The Historic Christ', in Streeter [ed.], *Foundations*, pp. 73-146,
here p. 77).

    82. Schweitzer, *The Quest of the Historical Jesus*, p. 399. Schweitzer's
hermeneutics are discussed at length by Henning Pleitner (in *Das Ende*, pp. 180-
262), who sees him far more as a metaphysician than an historian, and relates his
New Testament work to his philosophical system. In many ways, according to
Pleitner, he is far closer to liberalism than has hitherto been recognized. There are
indeed close parallels with the prevailing liberal metaphysics of personality, which
was (perhaps ironically) also the basis of Harnack's interpretation of Jesus (pp. 230-
31).

    83. Schweitzer, *The Quest of the Historical Jesus*, p. 400.

Jesus' Proclamation: indeed the only English-language review was of the second edition by Edward I. Bosworth in the *American Journal of Theology*, which is highly descriptive and which offers virtually no critical comment.[84] A couple of years later Weiss's *Die Idee des Reiches Gottes in der Theologie*, was reviewed by S.C. Gayford in the English-based *Journal of Theological Studies*,[85] but without any mention of Weiss's own eschatological interpretation of Jesus.

Thus even though Weiss's historical scholarship, at least in respect of New Testament origins, was far more rigorous and critical than Schweitzer's, it was through *Von Reimarus zu Wrede* that Weiss's influence in England was mediated.[86] Thus William Sanday, in *The Life of Christ in Recent Research*, admits that he was only able to base his sketch of Weiss on Schweitzer's summary 'checked by the second edition of Weiss's book which appeared in 1900. I unfortunately missed the first edition when it came out; there is no copy in the Bodleian, and I have not been able to find one in Oxford'.[87] Schweitzer was thus significantly more influential than Weiss in the reception of 'thoroughgoing' eschatology in England.[88]

84. Edward I Bosworth, Review of Weiss, *Predigt Jesu*, *AJT* (1901), pp. 357-58: 'Whatever be one's opinion of the author's main contention, he will find in the book many valuable exegetical suggestions and a wholesome emphasis of the reality of Jesus's religious experience.'

85. S.C. Gayford, Review of Weiss, *Die Idee des Reiches Gottes in der Theologie*, *JTS* 4 (1903), pp. 466-68.

86. It is also not implausible to suggest that Albert Schweitzer was also responsible for mediating Weiss's eschatological interpretation in Germany. Cf. Lannert, *Die Wiederentdeckung*, pp. 252-59.

87. Sanday, *The Life of Christ in Recent Research*, p. 59. He adds a footnote on the same page thanking Burkitt that he had been able to consult a copy 'in the Cambridge Library'. H.R. Mackintosh, Professor of Systematic Theology at New College, Edinburgh, and a leading interpreter of German theology, wrote to Sanday on 16 Oct. 1907 thanking him for his *Life of Christ in Recent Research* (BOD MS Eng. misc. d. 124 (2) no. 341): 'I am sorry to learn that you found it troublesome to get the first edition of Weiss' *Predigt*... I have a copy and it would have been an immense satisfaction to hand it to you. I have a fairly good connection with German booksellers, let me interpolate, which I should be extremely glad to make use of in your behalf, if you feel that it would be of service.'

88. Sanday later corresponded with Weiss, and during the First World War, after Weiss's premature death, he was able to send his message of condolence to Weiss's widow through the mediation of H. Latimer Jackson, who wrote to Sanday on 28 Dec. 1914 (BOD MS Eng. misc. d. 124 (I) no. 44) that 'Your sympathetic

Sanday discusses Schweitzer for 'a full half of these lectures'[89] in *The Life of Christ in Recent Research*, seeing *Von Reimarus zu Wrede* as 'the most striking work of its kind that I have read for some time... Perhaps the most noticeable thing about [Schweitzer] is the sturdy individuality with which he has chosen his own line and holds to it through thick and thin'.[90] Although he was not prepared to 'endorse all the novelties of detailed interpretation that Schweitzer puts forward', Sanday nevertheless suggests that 'on broad, general grounds, he and his school have a great deal to say for themselves'.[91] The chief reason for this positive estimation becomes clear at the end of the third chapter, where Sanday observes that Schweitzer places far greater weight on the historical trustworthiness of the gospels than most critics. Unlike the liberals, he does not seek to reduce 'the Person of Christ to the common measures of humanity, but leaves it at the transcendental height at which he finds it' and thereby allows a link to be made to the eschatology of Paul and John.[92] More importantly perhaps, Sanday also agrees with Schweitzer in his criticism of the modern 'tendency to minimize or explain away everything that is not congenial to our modern point of view'.[93] Thus, according to Sanday, we need to explore Jesus by accustoming 'ourselves to the recognition of a large acceptance on the part of our Lord of the ideas that He found in existence all around him'.[94]

However, even though Sanday acknowledges this need to contextualize Jesus's teaching, he is less willing to accept Schweitzer's opinion that Jesus never really thought of himself as a teacher,[95] or that he merely accepted the prevailing Jewish ideas of his time.[96] Indeed, Sanday wrote: 'I believe it to be, on the whole, as great a mistake to try to explain everything in the Life of our Lord in terms of eschatology, as

words have gone to the Joh. Weiss family. Weiss died, after much suffering, on Aug. 24th at the age of 50—leaving the widow, 2 daughters and 2 sons, one of whom has since been killed in action'.

89. Sanday, *Life of Christ in Recent Research*, p. 45. Schweitzer is discussed in detail on pp. 79-89, 91-118.

90. Sanday, *Life of Christ in Recent Research*, pp. 44, 45.

91. Sanday, *Life of Christ in Recent Research*, p. 88.

92. Sanday, *Life of Christ in Recent Research*, pp. 88-89.

93. Sanday, *Life of Christ in Recent Research*, p. 96.

94. Sanday, *Life of Christ in Recent Research*, pp. 108-109.

95. Sanday, *Life of Christ in Recent Research*, p. 97.

96. Sanday, *Life of Christ in Recent Research*, p. 127.

it is to treat the eschatology as a mere appendage'.[97] Despite this criticism, however, he nevertheless accepts the main outline of Schweitzer's
position and then goes on to look at eschatological themes elsewhere in
the New Testament.

Towards the end of the fourth chapter Sanday, in discussing the
relationship of the teachings of the early church to the ministry and
teaching of Christ himself, reveals his own conservative and basically
idealist method.[98] Although he is able to find a close connection
between Jesus and the church, he does so only by means of spiritualizing the eschatological message itself.[99] Thus he asks: 'What is the
essential meaning of the Kingdom of God?' and responds with a
question:

> Is it not the asserted and realised sovereignty of God, Divine influence
> and Divine power felt as energising in the souls of men? Is not this the
> eternal reality—as distinct from any temporary expression of what we
> mean by the phrase?[100]

Here, as John Riches points out, Sanday has constructed an

> historical apologetic out of the work of the apocalyptic school, by dint of
> spiritualising the sense of the apocalyptic terminology used by Jesus,
> claiming, of course, that this was indeed its intended sense. Thus in a
> surprising transformation, Schweitzer's work is used to buttress the very
> orthodoxy that he had sought to confound.[101]

Later, in his constructive Christology, *Christologies Ancient and
Modern*, Sanday continued to maintain that apocalyptic language was
the only language available to Jesus, but that latent within his personality
were deeper powers which expressed themselves in abundance
throughout his ministry. Thus rather than apocalyptic language being
of the very essence of Jesus' message (as it was for Schweitzer held), it

97. Sanday, *Life of Christ in Recent Research*, p. 100.

98. Sanday, *Life of Christ in Recent Research*, p. 114.

99. Paul Wernle in his review of *Life of Christ* observed how Sanday had
removed the difficulties of history by spiritualizing Jesus' message (col. 100).

100. Sanday, *Life of Christ in Recent Research*, p. 115.

101. Riches, *A Century of New Testament Study*, p. 28. Paul Wernle similarly
observed how Sanday had used Schweitzer to buttress the creeds thereby failing to
note the 'crisis' engendered by an eschatological position (Review of *Life of Christ*,
col. 100). Because of his failure to embrace criticism, Sanday could only really be
said to be preparing the way for critical scholarship rather than carrying it out
himself (col. 101).

was an example of the 'inadequacy and relativity of utterance which attaches to all that is human', and masked the true, though historically subconscious, message of Jesus.[102]

There are two crucial points to be drawn out of this discussion of Sanday's *Life of Christ in Recent Research*: firstly, Schweitzer offered a relatively straightforward (if, for Sanday, ultimately implausible) historical account of Jesus, which presented a way out of the sceptical quagmire of Wrede. Secondly, however, Schweitzer also pointed to the problems involved in modernizing Jesus. If contemporary criteria for truth could not explain much about the historical Jesus, how could Jesus be of abiding significance for faith? Although Sanday himself was most often content to wallow in a somewhat unsatisfactory spiritualism in his own interpretation of Jesus, he nevertheless shared Schweitzer's estimation that familiarity breeds contempt. Others, however, were rather more willing than Sanday to latch on to Schweitzer's understanding of Jesus as stranger, as a critique of all theological rationalizations, as will be discussed in the next Chapter. Sanday, however, by treating Schweitzer with such a degree of sympathy, opened himself up to a barrage of criticism from many quarters. This will be discussed in detail in Chapter 5.

102. Sanday, *Christologies Ancient and Modern* (Oxford: Clarendon Press, 1910), p. 18.

Chapter 4

F.C. BURKITT AND THE FAILURE OF LIBERAL THEOLOGY

The importance of William Sanday in the reception of Albert Schweitzer's ideas in England should by now be clear. Sanday, however, was not the only English scholar of some standing to take up the cause of eschatology in the aftermath of Schweitzer's *Von Reimarus zu Wrede*. Far more consistent and unequivocal was F.C. Burkitt who, as early as 1907, was introduced by Sanday to Schweitzer's book, which, he remarked 'was indeed both instructive and exciting'.[1] Burkitt later observed that the dilemma revealed by Schweitzer was this: 'If Jesus Christ be historical he belongs to his own age; if on the other hand, we persist in asking for a Jesus Christ who is up-to-date we can only get it by constructing a Jesus who is not historical'.[2] Burkitt addressed this dilemma in his wide-ranging studies of the New Testament throughout his career. Moreover he sought to tackle the wider implications of an eschatological view of the New Testament for theology.

Burkitt's Reception of Eschatology

Francis Crawford Burkitt (1864–1935)[3] had been educated at Harrow before going to Trinity College, Cambridge. He gained a First, and in

---

1. F.C. Burkitt to Sanday (16 Oct. 1907) (BOD MS Eng. misc. d. 122 (I) no. 259). He claimed that Schweitzer had 'done justice to Mk X45 which so few "liberals" have done justice to'. In another letter of 12 Oct. 1908 (BOD MS Eng. misc. d. 122 (I) no. 261), Burkitt expresses close agreement with Sanday on eschatology. Michael Ramsey (in *From Gore to Temple*, p. 171) fails to observe the direct influence of Sanday on Burkitt.

2. Burkitt, 'Twenty-five years of Theological Study', p. 12. Burkitt was influential on a range of scholars, not least his friend H. Latimer Jackson (Rector of Little Canfield, Essex). See Jackson, *The Eschatology of Jesus*, pp. xi, 352, 356.

1903 became university lecturer in Palaeography. Although a layman he was elected to the Norrisian Professor of Divinity in 1905, holding the post (which became the Norris-Hulse Professorship in 1934) until his death. He did not become a Fellow of Trinity College until 1926. Burkitt was an extraordinarily gifted theological polymath, who specialized in a wide range of subjects from Syriac (his first love), through the life of St Francis, to liturgy, becoming in the 1920s a vigorous opponent of the revised prayer book.[4]

As one of the leading British experts on apocalyptic writing, and the natural choice of James Hastings to contribute several articles on apocalyptic as well as the article on Eschatology for the *Dictionary of the Apostolic Church*,[5] Burkitt had come to the conclusion that it was impossible to understand the message of Jesus without some understanding of Jewish apocalyptic (a position he reached quite independently of Weiss and Schweitzer): 'I venture to think', he wrote, 'we can go so far as to say that without some knowledge of Jewish Apocalypses, and a fairly clear realization of the state of mind in which they were composed, it is impossible to understand the earliest Christianity'.[6] Indeed eschatology provided, he believed, sufficient ammunition for a threefold assault on the moralizing of Jesus' message prevalent in some liberal circles, along with the highly sceptical approach of Wrede, as well as the charlatanism of Arthur Drews's *Christusmythe* which questioned Jesus' very existence. In this he shows some similarities to Loisy.[7]

3.   Burkitt's correspondence is in the University Library, Cambridge (CUL): MS Add. 7658. Obituaries by various hands in *JTS* 36 (1935), pp. 225-54; J.F. Bethune-Baker in *DNB* (1931–40), pp. 124-25. There is a fairly complete bibliography in *JTS* 36 (1935), pp. 337-46. See also 'Burkitt, Francis Crawford', by Mark Glasswell in *TRE* 7, pp. 424-28.

4.   It is reported that the only change he sanctioned in the communion service was the substitution of 'and' for 'or' between the prayer of oblation and the prayer of thanksgiving after the Lord's Prayer.

5.   Hastings was clear that the articles should deal only with the apostolic age and not with the Gospels (letter to Burkitt, 14 Nov. 1912, MS Add. 7658 B. 245).

6.   Burkitt, 'The Apocalypses: Their Place in Jewish History', in A. Cohen *et al.*, *Judaism and the Beginnings of Christianity* (London: Routledge, 1923), pp. 49-90 (51-52).

7.   Burkitt was sympathetic throughout his career to Loisy and his papers contain two letters from Loisy (CUL MS Add. 7658 B. 605 of 1904 and 1909). He wrote to Loisy after his excommunication in 1908, expressing his 'very sincere

Burkitt's adoption of thoroughgoing eschatology is already clear in his contribution to the Oxford Congress of the History of Religions which took place from 15–18 September 1908, where he discussed the differences between the parable of the wicked husbandmen (Mk 12.1-12) and the doctrine of St Paul.[8] Jesus goes to his death, according to Burkitt,

> believing that by so doing He was bringing in the Kingdom of God. As a matter of history, it brought into being the Christian Church. And to those who believe that, notwithstanding all shortcomings and imperfections, the Church is really animated by the Divine Spirit, the result stands as the justification of the course decided on and of the expectation cherished. It is only the translation of the phraseology of Jewish aspiration into terms and conceptions suitable for other lands and a new age.[9]

While admitting that Jesus might well have been mistaken, Burkitt nevertheless allows a broad role for the Church in drawing contemporary Christians into union with Christ. This conception was later to dominate his thinking.

Burkitt's most important contribution to the eschatological debate, however, was his sparkling essay 'The Eschatological Idea in the Gospel', which impressed Sanday with its 'excellence simply as literature',[10] and which was included in the collection edited by H.B. Swete, *Essays on Some Biblical Questions of the Day by Members of the University of Cambridge*.[11] In this essay Burkitt makes a plea to study the ideas and language of Jesus in the thought-forms of his own

sympathy with you...and...to express the sense of personal fellowship many Liberal Christians feel with you... I know perfectly well that both as an English Churchman and as a Historical Critic my inherited and personal views are different in many ways from yours; but for all that, you are fighting for us the great battle. You and I do from our hearts believe in the reality and the irrevocability of history, of the *fait historique*, a thing which no decree on earth or in heaven can change' (Burkitt to Loisy, 17 March 1908, cited in Vidler, *A Variety of Catholic Modernists*, p. 186).

8. F.C. Burkitt, 'The Parable of the Wicked Husbandmen', in P.S. Allen (ed.), *Transactions of the Third International Congress for the History of Religions*, II (2 vols.; Oxford: Clarendon Press, 1908), pp. 321-28.

9. Burkitt, 'The Parable', p. 328.

10. William Sanday, 'The Cambridge Biblical Essays', *JTS* 11 (1910), pp. 161-79 (169).

11. Burkitt, 'The Eschatological Idea in the Gospel', in H.B. Swete (ed.), *Essays on Some Biblical Questions of the Day by Members of the University of Cambridge* (London: Macmillan, 1909), pp. 193-214.

age, to 'place ourselves mentally upon the standpoint of the Palestinian Jew of the first century A.D., to realize in some degree what the Gospel ideal would mean to him; and to do this, in order to be able to translate the Gospel ideal properly into the thought and action of to-day'.[12] Burkitt's intention was to expose the Christian Gospels to a thorough-going historical analysis which resisted making concessions to the presupposed absoluteness of their theological or ethical presupposi-tions, and which refused to make them conform to the contemporary canons of reason or ethics. Such a method, while 'liberal' in the sense of claiming a value-neutral presuppositionlessness, was far from liberal in the more deist sense of seeing universal moral principles embodied in Scripture. Indeed, although Burkitt's method was hardly original and stood in the line of Reimarus,[13] his downplaying of the uniqueness, and even the importance, of the Golden Rule,[14] was unlikely to win him many friends, as became clear in the subsequent debates which are discussed in Chapter 5.

Burkitt makes his method clear in a striking passage where he con-demns the very notion of an absolute, or unique religion as little short of an anti-semitic heresy.[15] '[I]f Christianity as a whole is not properly to be regarded as the absolute religion, still less is the Gospel a mess-age of "absolute" truth. Its real characteristics are totally different: it is intensely coloured by the historical circumstances of the time and place in which it first saw the light.'[16] Burkitt maintained, however, that his refusal to isolate Christianity dogmatically from its historical nexus could nevertheless provide the foundation for a Christianity as a thoroughly historical faith: indeed, an unprejudiced study of the message

12. Burkitt, 'The Eschatological Idea', p. 200.

13. In Burkitt's lectures on *Christian Beginnings* (London: University of London Press, 1924) he consciously places himself in the line of 'Semler and Herder and Reimarus and Lessing' and the 'wonderful century-and-a-half' since their writings (p. 140).

14. Burkitt, 'The Eschatological Idea', p. 199.

15. In a letter to William Sanday of 16 Oct. 1907, Burkitt was clear about the connections between the isolation of Christianity from its Jewish historical background and rampant German nationalism: 'As far as our friends over the water, especially Dr Kaftan and Prof. Seeberg, I am still of the opinion that they are disciples of Marcion. By the way, have the Pan-Germans never claimed him? Pontus—Galatia—Kelts—i.e. fair-haired tall Northerners—i.e. Germans. It's all clear as can be' (BOD MS Eng. misc. d. 122 (I) no. 259).

16. Burkitt, 'The Eschatological Idea', p. 201.

of Christ yielded something 'very simple and very familiar. In England the common expression for it is the belief in a good time coming'.

Later in the same paragraph he attaches capital letters to the phrase, identifying it with the 'popular expectation of the Kingdom of God'.[17] Although there is a quaintness and undoubtedly a certain tongue-in-cheek quality to this comparison, Burkitt insists that it is at the heart of the message of Christ. Indeed there cannot be 'any justification for its existence apart from belief in the power and goodness of God, and that the notion survives is a proof that belief in the power and the goodness of God still survives among us in a practical form'.[18] Thus the survival of Christianity, Burkitt held, did not depend on its specific ethical code, but rather on its being equipped for catastrophe. Whereas the modern world was something based on 'gradual and progressive evolution', the preaching of Jesus was founded upon the expectation of a 'sudden and complete catastrophe',[19] and such a difference was not something that mere 're-translation or emendation or archaeological research could overcome'.

It was trust in Jesus' message, according to Burkitt, that allowed early Christians to survive calamity and whereas all other aspects of the Roman Empire collapsed, Christianity alone survived because of its resilience and its message of the Good Time Coming. And that, Burkitt maintained, pointed to its abiding significance today. Although the world might appear stable, and might seem to be a long way removed from the world of the first century, it was in reality just as vulnerable as the Roman Empire:

> Our machine-made system is not really self-sustaining; it depends on the brains of the men who have set it going, and there are not wanting [*sic*] indications that our race, like the ruling race in the time of the Antonines, is beginning to get tired.[20]

It was because of the inherent instability of a world which was beginning to totter that Burkitt felt the real message of the Gospel could provide a support which no liberal moralism could supply. Here it becomes clear that eschatology functioned as a critique of Edwardian

17. Burkitt, 'The Eschatological Idea', p. 203. Burkitt retains this phrase in *Jesus Christ: An Historical Outline* (London: Blackie and Son, 1932). See esp. p. 6: 'for the historian it was the idea that was most decisively operative'.

18. Burkitt, 'The Eschatological Idea', p. 203.

19. Burkitt, 'The Eschatological Idea', p. 204.

20. Burkitt, 'The Eschatological Idea', p. 208.

complacency; it gave theological expression to that crisis experienced in so many other walks of life. Thus Burkitt wrote:

> If we are really confronted with disquieting signs of great and funda-
> mental changes in the social and political system that has lasted so long,
> it is the Gospel above all things that can reassure us. The Gospel is the
> great protest against the modern view that the really important thing is to
> be comfortable... If we have learnt the Gospel message, we shall at least
> escape the error of imagining that universal comfort and the Kingdom of
> God are synonymous.[21]

Burkitt seems to have regarded the eschatological interpretation of the Gospel with its focusing of attention beyond this world, as the means by which the Christian could relativize all the claims of the world:

> Without the belief in the Good Time Coming I do not see how we can be
> Christians at all. The belief in the Good Time Coming as the most
> important thing in the world, and therewith the duty of preparing
> ourselves and our fellow-men to be ready as the first duty and privilege
> of humanity—this is the foundation of the Gospel... As long as we
> believe in our hearts that our property, our arts, our institutions, our
> buildings, our trust-deeds, are the most permanent things in this world,
> so long we are not in sympathy with the Gospel message.[22]

Burkitt's eschatological interpretation of Jesus provided him with the basis for a radical application of an *unmodernized* message: it was not so much that the message of Jesus needed to be translated into the language of the 'cultivated modern man' (as Sanday had claimed during his notorious debate with the Bishop of Oxford shortly before the outbreak of war in 1914);[23] instead Jesus of Nazareth 'will not let himself be modernized'.[24] In turn, it was the Church's responsibility to proclaim the eschatological message and to resist simply identifying itself with any modern philosophy.[25] Burkitt concludes his article with

21. Burkitt, 'The Eschatological Idea', pp. 208-209.
22. Burkitt, 'The Eschatological Idea', pp. 210-11.
23. On this, see Chapman, 'The Socratic Subversion of Tradition'.
24. Burkitt, 'The Eschatological Idea', p. 211.
25. In a contribution to a discussion of 'The Limits of Biblical Criticism' at the Manchester Church Congress in October 1908 Burkitt made a similar point: 'If the Christian cause perishes at last, it will not be because historical critics have explained the Gospels away, but because the followers of the Christ are too faint-hearted to walk in the steps of their Master and venture everything for the sake of the Kingdom of God' (*Official Report of the Church Congress held at Manchester,*

a somewhat guarded prophecy:

> Whatever our own duties in our own times may be, and whatever we
> may believe as to the stability of our present civilization, the Gospels
> were written in times and circumstances when the civilization men saw
> around them was not stable, and when men's immediate duties were the
> duties of those who live in an unstable civilization. If we forget this
> when we study the Gospels, they become unreal for us and unmeaning.[26]

Burkitt's interpretation had far reaching consequences in a civilization
which was far from stable.

Burkitt's Defence of Eschatology

Unlike Sanday, Burkitt maintained an eschatological interpretation of
the historical Jesus for the rest of his life, retaining close links with
Schweitzer's position. He also got to know Schweitzer personally, and
it appears that he corresponded directly with him, although there is
only one (undated) postcard from Schweitzer in his correspondence.[27]
After the First World War Burkitt was instrumental in ensuring
Schweitzer a good hearing on his tour of England in 1921–22, a tour
which was greeted with much applause in Cambridge, as well as in
Oxford. C.H. Turner of Oxford wrote to Burkitt that 'Schweitzer was
most attractive. I heard him give the address on the message of
"apocalyptic" for the present day: and I also met him privately. I know
nothing of his medical ability but his personality is inspiring'.[28] In his
diaries, C.C.J. Webb, Oriel Professor of the Philosophy of Religion at
Oxford, wrote initially on 7 February 1922 that Schweitzer had not
much impressed him.[29] By 17 February, however, he had changed his
opinion, finding his lecture 'very vigorous', and after dining with him
he remarked that 'I liked him very much. He is only about 48. He
published "von Reimarus zur [*sic*] Wrede" at 28'.

October 1908 [London: Bemrose, 1908], p. 50). See also Jackson, *The Eschatology
of Jesus*, pp. 336-37.

   26. Burkitt, 'The Eschatological Idea', pp. 212-13.

   27. Schweitzer and his wife to Burkitt sent from Lambaréné, n.d. (CUL MS
Add. 7658 B. 898). In a letter of 21 Feb. 1925 (B550) Kirsopp Lake asked Burkitt
to send a letter to Schweitzer.

   28. C.H. Turner to Burkitt, 8 March 1922 (CUL MS Add. 7658 B. 965).

   29. Webb diaries (BOD MS Eng. misc. d. 1113).

On 3 March 1922 Schweitzer gave a paper to the Oxford Society of Historical Theology at Queen's College entitled: 'La signification de la conception eschatolique de la vie de Jésus et des croyances du christianisme primitif pour la religiosité moderne'. Webb commented that

> Schw.[eitzer] discoursed for more than an hour on the present significance of eschatology for our religious life—it was extremely interesting. He ended in a confession of inability to combine in one view the revelation of God in nature and that in our moral nature: we have to acknowledge a mystery here and live by the light of the love of God and obedience to his will with an 'optimism of the will' independent alike of optimism or pessimism with respect to the progress of the world.[30]

Elsewhere the reception of Schweitzer was a little less glowing. On 5 January 1922, Burkitt wrote to the Dean of Norwich (J.W. Witlink) with more than a hint of irony:

> Dear Mr Dean,
>
> No doubt it is better that Schweitzer should not come to Norwich, but it is a sad commentary on the standard of education in East Anglia that you can call him 'an utterly unknown man'.
>
> At the last C[ambridge] U[niversity] M[usic] S[ociety] Concert I attended Schweitzer's opinion on some phrases of Bach was quoted on the Programme, and you can hardly take up a number of the *C[hurch] T[imes]* or the *Guardian* without some mention of the 'eschatological problem' which he has made a living issue for theology…
>
> It is true that many of those who are interested in his theology do not know that he is a musician, and many musicians do not know that the author of the great book on Bach—as learned as Spitta's and nearly as big—is even more famous as a theological writer. But he is known to all students of theology as a theologian, and to all organists as a writer on Bach. I have been told also, on good authority, that he is really a brilliant organist, playing Bach almost exclusively.
>
> And to crown it all, this gifted man, Doctor of Theology, of Philosophy, and of Medicine, went away in 1912 and started a medical mission in Equatorial French Congo. Now he is going back there again, after having refused a Professorship of theology at Zürich.
>
> If you had said that Norwich folk did not care to listen to an Alsatian, who was therefore of German nationality before the War, or that you did not approve of 'The Quest of the Historical Jesus' on theological grounds, I could understand the tone of your letter; but to write of

---

30. Webb diaries (BOD MS Eng. misc. d. 1113).

Schweitzer as an utterly unknown man (even though you qualify it with 'to the Norwich public') is a curious revelation.

Yours v. faithfully,
F.C. Burkitt.[31]

As well as Schweitzer, Burkitt's name also continued to be associated with Weiss, and he was asked to write an obituary notice for the *Harvard Theological Review*: 'What I chiefly desire to do is to put on record the outstanding and permanent sense of respect and gratitude which all supporters of what Schweitzer calls "thoroughgoing eschatology" must feel towards the author of the *Predigt Jesu vom Reiche Gottes*'.[32] Incidentally, throughout the article Burkitt makes little effort to differentiate Weiss from Schweitzer.

It is also clear that Weiss read Burkitt. In a letter to Burkitt of 30 April 1922, H.N. Bate of Carlisle asked for copies of the obituary and also mentioned that he had been 'trying to find out whether anything has been written about him in Germany, but there seems to be next to nothing: and via Schweitzer and Klostermann I have found out from Frau Weiss she likes your articles best of all that has been written'.[33]

Burkitt's Later Thought

Burkitt's distinctive and radical position in comparison with at least some in the Anglican establishment is evident from his essay on 'The Eschatological Idea', and from a closer look at his writings it becomes clear that he appropriated Schweitzer's thought in a completely different manner from Sanday. He never displayed the same degree of utter scepticism about the fruits of historical research, nor indeed the extreme cultural relativity of Sanday's later thought. Instead, according to Burkitt, when approached without presuppositions, the study of history could be certain of one thing about Jesus: as an historical figure he remained utterly strange to modern categories of thought. Up-to-date and rationalist interpretations could never penetrate into the depths of the historical figure.

31. Burkitt to Witlink, 5 Jan. 1922 (CUL MS Add. 7658 A. 20).
32. F.C. Burkitt, 'Johannes Weiss: In Memoriam', *HTR* 8 (1915), pp. 291-97, here p. 291.
33. CUL MS Add. 7658 B. 51.

Burkitt continued to maintain this position throughout his career.[34] For instance, as late as 1932, he published a short life of Christ (*Jesus Christ: An Historical Outline*), in which he comments on the naivety of so much 'liberal' thought, emphasizing the need to approach the story of Jesus 'from without, as strangers'.[35] Echoing his earlier thought, he suggests that there is nothing 'dangerous' for the believer in adopting such a method, unless 'by "believer" is meant one who thinks he knows beforehand what must have happened'.[36] At the same time Burkitt is equally critical of those religious liberals, by which he means ' "progressive" and "up-to-date" and "broad-minded" and "philosophic" ',[37] who try to dispose of the centuries of ecclesiastical accretion in order to reveal an 'ideal Man'. What they lose in their idealist fantasies, he claims, is the vitality of the real man: 'What right have we to expect that counsel and warnings from so far-away a source will have much echo in our surroundings?'[38] Burkitt's interpretation, especially his dismissal of attempts at the modernization of Jesus' teaching, thus remains remarkably consistent.

Earlier in his career, as he came to develop this understanding, he had begun to question the modern emphasis on religious experience in both neo-Catholicism and many forms of Protestantism, feeling this in many cases to have become a substitute for history. In turn, he maintained that psychology had supplanted the impartial study of history.[39] However, even though Burkitt's own concerns were somewhat different from those of the liberals, he similarly refused to take refuge in any simplistic conservative appropriation of tradition: he was not looking for an idealized liberal Jesus, the 'wise Sage who saw by unerring instinct what was essential in human life and conduct',[40] nor yet for a Jesus who could be directly experienced in some unhistorical way, but for a Jesus who was true to his own times. This meant understanding Jesus as a Jew in first-century Palestine, however strange he might appear.

34. On Burkitt's position in the 1920s and 1930s, see Perrin, *The Kingdom of God*, pp. 52-54.
35. Burkitt, *Jesus Christ*, p. 2.
36. Burkitt, *Jesus Christ*, p. 3.
37. Burkitt, *Jesus Christ*, p. 4.
38. Burkitt, *Jesus Christ*, p. 4.
39. Burkitt, *Christian Beginnings*, p. 142.
40. Burkitt, *Jesus Christ*, p. 58.

This quest for the human Jesus, understood as the real stranger, dominates Burkitt's interpretation of the New Testament, providing the guiding thread through his many articles on synoptic themes (which on occasion made explicit use of Schweitzer). In 'The Historical Character of the Gospel of Mark',[41] for instance, he sought to diminish 'some of the weight' of Wrede, and in so doing made use of an eschatological view: 'there is a sense, on the eschatological view, in which it is true to say that Jesus had radically changed the messianic ideal. He had changed it, not by "spiritualizing" it, but by adding to it... He prefixed to it not a doctrine about Messiah, but the actual course of his own career'.[42] This use of Schweitzer provoked a critical response from von Dobschütz[43] who remarked:

> I am glad to see you combat Wrede's scepticism. That you follow the eschatological line of Schweitzer I knew before and you know that I do not go with you in this way. I cannot believe that Jesus thought his activity to be merely a *preparatory* one, he felt that he was bringing something more than only a way for repentance to mankind. He looked upon himself as the Messiah... So, going with you as regarding the outside form of his entry into Jerusalem, I nevertheless maintain, that he himself and for the small circle of his disciples wished to declare: Look! I am the Messiah, but quite another Messiah than you expect. Your very kind remarks on ministry tend to the same end and I think we will at last come to nearly the same mind.

41. F.C. Burkitt, 'The Historical Character of the Gospel of Mark', *AJT* 15 (1911) pp. 169-93. As is clear from the final sentence of a letter sent to Burkitt with the proofs of the article, the editor of the *AJT* seems not quite to have understood the significance of Burkitt's interpretation: 'We have here in America, as I think you have in Great Britain, a rather blind and tenacious unwillingness to view the New Testament historically, and to revise traditional theology to meet the demands of modern thinking... I had noted Lake's article in the HTR [Kirsopp Lake, 'The Shepherd of Hermas and Christian Life in Rome in the Second Century' (*HTR* 4 [1911], pp. 25-46)] for January. It seems as though we were gradually working our way through the eschatological problem, and would reach a historical viewpoint which will enable us to think of Jesus as showing much of the eschatological thought, perspectives and expectations of his day without its seriously interfering with our appreciation and use of his general moral-religious message and significance' (C.W. Votaw to Burkitt, 9 March 1911, CUL MS Add. 7658 B. 972).

42. Burkitt, 'The Historical Character', p. 193.

43. Von Dobschütz to Burkitt, 21 May 1911 (CUL MS Add. 7658. B. 276).

I have written for the same American Journal of Theology[44] on the motifs of activity in early Christianity—something anti-eschatologistic...

Believe me yours,
E. v. Dobschütz[45]

Similarly, in 'The Parables of the Kingdom of Heaven',[46] Burkitt speaks of the Kingdom of Heaven as the central theme of the Gospel

44. Ernst von Dobschütz, 'The Most Important Motives for Behavior in The Life of the Early Christians', *AJT* 15 (1911), pp. 505-524. Once again, von Dobschütz emphasizes the moral character of Jesus' teaching, and his anti-eschatological message. Eschatology was no more than a corruption of the purity of Jesus' message by the '*superstitio* of antiquity... And since it is no longer God and his salvation which are kept exclusively in view, but man and his accomplishments, asceticism, in the sense of meritorious action to help win salvation, very soon comes into Christianity' (p. 524). Von Dobschütz's attack on 'early Catholicism' is clear. See also 'The Lord's Prayer', *HTR* 7 (1914), pp. 293-321.

45. Von Dobschütz and Burkitt kept up a lively correspondence before the outbreak of the First World War and they became close friends, resuming contact after the armistice. Burkitt was invited to the 1911 Breslau Congress and was asked by von Dobschütz to bring some of his Doctor of Divinity hoods to show to 'the admiring people of Breslau. We are as you know simple folk' (von Dobschütz to Burkitt, 1911 (n.d.), CUL MS Add. 7658. B. 279A). During the First World War Burkitt received news of von Dobschütz from James Hardy Ropes of Harvard, where he had been a guest Professor (Ropes to Burkitt, 22 Sept. 1914, MS Add. 7658 B. 850). H. Latimer Jackson wrote to Burkitt (MS Add. 7658 B. 488) on 1 Oct. 1914 with news about von Dobschütz, which had been mediated by Mme Leeman of Leiden. Later in the war (9 May 1915) Jackson wrote to Sanday informing him that he had received a long letter from von Dobschütz which, '(ill informed gibes apart)...points to individuals from whom (so to say) he has received so much kindness; and the "stets Ihr" with which he finishes up is, I feel sure, significant of continued regard for old friends' (BOD MS Eng. misc. d. 124 (I) no. 52). Jackson received another long letter on 17 May (H. Latimer Jackson to Sanday (27 May 1915), BOD MS Eng. misc. d. 124 (I) no. 55). The tone quickly changed and by 29 June 1915, Jackson spoke of von Dobschütz's 'very sarcastic tone' which excited a desire to give him a 'piece of my mind' (BOD MS Eng. misc. d. 124 (I) no. 57). After the First World War von Dobschütz and Burkitt corresponded, although the tone was somewhat less familiar, marred as it was by the fact that 'there was too much "England ist der Feind", in Germany during the War for us over here to forget' (CUL MS Add. 7658 A. 10 [14 Jan. 1920]); See also B. 286 (30 Oct. 1923); and B. 288 (7 Jan. 1928). On Anglo-German relations during the war see my essays, 'The Sanday, Sherrington and Troeltsch Affair, pp. 40-71, esp. pp. 43-55; and 'Anglo-German Theological Relations', pp. 109-126.

46. Burkitt, 'The Parables of the Kingdom of Heaven', *The Interpreter* 7 (1911), pp. 131-48.

and offers a strict eschatological understanding.[47] He then proceeds to an exhortation to 'treat ancient documents historically... The first thing to do with the Parables of the Gospel is to see how they fit into the general history of the Christian movement: if there still remain some crumbs over for our own spiritual nourishment in the 20th century, so much the better. But that is a luxury beyond what we have any right to demand'.[48] While admitting it to be a luxury Burkitt nevertheless held that there could be some contemporary application of Jesus' message of the Kingdom. He concludes:

> According to the view I have taken, our Lord, like His contemporaries, thought of the Kingdom of God as something future, a new state of things which should follow on after the present state of things has vanished in catastrophe, after the day of God's Judgment. Nevertheless, even as God in this present time has not forsaken his people altogether, so it could be said that the sovereignty of God was to some extent actually in the process of becoming realised. And the duty and the privilege of the Saints was to work, even during the burden and heat of the day, for the wages of life, when the Kingdom should come at the end.[49]

Whatever Jesus might have thought, then, the realization of his message, his radical difference and otherness from our society, began to take root in the present through the activity of the church through its vocation to proclaim this otherness: thoroughgoing eschatology thereby opened the door to ecclesiology. Thus, although it had to stand constantly under God's judgment, the church and its saints could become the home to eschatological values.

Burkitt, Liberalism and Eschatology

As should already be clear from this brief analysis of some of Burkitt's discussions of New Testament themes, he drew altogether different implications from Sanday in his application of an eschatological interpretation of the New Testament. Although he similarly recognized that Schweitzer had perhaps been rather too one-sided,[50] Burkitt, instead of moving to a position of scepticism and relativism, emphasized the strangeness of Jesus as a counter to the prevailing liberal conceptions

47. Burkitt, 'The Parables', p. 135.
48. Burkitt, 'The Parables', p. 145.
49. Burkitt, 'The Parables', p. 148.
50. Burkitt, 'Twenty-five Years of Theological Study', p. 12.

of Jesus, using eschatology as a means of criticizing the vagueness and inadequacy of what he regarded as the flimsy synthesis of liberal Protestantism. In response, and recognizing that a liberal synthesis was no longer theologically defensible, Burkitt was nevertheless able to locate a new source of authority, not in the modernization of Jesus' ethical teaching, but in a church orientated away from theological and philosophical systems towards the future.

In a collection entitled *Anglican Liberalism*, published in 1908, Burkitt was already distancing himself from liberal compromise. 'Liberalism', he claimed,

> is a word that is losing its charm as a popular label, and many people may think its association with Theology altogether incongruous... Liberalism now-a-days conveys to some minds a notion of flatness and vagueness, a notion of halting in a half-way house.[51]

As J. Warschauer pertinently observed in a discussion of 'Liberal Theology in Great Britain' in the *American Journal of Theology*: 'The eschatological hypothesis was welcomed in England because it seemed to signify "the failure of liberal Christianity"'.[52] The situation was, however, perhaps rather more subtle than Warschauer realized.

Far from merely returning to the conservative settlement of the past, Burkitt maintained that the task of the theologian had to be to 'restate the Christian message that it can be understood by modern man'.[53] Nevertheless he felt it was impossible for 'Christian philosophy' to be 'satisfied to regard Jesus merely as a legislator and an example; in fact, it does not chiefly regard Him as a legislator and example'.[54] The task was instead to

> carry on the hope of the Kingdom of God and the preparation for it through a new and unsurveyed region...If the church be really guided by the Divine Spirit, as Christians believe, the *via media* will open before us, and those whose ears are attuned aright will hear the word behind them, saying: 'This is the way, walk ye in it'.[55]

---

51. Burkitt, 'Theological Liberalism', in Hubert Handley (ed.), *Anglican Liberalism, by Twelve Churchmen* (London: Williams and Norgate, 1908), pp. 18-34, here p. 18.

52. J. Warschauer, 'Liberal Theology in Great Britain', *AJT* 16 (1912) pp. 333-58, here p. 351.

53. Burkitt, 'Theological Liberalism', p. 22.

54. Burkitt, 'Theological Liberalism', p. 30.

55. Burkitt, 'Theological Liberalism', p. 34.

For Burkitt, then, Christianity was a religion of preparation, and it was in this way that the link was retained with the historical Jesus and the Kingdom he proclaimed. Indeed it was precisely in its role as proclaimer of an urgent eschatological message that the Church was given its contemporary task.

In a lecture,[56] which J.N. Figgis described as 'epoch-making',[57] given to the Cambridge branch of the conservative Anglo-Catholic English Church Union (ECU) held in the Henry Martyn Hall on 12 May 1910, Burkitt boldly proclaimed 'The Failure of Liberal Christianity'. Although he had little sympathy with the conservatism of the ECU itself,[58] Burkitt was nonetheless deeply critical of liberal attempts to remove 'superstitious' accretions in order to reach a Christ 'freed from all external and particularist elements'.[59] The historians of early Christianity, he went on:

> are beginning to feel that this sort of procedure is unscientific, and they are beginning to trust their documents more, even at the cost of recognising that the expectations of the future which we read in the Gospels were not literally fulfilled.[60]

Burkitt then goes on to challenge his audience to find the all-wise, all-powerful or all-good hero in the historical material; instead, he remarked in a somewhat provocative manner, an unprejudiced observer might be forced to use 'old fashioned words like "fanaticism" or "megalomania"'.[61] Although he believed that the old liberal compromise which failed to grasp this view of history was bound to collapse, he also gave a salutary warning to the conservatives not to 'be too cheerful at the failure of liberal Christianity'. Thus he claimed:

56. F.C. Burkitt, *The Failure of Liberal Christianity and Some Thoughts on the Athanasian Creed* (Cambridge: Bowes and Bowes, 1910).

57. J.N. Figgis, *Civilisation at the Cross Roads* (London: Longmans, 1912), pp. 192-93.

58. Burkitt's decision to lecture to the ECU may well have been a highly provocative act in itself, at least to his fellow liberal churchmen in Cambridge. W.R. Inge wrote to Rashdall in 1909: 'I am working mainly with the Evangelicals here. If they can tolerate my liberalism I am well content with their company. The ECU party are laying siege to Cambridge with extreme vigour, and our good folk are so simple that they are easily captured' (Rashdall Papers, BOD MS Eng. Lett. d. 361 fol. 163-64).

59. Burkitt, *The Failure of Liberal Christianity*, p. 13.

60. Burkitt, *The Failure of Liberal Christianity*, p. 15.

61. Burkitt, *The Failure of Liberal Christianity*, p. 19.

> The fact is that Liberal Christianity was a compromise between
> traditional Christianity and present-day philosophy, formed by taking
> some things out of Christianity and some things out of our modern
> world. It is not wonderful that the two elements are beginning to refuse
> to cohere, and there is not enough of either element to stand by itself.[62]

It was this position which was equally directed against both liberals
and conservatives that gradually began to consolidate into a distinctively 'Modernist' position. Thus, citing Peabody's paper to the 1908
Oxford Congress on the History of Religions as a specific example
(which will be discussed in the next chapter), Burkitt maintains that
liberal Christianity had been trying to find a Jesus who was in touch
with our age, with its social ethics and philanthropy. This, however,
was little more than an attempt to come to terms with the prevailing
Zeitgeist, an effort that was proving impossible as contemporary human
beings gradually began to recognize the limits of their own times:

> Perhaps the *Zeitgeist* has heard some whisper about the limits of
> profitable philanthropy, and so lost interest in its task of liberalising the
> Gospels. Perhaps it is beginning to find out that the only thing that will
> turn the unemployable into the effective is a change of *mind*—the poor
> benighted Semites called it a change of heart. However that may be, the
> trend of research has shifted. And the liberal Christian is left alone.[63]

Liberalism could thus find little place for repentance; the only solution
to this impasse faced by liberalism, according to Burkitt, was to
recognize that none of the 'phrases and formulae' we might use about
Christ would ever communicate the whole truth. Instead all were
approximations attempting to express what no words or terms have yet
been found adequate to cover. At the same time, however, the Christian
expressed a faith that the 'power behind human phenomena has been
and still is working in the Church' which meant that 'the imperfection
of the human members will not fatally injure the life of the whole. If its
life be Divine, it will continue to live'.[64] Here, then, as a direct

---

62. Burkitt, *The Failure of Liberal Christianity*, p. 20.
63. Burkitt, *The Failure of Liberal Christianity*, pp. 25-26.
64. Burkitt, *The Failure of Liberal Christianity*, p. 27. Burkitt exerted a strong
influence on his friend, Latimer Jackson, who, after a long and finely-balanced
account of eschatology, concludes: 'And inasmuch as—with the proviso that, in this
earthly life, He was not consciously its founder—it is safe to say that Jesus
"inspired the activities of His Church", it is meet [*sic*] and right to see in Him the
Sower of His own parable who goes forth to sow the seed of His teaching and of

consequence of his understanding of the historical Jesus, Burkitt directed his attention against any form of liberal compromise, affirming the power and necessity of the supernatural element of religion, and, in turn, of the church as the agent of this supernatural power.

Later in 1910, Burkitt gave a lecture at the conference of the (liberal) Churchmen's Union,[65] in which, referring to his ECU lecture, he clarified his attitude towards liberalism in the context of a markedly different audience:

> Whereas to the professed Catholicks [*sic*] I tried to point out that some of their cherished watchwords seemed to offer a better and safer approach to a scientific view of religion than much of the shallow and sentimental liberalism of the street and the newspaper, to you this afternoon I shall rather ask for a reconsideration of some Catholick [*sic*] watchwords in the name of History and Science, watchwords that are generally unpopular, however clear they may be to the conservative minority of English men and women.[66]

Liberals were misguided, Burkitt claimed, chiefly in their attempts to reduce Christianity to a rational system, as was instanced in their desire to remove the Athanasian Creed from the Prayer Book; their error lay, he felt, in what they saw as 'the necessity for simplification, for compromise, for concession,—concession not necessarily from the side of one who holds fast to the "Godhead" of "Christ", but certainly from one side or the other'.[67] Against such a conception, Jesus was, for Burkitt, a figure who simply could not be understood without grasping the supernatural: indeed any reduction to contemporary modes of thought was likely to destroy the distinctiveness and essence of his message.

There was a great deal of discussion of Burkitt's lecture. Hastings Rashdall, one of the leading Modernists of the time, responded at length in the first edition of the *Modern Churchman*.[68] Although he was critical of Burkitt, it would appear that he was soon having second thoughts about the importance of eschatology for understanding Jesus, a fact noted by Hewlett Johnson in a postcard to Burkitt in 1911: 'I

Himself in the immeasurable field of time' (*The Eschatology of Jesus*, pp. 336-37).

65. Burkitt, 'Some Thoughts on the Athanasian Creed', in *idem*, *The Failure of Liberal Christianity*, pp. 31-40.

66. Burkitt, *The Failure of Liberal Christianity*, p. 31.

67. Burkitt, *The Failure of Liberal Christianity*, p. 38.

68. Untitled article in *Modern Churchman* 1 (1911–12), pp. 23-35.

happen to know, not directly, but indirectly that Rashdall is v[er]y. [*sic*] much impressed with your "Schweitzerian views" as he terms them, and they are raising awkward questionings in his mind'.[69] By 1913, however, Rashdall lectured at Oberlin College, Ohio in a manner suggesting any such questionings had received distinctively liberal answers.[70] Similarly, in 1914, Rashdall remarked at the first Conference of the Churchmen's Union at Ripon that 'I do not see how the Christ of Schweitzer or of Tyrrell can be "the Way, the Truth and the Life" to anybody'.[71]

Israel Abrahams, a liberal Jew, also responded to Burkitt's pamphlet,[72] which provoked C.W. Votaw, of the *American Journal of Theology*, to write to Burkitt.[73] This letter reveals much about the significant differences between American 'scientific' re-interpretations and English supernaturalism:

> I do not quite understand why Abrahams spoke unsympathetically of your thoughts on the 'Failure of Liberal Christianity'. Reformed Judaism has nothing to lose, but much to gain, when Christians assume an *historical* instead of a *dogmatic* attitude towards Jesus.
>
> It was quite inevitable that the first stage away from the traditional interpretation of Jesus should be a *modernization* of him (that is the 'liberal Jesus'). But as you point out, that is only a transition stage. We are moving toward the *historical* interpretation of Jesus, in which we shall be *detached* from the Christological doctrines of the past, and shall view Jesus in the category of humanity. Then he will appear, I think, as a very ardent Jew of the first century, of the prophetic-apocalyptic type, who sought to reform the scribal and priestly Judaism by restoring and advancing the highest ethical and religious quality of Judaism. He certainly appears, not less significant, but more significant, when viewed historically than when viewed dogmatically, except to those minds that are not yet modernized. A scientifically trained man cannot find satisfaction in the classical Christian doctrine, but requires a rereading of

69. Postcard from Hewlett Johnson to Burkitt, 15 July 1911 (CUL MS Add. 7658 B. 500).

70. Rashdall, 'Ethics and Eschatology', in *idem, Conscience and Christ: Six Lectures on Christian Ethics* (London: Gerald Duckworth, 1916), pp. 36-76. See below, Chapter 5.

71. Rashdall, 'The Creeds', *Modern Churchman* 4 (1914), pp. 204-214, here p. 211.

72. Abrahams had written to Burkitt privately on 12 Dec. 1912 linking his name with Schweitzer (CUL MS Add. 7658 B. 2).

73. 17 Feb. 1913 (CUL MS Add. 7658 B. 973).

first-century history according to modern world-view and thought-forms.

America yields slowly to the historical interpretation of Jesus. Christianity is so wonderfully inwoven with the dogma of the centuries. I do not suppose that we shall have *more* difficulty than England or Germany in achieving freedom from the ancient world-view and theology, but it will be a long time before an *historical* attitude toward Jesus will be regarded as permissible or right. Those who assume this attitude find it a difficult task to present it to others helpfully.

Meanwhile, as you state on p. 20, the majority of the people who think themselves beyond the orthodox Christianity, instead of becoming Unitarian, either leave the churches, or stay in them in the hope of modernizing not Jesus, but Christianity.

Of course we can be patient and work quietly to bring about a scientific conception of life, present and past. I wonder that so few scholars in the foremost universities are really seeing the matter clearly, and moving in the direction of a modern Christianity with a scientific view of the universe and a biological view of life.

Yours,

C.W. Votaw.

It is clear from such a letter that Burkitt's position was somewhat different from the American scientific modernizers for whom Jesus was to be understood in modern thought-forms. For Burkitt, Jesus was a stranger, to his own day, and, what was equally important, also to ours.

Eschatology and the Modernist Identity

In a survey published in 1927, Henry Major, the most important figure in English liberal theological education and Principal of Ripon Hall, Oxford, the Modernist training college, looked back to the ten years or so before the first World War which saw the rise of Modernism.[74] He recognized that Burkitt had contributed to the questioning by many who identified themselves as 'Modernists' of liberal protestantism, which he acknowledged had been up till then 'the dominant note of English Liberal Churchmanship'.[75] The Modernist's criticism of the New Testament, he claimed, was

74. On Henry Major, see Alan Stephenson, *The Rise and Decline of English Modernism* (London: SPCK, 1984), ch. 4.

75. Major, *English Modernism*, p. 29. In a perhaps rather prophetic letter to Arthur Boutwood of 13 January 1909, George Tyrrell remarked that if modernism was to have a future it would have to be within the Church of England (Maude Petre [ed.], *George Tyrrell's Letters* [London: T. Fisher Unwin, 1920], p. 119).

more strictly critical than the Liberal's. Presuppositions, if not altogether excluded by the Modernists, are at least more rigorously kept in check. Although the conclusions of the extreme eschatologists with their *Interimsethik* are for the most part not accepted by English Modernists yet Modernists find Jesus less familiar in some ways and less comprehensible than the Son of Man in German Protestant Liberalism.[76]

In what is perhaps an overstatement, but one which undoubtedly contains an element of truth, Major then goes on to claim that 'after Schweitzer's book, *Von Reimarus zu Wrede*, became known in England, the ecclesiastical use of the word Liberal came to mean among younger scholarly Churchmen little more than anti-eschatological'.[77] Burkitt, in his oft-repeated claim that Jesus had to be true to his own day, thus helped redirect critical theology away from liberal reductionism towards a position which could no longer rest content with artificial rationalist reconstruction. Thus, according to Major:

> The Liberal was accused by the eschatologists of being afraid to face and accept historical and critical conclusions which were subversive of his liberal theology. The Liberal's critical method...[of] exorcising or eliminating...whatever did not appeal to the Liberal mind...was declared to be unsound.[78]

Major, although refusing to accept the eschatological position in its completeness, nevertheless sided with a view which was 'prepared to let historical criticism have full play'.[79] And in turn, like Schweitzer, and many Modernists, he emphasized the importance of the mysterious 'Spirit of Jesus' which transcended history. Whatever his exaggerations, Henry Major is without doubt accurate in pointing to the importance of eschatology, and in particular, to Burkitt, in consolidating a position which is recognizably Modernist in distinction from the older forms of liberalism which are characterized by the efforts to harmonize Jesus with the thought forms of the modern day.

---

76. Major, *English Modernism*, p. 36. In *The Lord of Thought* (London: SCM Press, 1921), for instance, C.W. Emmet and Lily Dougall argue against Schweitzer's *Interimsethik* (p. 268) chiefly because of the stress on individual reward. See also Emmet's article 'Is the Teaching of Jesus an Interimsethik?', pp. 423-34, esp. p. 434: 'the theory gives a low and unworthy colouring to the teaching of Jesus, since it represents Him as laying the whole stress on the self-centred desire of the individual for his own salvation'.

77. Major, *English Modernism*, p. 36 n. 2.

78. Major, *English Modernism*, p. 33.

79. Major, *English Modernism*, p. 75.

An eschatological interpretation of Jesus thus made an impact far wider than the specialist field of New Testament studies: indeed it soon spread out to permeate all aspects of theology. Moreover some of the figures who adopted an eschatological starting point in their christo-logical position (who will be discussed in more detail in Chapters 6 and 7) can perhaps be understood as paving the way for the radical critical eschatological theology which emerged after the First World War.

Chapter 5

ETHICS AND ESCHATOLOGY

William Sanday and Ernst von Dobschütz[1]

Almost immediately after the publication of *The Life of Christ in Recent Research*, William Sanday was subjected to a barrage of criticism from both Germany and England. As should already be clear, he had (perhaps unwittingly) entered a battle over the very future of liberal theology. To some, to side with Schweitzer was to question the contemporary relevance of Jesus' message and with it the ethical stability of the nation. The liberal synthesis of religion and ethics seemed to be shaking. Thus despite his far from unequivocal acceptance of Schweitzer in the *The Life of Christ in Recent Research*, Sanday was almost immediately plunged into a remarkably vigorous debate.

For instance, Ernst von Dobschütz, who was at the time Professor in Strasbourg and a colleague of Schweitzer's, wrote to Sanday on 21 October 1907, after receiving a copy of the *The Life of Christ in Recent Research*, expressing in somewhat harsh tones, his surprise that he should have attached

> so much importance to the book of Albert Schweitzer. I could almost believe that you had let yourself be misled by his anti-liberal attitude. I know him—perhaps only too well. The conservative turns of expression with him are only decorative: he is a leader of our extreme liberals here, and coquets with a certain independence over against his own party. He is highly gifted, but unfortunately while still too young has attained to a position of so much importance in Church affairs that it has turned his head; he is afflicted with a degree of self-conceit which is almost

1. Ernst A.A.O.A. von Dobschütz (1870–1934) was extraordinary Professor in Jena from 1898, becoming ordinary professor in Strasbourg (1904); in Breslau (1910); in Halle (1913). Under the combined influence of Harnack and Martin Kähler he sought to combine the best of both traditions, trying to continue Kähler's plan to write a history of the Bible in the Church.

insufferable. At the same time his influence as it seems to me is almost entirely destructive: he throws out questions to people which he cannot answer himself, which nobody can answer, and then plays the part of an independent sceptic; with a *salto mortale* (desperate leap) he then again suddenly takes his stand on the ground of an altogether mystical reverence for Christ. But let me ask you yourself: can the Jesus who is drawn for us by Schweitzer, this enthusiast who ends by being wrecked on the delusions of his own greatness (p. 367) be really He upon whom our faith rests? Schweitzer himself says on p. 199: 'not the Jesus whom we recognise in history, but only the Jesus who has risen again spiritually in humanity, can mean anything for our time and be a help to it': that is, precisely not Jesus as God has given him to us but only a figment of man's imagination: we are standing with both feet in the middle of Gnosticism!

Schweitzer's book has been with us generally repudiated, and Jülicher in my opinion has dealt with him quite justly.[2] And one who like Schweitzer looks down with such supreme contempt on all the work that has been done before him deserves to be dealt with. His book is not a history but a criticism of Research on the life of Christ, in which for the history Hase in his edition of 1876[3] had materially prepared the way for him; Schweitzer adds only the two criteria, [*sic*] Whatever is eschatological is good, whatever is not eschatological must be bad...

What I personally blame Schweitzer for most (because he corrupts my own students with it) is his supreme contempt for the work of literary criticism—and that in a pupil of Holtzmann's![4] Matt. X as originally a unity? And on this foundation he builds far reaching conclusions.

And then this playing the conservative with contemptuous onslaughts upon liberalism. He makes merry over the facts that liberals (as by the way does also Bernhard Weiss) still hold to naturalistic explanations of miracle, as for instance, in the case of the feeding. He retains the whole miracle, only without the miracle, and imagines for himself an eschatological sacrament, of which there is not the slightest hint in the texts. By the way, what can be the significance of an eschatological

---

2.   Schweitzer had been highly critical of Adolf Jülicher's subjective reading of the parables (*The Quest of the Historical Jesus*, pp. 40-69). In response Jülicher wrote a brief pamphlet attacking Schweitzer, *Neue Linien in der Kritik der evangelishen Überlieferung* (Giessen: Adolf Topelmann, 1906), suggesting that the fruit of the new epoch in Life of Jesus Research should be a 'peaceful separation of religion and historical knowledge' (p. 76).

3.   Karl Hase, *Geschichte Jesu* (Leipzig: Breitkopf und Hartel, 1876).

4.   H.J. Holtzmann (1832–1910). Taught at Heidelberg (1858–1874) and Strasbourg (1874–1904). He strongly defended the Markan hypothesis and later argued for a psychological development in Jesus' self-consciousness.

sacrament, the significance of which Jesus alone understands, and neither his disciples nor the people [*sic*]. That is nonsense. And so throughout the positive construction: he finds fault with the psychological analysis of Liberal Theology, and with the help of psychology he builds up his own purely eschatological Jesus, only that by means of eschatological psychology (which we naturally have no means of checking) the greatest extravagances can be attributed to him.

The whole book is the carrying out of a fixed idea which will do great mischief, because it undermines confidence in solid historical work. And the blessing of God will only be given to careful work that is also accurate in detail (compare Harnack!), not to clever fancies (*genialen Phantasien*). Science does not tolerate artistic natures: it would rather have draymen.

I am afraid that the respect which you have paid to Schweitzer's book will tend to strengthen these dangerous influences, and that grieves me. You have got out of the book something altogether different (in a positive sense) from what most of those will get out of it into whose hands it comes. It is true that you tolerate in England much that with us would be far less tolerated.

But I must beg your pardon for detaining you so long with my ideas. Your beautiful book has stirred me to it. It would be delightful if we could talk things over by word of mouth. Perhaps one day you may find your way to Strassburg; it would be a great pleasure to me to welcome you here.[5]

In his reply to von Dobschütz of 30 October 1907,[6] which adopts a similar polemical tone, Sanday expressed his hope that his book 'would show that I have some conception of the extraordinarily high standard of intellectual sincerity characteristic of your theologians' and then pointed out some of the differences between the English and German way of scholarship (which were discussed in Chapter 3). In this letter Sanday's own conservatism comes out clearly, and he claims that 'the Church of to-day is still the same living Church as in the days of the Apostles'. He goes on to say, however, that while he admires Jülicher, he is also nevertheless prepared to defend his use of Schweitzer:

The only serious personal question between us is as to Schweitzer; and on this head I confess that your letter causes me some concern. When I read his book I knew nothing of the writer and had not even seen a review of it. Its literary style and the ability with which it was written interested me greatly; and I think that the spirit and courage in it

5.   BOD MS Eng. misc. d. 123 nos. 83-92.
6.   Sanday to von Dobschütz (BOD MS Eng. misc. d. 128 no. 46).

overshadowed the audacity which I am free to confess was not altogether unwelcome to me. He was attacking a strongly established school, which seemed to me to be doing what it could to rob the world of things that it ought not to be robbed of. I had some thought of a youthful David, not perhaps with all the wisdom of a maturer combatant, but with a sling and a stone and a nervous arm.

It is true that I gave him the benefit of the doubt where I could. It is true also that I tried to extract from his book what I could assimilate myself and what I thought that others of my countrymen might assimilate. The book really taught me much. It gave point and coherence to not a little that lay half-developed in my own mind. (pp. 119, 122).[7]

And then, my dear Professor, I cannot help asking, Are you yourself quite just to the man or (still more) to the book? Is your own diagnosis either psychologically possible or consistent with the facts? I am sure that you would not want to say that the writer is consciously insincere. I cannot for a moment admit that the conservative turns of his thought are 'merely conservative'. They have cost him far too much trouble for that, and they are too consistent with themselves. I do not mean that there is no more inconsistency. I have warned my own readers that there are sceptical presuppositions in his book that he does not disguise (pp. 100, 109). But the point on which I am most inclined to question your own estimate is that you put aside the whole mystical element in his thought as though it meant nothing to him, not because it is insincere but because you are out of sympathy with it yourself. In all this, I must confess, that I am very much on Schweitzer's side!... Believe me it is not Gnosticism, but an attempt,—perhaps slightly peculiar in the way it is expressed, but quite innocent in intention—to paraphrase St. Paul. (2 Cor. V.16, which has been quoted just before).

If I may venture to say so, it is just on this side that I feel my own divergence from you most acutely: it is the reverse or negative side of your insistence upon the historical Jesus. This really, I should say, needs to be supplemented by the Pauline doctrine of the Holy Spirit. I would not accuse you of omitting this: but there is at least a great tendency to omit it among your allies.

7.   In these pages Sanday uses Schweitzer to defend what amounts to a very traditional doctrine of the Holy Spirit: 'I am inclined to believe—though this is speculation, that I would not express otherwise than very tentatively—that the real coming of the Kingdom—the fact corresponding to it in the field of ultimate realities—is what we are in the habit of calling the work of the Holy Spirit, from the day of Pentecost onwards; the presence of a divine force, drawing and annexing (so far as the resistance of human wills allows it) the world to itself, but as yet still in mid process, and with possibilities in the future of which we perhaps hardly dream' (Sanday, *Life of Christ in Recent Research*, p. 122).

I am afraid that I may have taken some liberties in what I have written. But I know that you would wish me to write frankly as you have written yourself. I hope that only good can come of such an interchange as ours.
    With sincere regards,
            Believe me,
                    Yours very truly,
                        W. Sanday.

The Oxford Congress of the History of Religions, 1908

In another letter of 11 December 1907[8] Sanday invited von Dobschütz to stay with him during the Oxford Congress of the History of Religions in 1908, where discussion of eschatology was to dominate the section on Christianity. In his Presidential address to this Section, which was a masterly summary of an enormous range of primarily continental learning published in the previous four years, Sanday expressed his admiration of *Von Reimarus zu Wrede*, describing it as a 'combative book, [which] has passed rather like a storm cloud across the sky'. It would appear, however, that von Dobschütz's letters had had some effect on Sanday's thought, and in his brief summary of Schweitzer's book he was far more willing than he had been in his *Life of Christ in Recent Research* to point to its faults, which, he felt, were twofold. Firstly, it did not 'take sufficient account of the literary criticism of the Gospels' and secondly, 'it does not allow enough for the extent to which Christ, in adopting the current ideas of the time, also transformed them. I think we may say that the extent to which He did transform this particular group of ideas is one of the leading problems that the student of the New Testament has to consider'.[9] This observation was borne out in a number of papers at the Congress which addressed this problem of Jesus' own individual creativity.

Von Dobschütz, for instance, in his paper on 'The Significance of Early Christian Eschatology',[10] discussed the 'over-estimation of the

8.   BOD MS Eng. misc. d. 128 no. 59. At about the same time von Dobschütz also kept up a lively and often intimate correspondence with Hastings Rashdall of New College, Oxford. They often exchanged students with one another, and invited one another to stay. See BOD MS Eng. lett. d. 391 fols. 27, 185-86, 198.

9.   Sanday's Presidential Address to 'Section VIII: The Christian Religion', in P.S. Allen (ed.), *Transactions of the Third International Congress for the History of Religions*, II (2 vols.; Oxford: Clarendon Press, 1908), pp. 263-82 (278).

10.   Von Dobschütz, 'The Significance of Early Christian Eschatology', in Allen (ed.), *Transactions of the Third International Congress*, II, pp. 312-20.

significance of eschatology on the part of a considerable number of scholars'.[11] Although he recognizes the importance of eschatology as a characteristic of 'Jewish thought as contrasted with Greek philosophy', he goes on to claim that '[w]hen we ask what is the kernel of early Christian religious feeling, we shall find that there is nothing eschatological about it'. Whereas the Jewish religion conceived of God as a distant Being, Jesus speaks of the intimacy of God as Father. Thus instead of the Kingdom of God being a completely future event, 'Jesus Himself by His complete union with God brings in this domination of God'.[12] Although eschatology 'is at the background of all this, it has changed its significance'. Jesus is thus not imprisoned within his own world, but is able to contribute something decisively new: he 'was at once progressive and eminently conservative'.[13] Though undoubtedly important, eschatology could not be seen as 'of the essence of Christian faith, this being rather confidence in a present activity of God and an already accomplished salvation'.[14] Thus, von Dobschütz concluded, 'wherever there is a revival of the Gospel, (e.g. in Augustine, St. Francis, Luther and the other heroes of the Reformation) we meet again the joyful confidence and assurance of salvation combined with a secure hope of still greater things'.[15] Jesus' own creativity was thus of the essence of the Gospel.

In another contribution to the Congress, the American scholar F.G. Peabody,[16] discussed 'New Testament Eschatology and New Testament Ethics' and criticized Schweitzer, Sanday and H.W. Garrod[17] directly, setting them against the dominant ethical interpretations of modern liberal theology. In his paper, Peabody addresses Garrod's question: 'Can any moralist, firmly persuaded of the imminent dissolution of the world and all things in it, frame an ethical code adequate for all

11. Von Dobschütz, 'The Significance', p. 312.
12. Von Dobschütz, 'The Significance', p. 316.
13. Von Dobschütz, 'The Significance', p. 317.
14. Von Dobschütz, 'The Significance', p. 319.
15. Von Dobschütz, 'The Significance', p. 320.
16. Francis Greenwood Peabody (1847–1936). Unitarian Professor at Harvard from 1881–1913. Dean from 1901–1906 and founder Professor in the Dept. of Social Ethics in 1906.
17. See esp. H.W. Garrod (of Merton College, Oxford), 'Christ the Forerunner', in *idem*, *The Religion of All Good Men and Other Studies in Christian Ethics* (London: Constable, 1906). Garrod does not display any knowledge of Schweitzer.

time?'[18] So powerful are the ethical ideas in the Gospels, according to Peabody, that they 'provide a test which is likely to modify in limit an extreme application of eschatology to their interpretation'.[19] Though he admits that eschatology had served as a 'corrective influence', it had certainly not replaced all conceptions of New Testament ethics which focused on obedience and discipleship. Peabody then goes on to outline the historical problem in a manner reminiscent of Sanday, which, he suggests

> has to consider whether the secret of Jesus lay in His reflection of con-
> temporary ideals or in His creation of new ideals; whether His apocalyp-
> tic expectation was His master or whether it was His servant; whether He
> reiterated the current eschatology or utilized and spiritualized it; whether
> in a word the central motive of His teaching was dramatic or didactic, the
> work of a herald or the work of a teacher.[20]

Drawing from Wellhausen, Peabody concludes that '[it] is the non-Jewish and human, rather than the Jewish in Him, which stamps [Jesus'] character'.[21] As is clear from both of these contributions to the Congress, the question of eschatology brought to a head a central historical problem faced by all who sought to place Jesus in his contemporary nexus of ideas, from whatever school of thought: how far did he merely express the hopes and expectations of the time, and how far was he a creative genius able to modify and stand above current ideas?[22]

---

18. Garrod, *The Religion*, pp. 60, 61 cited in Peabody, 'New Testament Eschatology and New Testament Ethics', in Allen (ed.), *Transactions of the Third International Congress*, II, pp. 305-312 (308).

19. Peabody, 'New Testament Eschatology', p. 310.

20. Peabody, 'New Testament Eschatology', p. 310.

21. Peabody, 'New Testament Eschatology', p. 311, citing Wellhausen's *Einleitung in die drei ersten Evangelien* (Berlin: Reimer, 1905), p. 114.

22. Wilhelm Bousset, one of the most important scholars in the so-called *Religionsgeschichtliche Schule* observed, for instance, that historical research was in 'danger of placing Christianity in the flux of development', thereby 'failing to give due worth to its special character and unique meaning, and thereby neutralising and relativising everything' ('Die Religionsgeschichte und das neue Testament', *TRu* 7 (1904), pp. 265-77, 311-18, 353-65, here pp. 364-65). On this see my essay 'Religion, Ethics and the History of Religion School', pp. 43-78.

The Debate Widens

Discussion of eschatology continued later in 1908 spreading outside the confines of the academic world. The Church of England Church Congress, meeting at Manchester, devoted its morning session on 8 October to a discussion of 'Eschatology of the New Testament' under the chairmanship of the Bishop of Derry, G.A. Chadwick. William Sanday was the principal speaker and, although he observed that at the Oxford Congress 'there was an admirable discussion of the subject which seemed to me to present it in a better form, and, indeed, to bring the whole discussion perceptibly nearer to a solution',[23] he nevertheless offered his own thoughts on the subject. In his paper, which 'was listened to with the deepest attention throughout',[24] Sanday's conservatism becomes clear: although he points to the vital importance of apocalyptic for Jesus, he is once again able to avoid any difficult questions by spiritualizing the message. He could write, for instance, that 'although we believe that the mind of the Son was in perfect unison with the mind of the Father, still there is room for difference between the truth of things absolutely as they are and the truth of things humanly apprehended...in other words there may well be an element of type and symbol; and to say precisely how far this element of type and symbol extended in the case of our Lord may perhaps be beyond our power'. He concludes: 'although the imagery in which the judgment is described is imagery, and is not to be taken too literally, yet we may be sure that it has a solid foundation in the eternal law of God's Providence and of His dealing with the souls of men'.[25]

R.H. Charles[26] spoke next, presenting a detailed discussion of the Old Testament background to New Testament eschatology. He finished by claiming that it was impossible to reach any conclusion on the nature of the New Testament without taking into account its radically

23. *Official Report of the Church Congress held at Manchester*, October, 1908, p. 380. Sanday had von Dobschütz in mind.

24. *The Guardian* (14 October 1908), p. 1718.

25. *1908 Report*, p. 384. For Sanday's conservatism, see also 'The Bearing of Critics upon the Gospel History', *ExpTim* 20 (1908–1909), pp. 103-114; 152-62, esp. p. 162.

26. Robert Henry Charles (1855–1931). Professor of Biblical Greek in Dublin (1898); Grinfield lecturer in the Septuagint at Oxford (1906–1913); Canon and later Archdeacon of Westminster (1913). Leading expert on apocalyptic literature.

new spiritualized understanding of God and Christ, 'for the Messiah assumes a position undreamt of in the past, and membership of the Kingdom is constituted firstly and predominatingly [*sic*] through formal relationship to its Divine Head'.[27] Other contributions (on Pauline themes) came from Professor R.J. Knowling of Durham and W.H. Fremantle, Dean of Ripon, and in the lively discussion that followed, Canon Harford of Liverpool remarked that 'the crowded attendance at this meeting proves the profound interest that the subject of the future excites in the minds of Christian men and women'.[28] Both Sanday and Charles, however, placed little emphasis on the radical strangeness of Jesus' message choosing instead to spiritualize the religion of Jesus, as if the future, and its coming judgment, did not much matter.

In the years that followed the publication of Sanday's *The Life of Christ in Recent Research*, von Dobschütz was not the only Continental scholar to make contact with Sanday over his positive estimation of Schweitzer. Paul Wernle,[29] who had originally reviewed *Von Reimarus zu Wrede* for the *TLZ*[30] wrote to Sanday on 21 February 1909, after eventually receiving a review copy of *The Life of Christ in Recent Research* for the *TLZ*.[31]

> I find your book a good example of how we can engage with one another from a different theological and ecclesiastical standpoint, and I have always had the distressing feeling of just how far you in England are from us, not merely in knowledge but also in understanding and judgement. We are in a very bad position through the fault of our booksellers. I fear that had I not obtained a review copy of your book from Schürer,[32] I would never have seen it[33]...We in Germany and

27. *1908 Report*, p. 388.

28. *1908 Report*, p. 403.

29. Paul Wernle (1872–1939). From 1900 Professor of Church History and History of Dogma at Basel. He also published works on New Testament.

30. *TLZ* 31 (1906), cols. 516-19. Though he had been an object of Schweitzer's attack, Wernle reluctantly admired the book, noting that 'the title ought to read *Von Reimarus zu Schweitzer*, for Wrede is also one of the many corpses on the vast life-of-Jesus battlefield on which Schweitzer is the sole survivor'.

31. Review of Sanday, *Life of Christ*, *TLZ* 34 (13 Feb. 1909), cols. 98-101.

32. E. Schürer, editor of the *TLZ*.

33. In the review itself, Wernle lamented the fact that he could not introduce his students to English scholarship in the way Sanday had introduced his to German scholarship because of the difficulty of obtaining foreign titles (Review of Sanday, col. 98).

Switzerland have to carry the bad consequences of our radicalism along with the good, and I sincerely hope that you and your church might be spared the same thing. I usually sharply play up the negative in my books, often more sharply than it is good to do... I personally got to know Albert Schweitzer and I looked on with distress as he only listened to himself and his own ideas and was not open to anything else. He is extraordinarily gifted, but where will that take him, if he only listens to himself and finds only his own ideas in all the Gospels? You have made so many concessions to him that his one-sidedness can scarcely come to the surface.[34]

Such letters evidently had some effect on Sanday, and he soon began to rethink his views on eschatology.

The Oxford Summer School in Theology, 1909

Equally influential were the four 'exceedingly important lectures'[35] on 'The Eschatology of the Gospels' which von Dobschütz gave at the Oxford Summer School in Theology from 11–22 September 1909.[36] *The Guardian* reporter noted that

no one could follow the lectures without noticing the cross-currents on this subject. On the one hand those who are theologically conservative are inclined to minimize the eschatological element in the Gospels, and for this purpose are prepared to go to further lengths in the use of the critical knife than was formerly the case, whereas those who are theologically quite radical are too prepared to accept these passages, and even to emphasize their importance. This is a new phenomenon, and probably means that radical theology and extreme criticism will not go together in the future in the way in which they have in the past.[37]

34. BOD MS Eng. misc. d. 140 no. 339. My translation.
35. *The Guardian* (29 Sept. 1909), p. 1507. Von Dobschütz, 'The Eschatology of the Gospels', pp. 97-113; 193-209; 333-47; 398-417. These lectures were also published in book form together with the address to the Oxford Congress: *The Eschatology of the Gospels* (London: Hodder & Stoughton, 1910).
36. *The Guardian* (15 Sept. 1909), p. 1440. The sessions on eschatology were attended by Sanday, Burkitt, Kirsopp Lake (of Leiden), Percy Gardner (Professor of Classics at Oxford) and Claude Montefiore, one of the leading liberal Jewish scholars of the time. In a letter to Sanday of 4 July 1909, von Dobschütz remarked that he was looking forward to discussing the subject of eschatology (BOD MS Eng. misc. d. 123 no. 94).
37. *The Guardian* (29 Sept. 1909), p. 1507.

This observation reflects something of the strange dynamic exerted by eschatology. However, it was not merely conservative scholars who were to try and explain away the eschatological passages. More liberal scholars were equally critical of eschatology because of its effects on the perception of Christ as universal ethical teacher, as von Dobschütz's lectures make clear.

He opens with a lengthy discussion of the history of the problem up to Schweitzer who, he suggests, 'met with much more appreciation in England than in Germany, where even Schweitzer's friends were rather surprised by the one-sidedness of his views'.[38] He goes on to point out that 'Professor W. Sanday's treatment of the book in his work, *The Life of Christ in Recent Research* (1907), gave Dr. Schweitzer's book a splendid advertisement in this country and, at the Oxford Congress for the history of religions in 1908, Professor F.C. Burkitt made himself a champion of this theory of consistent eschatology, which I myself would prefer to call radical eschatology'.[39] Von Dobschütz then goes on to outline his own approach to eschatology, pointing to Kirsopp Lake[40] and Shailer Mathews[41] as English-speakers who shared his 'sounder' method. 'The problem before us', he suggests at the conclusion of the first lecture, 'is whether the eschatology of the Gospels belongs to the original stock of the Jesus-tradition, or is due to this later eschatological inclination of Christianity, which, borrowing from Judaism, transformed the gospel into a rather eschatological teaching'. Once again he asks whether Jesus was dependent on Judaism, or whether he should be 'regarded as an exceptional being outside the operation of this law'.[42]

In later lectures he surveys the eschatological material in greater depth, suggesting that the non-eschatological sayings have to be regarded as of the essence of the Gospel, since it is their 'permanent

38. Von Dobschütz, 'The Eschatology', p. 105.

39. Von Dobschütz, 'The Eschatology', p. 106. In a footnote, von Dobschütz remarks, however: 'Unnecessary to say, that Prof. Burkitt does not share all the conclusions of Dr. Schweitzer!'

40. Kirsopp Lake (1872–1946). Professor at Leiden (1904–1914) and later at Harvard. He edited (with Foakes Jackson) a five volume work on *The Beginnings of Christianity* (London: Macmillan, 1920), and was, like Burkitt, a student of palaeography.

41. See esp. *The Messianic Hope in the New Testament* (Chicago: Chicago University Press, 1905).

42. Von Dobschütz, 'The Eschatology', p. 113.

value' that 'causes us to put them in the first rank... It is, lastly...the history of the Christian Church, from its beginning in the apostolic age to our own time, that proves the non-eschatological element to be essential. This statement does not include, however, the opposite thesis, that eschatology has no place at all in Jesus' mind. A sound and sober interpretation will be found to be one which gives to every group of sayings its own value and weight'.[43] Von Dobschütz goes on to maintain that Jesus speaks of a 'transmuted eschatology...in the sense that what was spoken of in Jewish eschatology as to come in the last days is taken here as already at hand in the lifetime of Jesus'.[44] This is to be preferred to consistent eschatology which does 'violence to Jesus' moral teaching' as well as to those statements which speak of Messiahship and the kingdom as already present.[45] Finally, after a survey of the Johannine literature, von Dobschütz concludes that 'however strong Jesus' belief in eschatology might have been, it was only of secondary importance for His religious life, and for His teaching'.[46] Salvation, according to von Dobschütz, was thus experienced in the present since Jesus

> realised in Himself the complete and supreme communion with God, and yet he looked forward to a time of final salvation...Jesus' victory over Satan, His casting out of devils, was only an anticipation...The Christian is a new creature, but he looks for a new heaven and a new earth, and his prayer will be for ever as His Lord taught him: '*Thy Kingdom come*'.[47]

Von Dobschütz consequently argues against Schweitzer on three counts: firstly, an explanation solely in terms of eschatology reduces Jesus completely to his Jewish milieu thereby denying his creativity; secondly, consistent eschatology downplays Jesus' ethical teaching; and finally, the focus on the future denies the realized character of salvation.[48]

---

43. Von Dobschütz, 'The Eschatology', p. 347.
44. Von Dobschütz, 'The Eschatology', p. 344.
45. Von Dobschütz, 'The Eschatology', p. 346.
46. Von Dobschütz, 'The Eschatology', p. 416.
47. Von Dobschütz, 'The Eschatology', p. 417.
48. These various strands of criticism were emphasized later by many other writers. See, for example, Dewick, *Primitive Christian Eschatology*, p. 390: 'If Jesus was simply a Jew and nothing more, it is inconceivable that he should be the permanent Centre of the Absolute Religion for all mankind'. Cf. Perrin, *The Kingdom of God*, pp. 41-45.

The Translation: The Quest of the Historical Jesus

All three arguments were to re-emerge in the following year, which saw the publication, at Burkitt's instigation, of the English translation of *The Quest of the Historical Jesus* by William Montgomery,[49] one of his former pupils, and which served to rekindle interest in Schweitzer's ideas.[50] Reviewing the book for the *Journal of Theological Studies*, J.F. Bethune-Baker remarked:

> Professor Burkitt has at least done good service to the English-reading public in giving them an opportunity of judging for themselves whether after all the Catholic Church has not preserved an interpretation of the Person of her Lord more adequate to account for all the facts than any of the modern investigators, whose results are recorded here, has produced.[51]

Soon after the publication, however, W.R. Inge, by now Lady Margaret Professor at Cambridge, added his weight to the critics of eschatology, developing a variant of the moral argument in a Cambridge University sermon preached in May 1910 on 'The Apocalyptic Element in Christ's Teaching'.[52] Later in the summer, in a review of Sanday's *Christologies Ancient and Modern*, he openly challenged Sanday to make a public recantation of Schweitzer.[53] In the University sermon Inge issued something of a war-cry against Schweitzer but approached the subject from a rather different direction from most of the earlier critics. 'It is enough to say', he suggested

49. In a letter to Burkitt, Montgomery remarked that he liked Burkitt's introduction to the volume 'very much. So far as my judgment goes it says just what needs to be said and says it in the right way. It is as well calculated as anything could be to avoid "serious stumbling blocks"' (Montgomery to Burkitt, CUL MS Add. 7658 B. 683, 12 June 1909).

50. *The Quest of the Historical Jesus* was reviewed at length by Hewlett Johnson in *The Interpreter* 6 (1910), pp. 337-47. In a letter to Sanday dated Easter 1910 (BOD MS Eng. misc. d. 122 (I) no. 268), Burkitt remarks that eschatology was the talk of the day.

51. J.F. Bethune-Baker, review of Schweitzer, *The Quest of the Historical Jesus*, *JTS* 12 (1911), p. 148.

52. Inge, 'The Apocalyptic Element in Christ's Teaching', *The Guardian* (13 May 1910), p. 680.

53. Inge, review of Sanday, *Christologies Ancient and Modern*, *JTS* 11 (1910), pp. 584-86.

that since the alleged predictions were falsified in every particular, and since outside these predictions we are allowed by these critics to claim very little as the authentic teaching of our Lord, Christianity as based on the Incarnation of the Son of God in the Person of the historical Jesus Christ, is torn up by its roots.

The truth is, Inge went on, that 'Greek metaphysics' is 'either implicit or explicit in every book of the New Testament'. This meant that the whole notion of a temporal eschatology was superseded; indeed beliefs in the imminent coming of the Kingdom of God were

the reflection of the soul's deepest intuitions, their substance is felt to be independent of their form to a degree quite unique... And so, though the early Christians thought they believed in the approaching end of the age, they did not behave as if they really believed it, and when the Kingdom of God changed into the ideal of a Christian Church, the second coming into the gift of the Holy Spirit, and the passing away of the earth into the passing away of each individual in turn from the earth, they were conscious of no shock, and in fact found that the teaching of Christ was much better adapted to the new belief than the old. The new wine of Christianity burst the wineskins of Messianism in a very short time; but no wine was lost—the treasure was transferred to other vessels.

Inge then goes on to defend his views, concluding with a 'faithful picture' of Jesus Christ

as our perfect Teacher and our perfect Example. [Liberal scholarship especially in Germany] has shown us, far more clearly than we saw before, that the real source of Christian faith was the profound and wholly unique impression which the personality of our Blessed Lord made upon those who saw and heard Him.[54]

Although he argues from explicitly Platonist grounds he reaches the same conclusion as the other critics: eschatology both removes the ethical potency of Jesus and at the same time reduces him to a product of his Jewish environment thereby robbing him of his universal significance.

In his review of Sanday's *Christologies Ancient and Modern*, Inge points to his judicious scholarship 'of comprehension and acceptance' and his reluctance to adopt 'the *Entweder-Oder* argument, of which the Germans are so fond',[55] before going on, not surprisingly, to rejoice in

54. Inge, 'The Apocalyptic Element', p. 680.
55. Inge, Review of Sanday, p. 584.

Sanday's repristination of the *unio mystica*.[56] At the end of the review, however, he discusses *The Life of Christ in Recent Research*, expressing rather slyly his hope

> that Dr Sanday will dissociate himself more explicitly from the school of Schweitzer. The praise which he then [i.e. in 1907] bestowed on this writer, guarded as it was, gained for a production which I am old-fashioned enough to think blasphemous,[57] a vogue which it would not otherwise have obtained in this country... Here is surely a case when the *Entweder-Oder* must be faced, and I cannot doubt that Dr Sanday will vindicate the 'existence', and a good deal more, of the historical figure with whom the Christian Church stands or falls, and will assure us, with the weight of his unrivalled authority, that the foundation of our faith in Him standeth sure.[58]

The irony of Inge's attack on Sanday was noted by J.H. Moulton[59] in a letter to Burkitt, where he also points to his own sympathy to the 'considerable residuum' in the *Quest* even after criticism:

> What a queer mixture your colleague Inge is! For a heretic like him (as most 'old fashioned' people regard him on reading C[ambridge] B[iblical] E[ssays])[60] to talk of Schweitzer as a blasphemer is rather comic.[61] And unless my only just completed reading of *Quest* is all

56. In a letter to Sanday of 10 May 1910, von Dobschütz (BOD MS Eng. misc. d. 140 no. 109) welcomed his *Christologies Ancient and Modern* but also expressed his dissatisfaction with those English theologians who turn to ancient philosophy to defend their position (which proves something about the lack of clarity in Sanday's book). He goes on to say that 'if theology needs philosophical aid for getting definitions, it must be the philosophy of our time, and not that of Plato and Aristotle, which guided the fathers. Oxford men, it is true, live in this old philosophy, but this is an anachronism, and by calling to the help of psychology you yourself left this field and passed into ours'.

57. Inge cites pages from *Von Reimarus zu Wrede* (pp. 396-99) where Schweitzer appears to deny the existence of Jesus as the Messiah who preached the ethical kingdom.

58. Inge, Review of Sanday, p. 586.

59. J.H. Moulton (1863–1917). Methodist Professor of Hellenistic Greek and Indo-European Philology at Manchester University from 1908. One of the leading scholars of New Testament Greek of his generation.

60. Inge had written on 'The Theology of the Fourth Gospel', in H.B. Swete (ed.), *Essays on Some Biblical Questions of the Day by Members of the University of Cambridge* (London: Macmillan, 1909), pp. 251-88.

61. Inge was himself under suspicion after making some remarks which appeared to deny the incarnation at Exeter earlier in the summer.

wrong, Inge is…unfair to Schweitzer… I am rather interested in this eschatology business just now: I gave my men an address on it yesterday which I am repeating revised as an inaugural in Wales next month.[62] Percy Gardner has sufficiently shown Schweitzer's amusing dogmatism and one-sidedness,[63] but there is considerable residuum I think, and the book is unmistakably stimulating, and in its net result distinctly *anti-*sceptical. But it is easy to misread it—only Cambridge Professors oughtn't to do so. But I digress![64]

Inge's review provoked Sanday into a strongly-worded letter to *The Guardian* of 19 August 1910. However, although he attacked Inge, he was also prepared to acknowledge that he had moved on from his position in *The Life of Christ in Recent Research*. He began by commenting that Dr Inge 'seemed to be on the warpath' and had been

politely inviting allcomers to say 'shibboleth' without lisping. It happens that I myself am one of those who have received this invitation, and I should like to accept it. Not that I can frame my lips to say 'shibboleth', but I should like to say the truth. This is just the difficulty in these matters; one cannot always say the truth, however much one wishes. I could not say it three years ago, but I can perhaps come a little nearer to it now.

He then goes on to ask: 'Is not the question about Schweitzer a little dragged in?' He continues:

However, I shall not shirk it. I cannot say that I look back with satisfaction to the way in which I wrote on this subject three years ago. I made the mistake of trying to do two things at once—to give some account of Schweitzer, and at the same time to state what I thought could be assimilated of his book. In the double task I cannot think that I was successful. At the same time, I am conscious that I owe much to Schweitzer for compelling me to see things that I had not seen before or seen so clearly. I cannot retract anything of the acknowledgements that I made to him on this head. Neither can I retract anything that I said in praise of qualities which excited my genuine admiration. And yet I admit that the balance was not struck perfectly. I made allowance for the audacities of a young writer. There are one or two that I should not defend. Which of us sends out a book in which he has nothing to regret? But those quoted by Dr. Inge are not as bad as they may seem.

62. I have been unable to locate this lecture.

63. 'Present and Future Kingdom in the Gospels', *ExpTim* 21 (1910), pp. 535-538.

64. J.H. Moulton to Burkitt, 7 Sept. 1910 (CUL MS Add. 7658 B. 694).

Schweitzer does not deny the existence of our Lord Jesus Christ, but only the reality of a particular conception of Him ('*der liberale Jesus*'). If I am asked whether I wished to see his book translated, I do not think I did. I was not consulted on the subject. But the days are gone by for any attempt to hush up great questions. They must be met and directly grappled with. My own belief is that this group of questions is settling itself gradually, and that the clearer the discussion, the sooner it will be ended. I cannot say that it is freshly before my mind at this moment; but I am inclined to think that the most helpful thing I have seen is the series of articles by Professor von Dobschütz in the *Expositor* for the first half of this year.[65]

Though in a somewhat backhand manner, Sanday had thus revoked his former views and sided more directly with the moral position adopted by von Dobschütz in his lectures.

The Church Congress, 1910

Later in 1910 discussion of eschatology was still in the air, and at the Church Congress held at Cambridge at the end of September, a special session was devoted to 'The Apocalyptic Element in our Lord's Teaching: Its Significance for Christian Faith and Ethics' presided over by Dr A.J. Mason, now Vice Chancellor of Cambridge University.[66] Four eminent churchmen commented on eschatology including one of the leading scholars of the age, Bishop Charles Gore of Birmingham,[67] who, while recognizing the importance of eschatology, claimed 'we have no ground for believing him [Jesus] to be deluded'.[68] Dr J.H. Bernard,[69] Dean of St Patrick's Cathedral, Dublin, spoke next remarking that although 'Dr Schweitzer has revolted against the scepticism which has been masquerading under the garb of liberal protestantism',

65. *The Guardian* (19 August 1910), p. 1112. Inge's outspokenness on the doctrine of Christ provoked a hostile response from many other correspondents in the few weeks following.

66. *The Official Report of the Church Congress held at Cambridge* (ed. C. Dunkley; London: George Allen, 1910), pp. 60-64. The session was held on Tuesday 27 September at 8 p.m.

67. Charles Gore (1853–1932). First principal of Pusey House Oxford (1884); Canon of Westminster (1894–1902); Bishop of Worcester (1902); Birmingham (1905); Oxford (1911–19).

68. *1910 Report*, p. 69. (Also in *The Guardian* [30 Sept. 1910], p. 1356).

69. John Henry Bernard (1860–1927). He became Bishop of Ossory (1911); Archbishop of Dublin (1915); Provost of Trinity College (1919).

his own 'constructive theory' was unhappily 'even further removed from the historical faith of Christendom than the liberalism which he deprecates'.[70] The next speaker was R.H. Charles, who, developing his arguments from two years previously, argued against Schweitzer's work on the basis of his own wide knowledge of apocalyptic sources, claiming with a certain gusto that

> its bizarreness is only equalled by its cocksureness. He reminds one of the old Epicurean teachers who, according to Cicero, spoke with as much assurance as though they had just come down from the council chamber of the gods. I have shown incidentally that much of Schweitzer's structure is built on a foundation of sand. It is also in many cases built with untempered mortar, for he shows a halting knowledge of Apocalyptic.[71]

Like Sanday, Charles pointed to von Dobschütz's articles in the *Expositor* as the most convincing interpretations of Jesus' message. This meant that ultimately what was important was that Jesus' 'world-accepting ethics' formed a 'nucleus for a code valid for all time, in which Christ repeatedly sets aside the Mosaic rule and substitutes his own'. Finally V.H. Stanton, Ely Professor of Divinity at Cambridge, added his support for the need for an inner-worldly ethics: 'In the main and in substance [Jesus'] ethics were not those of a period of transition, but of that new and eternal order to the laws of which we may and ought even here to strive more and more to conform ourselves'.[72] The discussion after the lectures, which did not commence until 9.40 p.m., was rather curtailed. Walter Lock, Warden of Keble College, Oxford, suggested that the crisis language proclaimed by Jesus was 'fulfilled with the coming of the Spirit' and Canon Harford of Liverpool 'expressed gratitude for the way in which the home product of British scholarship had been vindicated'.[73]

The meeting proved so popular, however, that it was necessary to hold an overflow meeting under the chairmanship of S.A. Donaldson, Master of Magdalene College, Cambridge, where the papers were read in a different order from the main meeting. During the discussion which followed, Burkitt told the packed room: 'I am only here to speak

70. *1910 Report*, p. 61.
71. *1910 Report*, p. 74.
72. *1910 Report*, p. 81.
73. *The Guardian*, 30 Sept. 1910, p. 1317. There was some correspondence over the next few weeks in *The Guardian* with various learned clergymen offering definitive interpretations of specific passages of Scripture.

one short word in defence of Albert Schweitzer. Albert Schweitzer is still a young man, and perhaps his views are not correct. Perhaps he does not understand Jesus Christ; but who in this room dares to say he understands Jesus Christ?'[74] According to Burkitt, it was vital to come to some understanding of the eschatological sayings of Jesus without deliberately trying to modernize them, since 'these striking stumbling blocks—these startling words come, not from some heretical document excavated by the eschatological school, but they are from the Gospel'.[75] Burkitt urged his audience to read Schweitzer for themselves to see how he was able to combine an immense enthusiasm for the Gospel while maintaining an eschatological viewpoint. Indeed, according to Burkitt, the question of whether or not our Lord's teaching was apocalyptic had clouded the real issue of eschatology and ethics: an eschatological position certainly did not preclude a strong ethical position but could indeed lead to a strong sense of urgency and commitment.[76] This line of argument was continued by Gordon Selwyn of Corpus Christi College, Cambridge, who asked:

> Is it not the case that supposing tomorrow we were set down in a place of exile, we should begin as soon as possible to make it as pleasant a place as we could? And it seems to me perfectly possible, and a perfectly Christian thing, to look upon life in this world as an interim, wherein we dare to do our best in the practical difficulties which lie before us.[77]

74. *1910 Report*, p. 85.

75. *1910 Report*, p. 85.

76. *1910 Report*, p. 85. The opposite line was taken by C.W. Emmet in his article in the *Expositor*, 'Is the Teaching of Jesus an Interimsethik?' which had been an address given at the Fourth International Congress for the History of Religions at Leiden. Emmet suggests that understanding Jesus' desire for the Kingdom as the centre of his teaching means that this would make him care little for the effects of his actions on the world as a whole: 'We cannot indeed exclude from ethics the thought of reward, but it is psychologically false to regard it as the primary and consciously-realised motive of the life of self-sacrifice…we may fairly appeal to the…life and teaching of Jesus as a whole as a proof that self-interest, however enlightened and far-seeing, is not the true expression of His inmost mind' (p. 434).

77. *1910 Report*, p. 87. This line was later followed by Latimer Jackson in *The Eschatology of Jesus*, pp. 355-56:

'So, then, the call comes to all to fit themselves for the Kingdom—whether it be here on earth or in that hereafter which lies behind the inevitable "catastrophe" of death—and, as "God's fellow workers" to play their part in the accomplishment of these divine purposes which surely take account both of humanity and the environment of men.

Herein, it may be, some words of Jesus in and to the modern world'.

Theological Critics of Schweitzer

Such defences of Schweitzer, however, were the exception, and with the combined weight of the opposition, Sanday, while acknowledging his 'own sharing in the responsibility for calling attention rather markedly to' *Von Reimarus zu Wrede*, eventually chose to distance himself publicly from Schweitzer's eschatological position.[78] 'The fundamental mistake of Schweitzer's theory', he wrote in 1911, 'lies just in what he believes to be its special virtue, the rigorous application of logic'.[79] After acknowledging his debt of gratitude to von Dobschütz,[80] Sanday went on to discuss the place of Apocalyptic in the Gospels; he had gradually come to feel that the figure of Christ was not accessible to such an application of 'western' logic.[81] This criticism of the one-sidedness of Schweitzer's logic was shared by others. Thus, in an article in the *Expository Times* in 1910, Percy Gardner remarked:

> Systems of such extreme simplicity and logicality have drawbacks. They sometimes make up for the triumph of massacring *buts* and *notwithstandings*, and marching straight to their end, by outraging common sense, and constructing a house of cards which, however fine to look at, will not resist a breath of wind. If their principle is faulty, their

78. W. Sanday, 'The Apocalyptic Element in the Gospels', *Hibbert Journal* 10 (1911), pp. 83-109, here p. 83.

79. Sanday, 'The Apocalyptic Element', p. 103.

80. Sanday, 'The Apocalyptic Element', p. 85. Sanday also acknowledges B.H. Streeter's contribution to the discussion in the appendix ('Synoptic Criticism and the Eschatological Problem') to *Studies in the Synoptic Problem* which reached similar conclusions: 'Two great religious geniuses, St Paul and the author of the Fourth Gospel, stemmed the tide [of amplifying the element of Jewish apocalyptic in our Lord's teaching] and by a counter evolution brought back the Church to profounder and more spiritual conceptions; which, though often expressed in terms of a Hellenized philosophy foreign to the Master's own environment, surely present some aspects of His mind which in the Synoptic Gospels are almost buried under the picturesque materialism of Jewish Eschatology' (p. 436). Streeter later discussed the 'eschatological school's' contribution to scholarship in his essay 'The Historic Christ', in *idem* (ed.), *Foundations*, pp. 73-145. Another contributor to *Foundations*, William Temple, however, was deeply critical of the relative degree of acceptance of Schweitzer's views. See his letter to Ronald Knox of 29 October 1913, cited in F.A. Iremonger, *William Temple* (London: Oxford University Press, 1948), p. 163.

81. Sanday, 'The Apocalyptic Element', p. 105.

consistency only makes them the easier to refute... The question whether the primacy in the teaching and life of Jesus belongs to the practical or apocalyptic side of his beliefs is no doubt a matter as to which various opinions may be held. I am altogether on the side of those who regard the apocalyptic side as comparatively unessential, though I am aware that much may be argued to the contrary. But to assert, as does Dr. Schweitzer, that it is a question of *either-or*, and that the apocalyptic side of the teaching is the only side, seems to me a quite unmaintainable theory in the face of St. Paul's Epistles.[82]

This article presents a judicious and useful summary of the criticism offered of the one-sidedness of Schweitzer's interpretation. Similar interpretations were offered by Dewick, who in *Primitive Christian Eschatology* wrote that 'the great fault of the "consistent eschatologists" is—their consistency'.[83] The work of one of the leading Modern Churchmen of the time, Cyril W. Emmet, vicar of West Hendred, Berks, moved in a similar direction. Indeed he remarked that his book, *The Eschatological Element in the Gospels*, was written 'to remove the widespread impression that the position of Loisy and Schweitzer is somehow more compatible with a full and Catholic Christianity than that of the Liberal Protestants'.[84]

Hastings Rashdall similarly entered the debate over ethics and eschatology in his lectures *Conscience and Christ: Six Lectures on Christian Ethics* which he gave at Oberlin College in the autumn of 1913.[85] In his second lecture he presents the case for an eschatological Christ, and is critical of its one-sidedness. For Rashdall, Jesus' emphasis on the totality of commitment forced by the coming judgment was merely a minor aspect of his teaching which paled into insignificance when compared to his preaching of a universal moral kingdom. This alone was of contemporary importance:

> If we cannot make the Kingdom mean something modern, there is a large part of Jesus' teaching which will mean nothing at all for us. I have endeavoured to show you that, though the original conception was that of a future, catastrophic Kingdom, Jesus did also in all probability speak of a Kingdom which should come gradually...in a quiet, unobtrusive, uncatastrophic development, as individual souls listened to His message...

82. Percy Gardner, 'Present and Future Kingdom in the Gospels', *ExpTim* 21 (1910), pp. 535-38, here pp. 535, 537-38.

83. Dewick, *Primitive Christian Eschatology*, p. 230.

84. Emmet, *The Eschatological Element*, p. vii. Cf. p. 65.

85. Rashdall, *Conscience and Christ*.

If this meaning of the Kingdom was for Him, in a sense, a secondary meaning, it is clear to us it must be the primary one.[86]

Thus, for Rashdall, if the modern world found its Jesus uncongenial, or if it considered his message to be distorted merely on account of his Jewish surroundings, then it was necessary to rediscover an essential message compatible with modern conceptions:

> We can accept Jesus' fundamental idea that the supreme object of human life should be the promotion of the Kingdom in the sense of an ideal social state. That conception already implicitly involves the notion which...is developed in the actual teaching of Jesus—that the duty of mutual love is the best summary of human duty. The conception of the Kingdom of God may be regarded as expressing fundamentally the same idea as Kant's notion of the Categorical Imperative.[87]

For Rashdall, Jesus was a Kantian before Kant who presented a universal ethical message and whose emphasis on eschatology was a mere cultural constraint imposed by a long-dead world-view.

Sanday's Critique of Schweitzer

Sanday was by now equally prepared to criticize Schweitzer's eschatological position, yet his criticism went in a somewhat different direction from Gardner, Rashdall and the other liberals. Sanday admitted that Christ used apocalyptic language in so far as it 'supplied the forms under which our Lord expressed His conception of His own Person and Mission',[88] and yet, whatever language he may have used, what was crucial in any interpretation was that Christ remained ultimately mysterious. Sanday could thus not even share Schweitzer's confidence that Jesus was an apocalyptic fanatic. Indeed, according to Sanday, Schweitzer himself was guilty of reading his own criteria for truth into the past and his conclusions were thus self-destructive. Sanday finished his article on 'The Apocalyptic Element in the Gospels' on a sceptical note: 'I am afraid we must be content to recognise this confusion so far as it exists for a fact; the uncertainties that remain when criticism has exhausted its resources prevent it from being wholly disentangled'.[89]

86. Rashdall, *Conscience and Christ*, p. 66.
87. Rashdall, *Conscience and Christ*, p. 70.
88. Sanday, 'The Apocalyptic Element', p. 106.
89. Sanday, 'The Apocalyptic Element', p. 109.

Sanday thus attacked Schweitzer's logical one-sidedness and yet he did not revert to a simplistic and equally one-sided ethical interpretation: there could be no such clear delineation of the strands of thought present in Jesus' mind. Though eschatology may not have been the most important strand for Jesus Christ and in the Gospels, it was impossible to reach security or certainty as to what was the dominant theme in Christ's preaching and teaching, which 'in any case...have become more or less blurred and confused in the tradition that has come down to us...We must be content not to know, as the Son Himself was content not to know'.[90]

Sanday expressed similar scepticism in a letter to Schweitzer thanking him for a copy of his book on the mystery of the Kingdom of God.[91]

> [We] English, I'm afraid are illogical people, and my chief doubt, if I may say so, in regard to your views is whether after all they do not press logic rather too hard. Does not nature itself seem to be illogical? I quite allow that it 'seems to be' rather than 'is'. But does it not come round to much the same thing? There is a real logic no doubt in each chain of processes. But one chain is crossed and (in appearance) deflected by another chain, so that there seems to be inconsistency. But really it is not inconsistency, but only two distinct sets of facts existing at the same time. If we could take a perfectly clear and balanced view of all the facts, I believe we should see how the two trains can exist together. But because we do not always see this, we are apt to be one sided.
>
> That seems to me to be the danger. But at the same time I think that our debt to you is immense to those who follow out a logical train with so much clearness and incisiveness as yours [*sic*].

Criticism of Schweitzer's single-mindedness thus led Sanday into a position of utter scepticism, and in this his conclusions were quite different from those reached both by Schweitzer[92] as well as von

---

90. Sanday, 'The Apocalyptic Element', p. 109.

91. 31 Jan. 1912 (BOD MS Eng. misc. d. 128 no. 95). This book, which originated as part II of Schweitzer's, *Das Abendmahl im Zusammenhang mit dem Leben Jesu* (Tübingen: J.C.B. Mohr [Paul Siebeck], 1901) was Schweitzer's first statement of consistent eschatology although it made little initial impact in England. It was published in English as *The Mystery of the Kingdom of God* (trans. Walter Lowrie; London: A. & C. Black, 1914).

92. For a critique of Schweitzer's radically strange Jesus who makes little impact upon the social and political sphere, see Christopher Rowland, ' "Upon whom the Gods of the Ages have come". Apocalyptic and the Interpretation of the

Dobschütz and the English liberals. Indeed for Sanday, Christ eventually became so completely unknowable that he was forced to give up his lifelong project of writing a life of Jesus. It comes as little surprise that he rapidly moved to a position of utter relativism, becoming late in life the greatest champion of the 'Modernist' cause, even if his modernism was very different from Burkitt's.[93]

Eschatology and Liberalism

It should by now be clear that a great deal was at stake in the appropriation of eschatology for theology and for the church. The remainder of this book analyses the ways in which eschatology provided the means and impetus for several theologians from different traditions, most importantly J.N. Figgis (who is the subject of the next chapter) and George Tyrrell (the subject of Chapter 7), to offer critiques of liberal rationalism and reductionism. An eschatological interpretation of the historical Jesus soon expanded into little less than a defence of the supernatural against modern reductionism. In this way, eschatological thought moved far beyond the specialist field of New Testament studies (a fact which had been noted by Burkitt in his reference to Tyrrell in his Preface to *The Quest of the Historical Jesus*).[94] Indeed, the outspoken and prophetic cultural critique which will be discussed below, can hardly be distinguished from Edwyn Hoskyns's opinions developed in the 1920s.[95]

New Testament', in Malcolm Bull (ed.), *Apocalypse Theory and the Ends of the World* (Oxford: Basil Blackwell, 1995), pp. 38-57 (52).

93. Cf. Chapman, 'The Socratic Subversion of Tradition', pp. 105-116.

94. Schweitzer, *The Quest of the Historical Jesus*, p. vi.

95. Cf. E.C. Hoskyns, *Cambridge Sermons* (London: SPCK, 1938), p. 37. On Hoskyns and Schweitzer, see Parsons, *Sir Edwyn Hoskyns as Biblical Theologian*, esp. ch. 2.

Chapter 6

J.N. FIGGIS: ESCHATOLOGICAL CRITIQUE IN EDWARDIAN ENGLAND

Although I have touched on several of the broader theological themes that emerged out of the discussion of eschatology in England before the First World War, my main purpose in the previous chapters has been to give a detailed survey of the debate over the eschatological interpretation of the historical Jesus in English New Testament studies, and also to survey the controversies it provoked both in the universities and the churches. It should also have become clear, however, particularly from the discussion of Burkitt, that a great deal more was at stake than merely the character of the historical Jesus.

The remainder of this book discusses the appropriation of eschatology by some leading theological thinkers of the Edwardian period. In a story that contains some unlikely turns, an emphasis on eschatology became a feature of some of the more radical theological positions that were developed before the First World War. Such positions were equally critical of both liberalism and conservatism, and display, as I will show in the final chapter, striking continuity with the new theological movements which developed both in England and on the Continent after 1918.

John Neville Figgis (1866–1919)

The subject of this chapter is the work of the great, yet neglected political theorist and preacher, J. Neville Figgis, who combined a radical cultural critique with an eschatological interpretation of the historical Jesus. Figgis was the son of a Brighton minister of the Countess of Huntingdon's Connexion and was educated at St Catharine's College, Cambridge where he came under the influence of Mandell Creighton, the Dixie Professor of Ecclesiastical History, and afterwards bishop of

London, and F.W. Maitland, the great legal historian. He gained a brilliant First in 1889, winning a host of prizes including the Prince Consort Prize for his essay on the Divine Right of Kings which later evolved into a book.[1] He was received into the Church of England and ordained after a period at Wells Theological College in 1894. After a curacy in Kettering he became lecturer at his old college from 1896–1902, and in 1900 was Birkbeck Lecturer at Trinity College.[2] During this period he also served as Chaplain of Pembroke College and later of his own College, and lectured at the Clergy Training School. After experiencing a crisis in faith and health he became Rector of the College living of Marnhull in Dorset from 1902–1907. Figgis seems to have enjoyed his period as a Parish Priest, devoting much time to visiting and to entertaining his parishioners. He once responded to a friend with typical wit: 'Prigs would say that I waste my time [in visiting]. Yet old women have souls, like more interesting people. (Pause). But why were they made so incredibly dull?'[3] There are many other stories of Figgis's wit, his absent-mindedness and his boyish laugh.

In 1907 he was received into the Community of the Resurrection, founded by Charles Gore and presided over at the time by Walter Frere, after seeing a play by Bernard Shaw and, as an honorary Fellow of his old College, he alternated in a regular pendulum motion between Mirfield fasts and Cambridge feasts.[4] Freed from parochial and teaching duties he was able to devote himself to writing and preaching, his publications proceeding steadily from 1907. During his time as scholar-monk he gave the acclaimed Hulsean lectures in 1908–1909[5] and lectured on three occasions in the USA (at Harvard in 1911[6], in New York in 1913,[7] and in Illinois in 1915[8]). He was also much in

---

1.   *The Divine Right of Kings* (Cambridge: Cambridge University Press, 1896). This was republished with an introduction by G.R. Elton in 1965 (New York: Harper & Row).

2.   His lectures were published as *From Gerson to Grotius* (Cambridge: Cambridge University Press, 1907).

3.   This episode is cited in Maurice G. Tucker, *John Neville Figgis: A Study* (London: SPCK, 1950), p. 15.

4.   Cf. Tucker, *John Neville Figgis*, pp. 14-18.

5.   *The Gospel and Human Needs* (London: Longmans, 1909).

6.   *Civilisation at the Cross Roads*.

7.   *The Fellowship of the Mystery being the Bishop Paddock Lectures delivered at the General Theological Seminary, New York, during Lent 1913* (London: Longmans, 1914).

demand as a preacher and retreat conductor, particularly in more fashionable Anglo-Catholic churches, publishing many volumes of sermons,
most importantly, *Antichrist*.[9] His obituarist in *The Guardian* noted that
his 'graceful style, his gift of epigram, his devotion, combined with his
remarkable intellectual power' were able to fill churches in Oxford and
Cambridge.[10] In January 1918 while on his way to the USA he was
torpedoed and shipwrecked off the coast of Antrim, where his
manuscript on Bossuet was lost. He never recovered from the trauma of
this incident and spent his last days in a mental hospital in Virginia
Water, dying on Palm Sunday, 13 April 1919.[11]

Figgis's Apologetics

Figgis's many sermons and lectures offer fiery diatribes against the
spirit of the age and are often couched in apocalyptic phraseology.
Most important among these are the collection of sermons provoca-
tively entitled *Antichrist and other Sermons*, together with the Hulsean
lectures, *The Gospel and Human Needs* and, most crucially, *Civilisation at the Cross Roads*. Each of these is bold Christian apologetic, and

8.   *The Will to Freedom or The Gospel of Nietzsche and the Gospel of Christ
being the Bross Lectures delivered in Lake Forest College, Illinois* (London:
Longmans, 1917).

9.   *Antichrist and Other Sermons*.

10.   *The Guardian*, 24 April 1919, p. 430. On Figgis as a preacher, see Robert
Dolman, 'Forgotten Man of the Church of England: John Neville Figgis as
Preacher', *ExpTim* 107 (1996), pp. 169-72.

11.   The only lengthy biographical account is Tucker, *John Neville Figgis.* See
also the scanty sketch by Walter Frere in *DNB*, 1912–21 and the anonymous Anglo-
Catholic obituary in *The Guardian*, 24 April 1919, p. 430. There is much useful
biographical information, especially on Figgis at Mirfield, in Alan Wilkinson, *The
Community of the Resurrection: A Centenary History* (London: SCM Press, 1992),
passim. As well as his many pungent essays in cultural criticism, Figgis also wrote
widely on political theory and ecclesiology. There have been several recent attempts
to apply his thought, most notably by the late David Nicholls in *The Pluralist State*
(Basingstoke: Macmillan, 2nd rev. edn, 1994 [1975]). See also Paul Q. Hirst,
Associative Democracy (Cambridge: Polity Press, 1994), esp. ch. 2. I have also
surveyed the contemporary implications of Figgis's political thought in 'Tony Blair,
J.N. Figgis and the State of the Future', *Studies in Christian Ethics* 13 (2000), pp.
49-66. On Figgis's ecclesiology see my essay 'Concepts of the Voluntary Church in
England and Germany, 1890–1920: A Study of J.N. Figgis and Ernst Troeltsch',
Zeitschrift für neuere Theologiegeschichte 2 (1995), pp. 37-59.

in many ways taken together, they present Figgis's own efforts to fulfil the need he had expressed in an address of 1910. The contemporary church, he remarked, was called on to rise from its dogmatic slumbers and to engage in a modern apologetics

> that should be interesting and well-written, which shall show the beauty as well as the truth of the Christian faith and church; liberal in its openness to modern currents, but standing a little apart from them all, and vitally organic with the historic life of the church. Secondly, we want some systems of instruction which shall be definite and sacramental, at once thorough and attractive, and yet alive to the symbolic and provisional nature of every word we say; for we must always remember the words of an early Franciscan: 'All things that can be thought or seen or told or handled are as nothing in comparison with those things that can neither be thought nor seen nor told nor handled'.[12]

In this apologetic task Figgis, who was never averse to a nice turn of phrase, could be extremely outspoken and challenging. He began his Hulsean lectures, for instance, with an extraordinarily provocative remark about his chosen text from the Benedictus: 'Blessed be the Lord God of Israel, for He hath visited and redeemed his people'. The opening sentence of the lecture that followed was simply: 'Has He? That is the question we are all asking'.[13] This striking beginning made a lasting impression on the audience, among whom was F.J.E. Raby, who recalled in 1940: 'Who could forget the sudden beginning?' He went on: 'In short sentences incisively spoken, the pupil of Maitland told us, not of the achievements of historical criticism nor of ways and means of accommodating the Gospel to current philosophy, but of man's desperate need and God's redemption'.[14] Another hearer in 1908 was L.E. Elliott-Binns, who wrote: 'I considered among the greatest blessings that God has vouchsafed to me that I was allowed to hear those lectures and to enjoy some small measure of friendship with their author'.[15] E.G. Selwyn, who became Dean of Winchester, remarked that Figgis communicated a 'religion which was at once vital and critical, orthodox and up to date, Catholic and non-Roman, Anglican to

12. *Religion and English Society*, p. 22.
13. *The Gospel and Human Needs*, p. 1.
14. F.J.E. Raby, 'John Neville Figgis, Prophet, 1866–1919', *Theology* 40 (1940), pp. 325-32, here p. 325.
15. L.E. Elliott-Binns, 'The Apologetics of Neville Figgis', *Church Quarterly Review* 130 (1940), pp. 47-57, here p. 47.

the core!'[16] Because of his taut and pungent style, and his frequent unguarded and often rather purple pronouncements on the end of Victorian complacency, Figgis has been hailed as an 'Anglican Prophet', a 'kind of Tertullian of the early twentieth century running full tilt against those like Fr Tyrrell who appeared to make the thought of their day the yardstick by which to shape Christian apologetic'.[17] Similarly, Bernard Lord Manning had remarked that Figgis 'taught his congregation to see what the truth of the holy faith would be like in a world where, so far as they could judge, everything would have gone wrong'.[18] The parallels that Figgis himself drew with his intellectual precursors, however, were rather more modest; instead of Tertullian or any other great figure of the Christian past, it was none other than Disraeli who, Figgis believed, offered the most illuminating parallel.[19]

Figgis's departure point for his apologetics was his belief that Edwardian culture had outgrown the complacency and optimism which had characterized the Victorian period, at least in the popular imagination: as has already been discussed in relation to the Edwardian crisis in Chapter 1, the ' "Alexandrian" age of Westcott was gone'.[20] In an undated letter written before 1907 to Burkitt which announced his intention to write *Civilisation*, Figgis commented: 'I do think the clock is running down, the civilisation is revealing its own end times'.[21] Thus at the very outset of *Civilisation*, he wrote that '[s]omething is crumbling all around us. That is clearer every moment'.[22] As with Schweitzer, there is indeed a distinctly Nietzschean flavour to Figgis's critique, so much so that he announces the lectures to be 'so many "Unzeitgemässe Betrachtungen" '.[23] Indeed, Nietzsche features in a

16. E.G. Selwyn, 'The Outlook for English Theology', *Theology* 40 (1940), pp. 6-14, here p. 7.

17. J.M. Turner, 'J.N. Figgis: Anglican Prophet', *Theology* 78 (1975), pp. 538-44, here p. 539. As will be shown below, this is a somewhat misleading view of the relationship between Figgis and Tyrrell. See also David Newsome, 'The Assault on Mammon: Charles Gore and John Neville Figgis', *JEH* 17 (1966), pp. 227-41.

18. Lord Bernard Manning, *More Sermons of a Layman* (London: Independent Press, 1944), p. 34.

19. *Civilisation*, p. 17.

20. *Hopes for English Religion*, p. 24.

21. This letter is written on Marnhull Rectory notepaper and is therefore before 1907 (CUL MS Add. 7658 B. 314).

22. *Civilisation*, p. ix.

23. *Civilisation*, p. xi.

remarkably positive light in Figgis's work, not on account of his view of Christianity, but because of his refusal to be constrained by the superficiality of convention, and especially of conventional religion. Thus Figgis remarked in *The Fellowship of the Mystery*: 'We must live dangerously, said Nietzsche. Nowhere is this truer than religion',[24] and similarly, in an address on *Religion and English Society*, he said that '[e]ven people imbued with the ethics of Nietzsche are nearer to the Kingdom of God than men stricken with the gold fever'.[25] In the moral anarchy of the present, the old compromise of conventional religion had, according to Figgis, quite simply broken down:

> That siren-song which charmed men a generation back, as it allured them to peace and rest of spirit in scientific inquiry or idealist systems of benevolence, has changed for us its note; and it sounds to our ears only as the dirge of the nineteenth century, with its prosaic and complacent heterodoxy, or its thin and weary intellectualism.[26]

In short, according to Figgis, we 'live in a new age, to whose eyes "the Victorian era" has become an historical expression'.[27]

Similarly, in many of his sermons, especially those collected in *Antichrist*, Figgis was equally strident in his critique of cultural complacency. Thus, in a sermon preached at All Saints', Margaret Street, one of the most fashionable of London's Anglo-Catholic shrines, Figgis talks of the contemporary foe of Christianity as

> the spirit which often through a genuine and Christian desire to be sympathetic is ever ready to confuse Christianity with something else, and to surrender to a foe who is insatiable everything that invests the Church with charm, all that gives the unique appeal she still holds.

In equally challenging mode, Figgis went on to remind the congregation that '[t]he world has no use, never will have any use, for a faith whose meaning lies in the other world'.[28] And without Christ, Figgis continued, the forces of civilization were

> visibly dissolving. Its tall towers are shaking, and the splendid spires of the edifice of the western world are crumbling. Catastrophe is threatening. We can almost hear the thunders of the avalanche of war—war on a

24. *The Fellowship of the Mystery*, p. 107.
25. *Religion and English Society*, p. 33. See also, J.N. Figgis, *The Love of God* (London: Francis Griffiths, 1916), p. 24.
26. *The Gospel and Human Needs*, p. ix.
27. *The Gospel and Human Needs*, p. 3.
28. *Antichrist*, p. 21.

scale unknown. Hardly does the world even look stable any longer. It is not like the forties of Victorian complacency, but looks all tottering— tottering.[29]

To reassure his congregation in what must have seemed a rather bleak sermon, however, Figgis asserted that against the false hope placed in the absolutes of our own imaginings, Christians have the Christ who stands beyond any of these systems, and in whom rests the 'very secret of the universe'.[30]

Having had greater foresight than many of the politicians in forecasting the outbreak of war, Figgis returned to the same subject during the course of the War, preaching a sermon at London's Grosvenor Chapel which contextualized the theme, and which later proved tragically ironic: 'The intellectual baggage for life's cabin passage, which a little while did duty, has been torpedoed'.[31] And in the same book of sermons, as if to rub the point home, he remarked:

> Much that we deemed so secure is gone, the serene and gracious harmonies of ten years back are not for us... The carnival of Flanders has put an end to it. Progress, with a capital P, was torpedoed by the man who sank the *Lusitania*.[32]

In short, as he remarked in another sermon preached during the First World War:

---

29. *Antichrist*, p. 31. There is more than a passing resemblance to some of Ernst Troeltsch's more ephemeral writings, which are frequently similarly prophetic and equally gloomy in tone. The following notorious account with which Walter Köhler began his 1941 biography of Troeltsch illustrates the point. At a meeting in 1896 of the Friends of the liberal newspaper, *Die christliche Welt*, Troeltsch began his contribution with the outburst 'Es wackelt alles' ('Everything is tottering') and then left the room slamming the door behind him. This incident is reported in Walter Köhler, *Ernst Troeltsch* (Tübingen: J.C.B. Mohr, 1941), p. 1. On this, see my essay, 'Concepts of the Voluntary Church', p. 41.

30. *Antichrist*, p. 31.

31. *Hopes for English Religion*, p. 15. Figgis's thought underwent something of a revival at the outbreak of the Second World War, Raby writing that the 'problems he raised are precisely the problems that are facing the Church in this shattered world, and they are the problems that Christian thinkers are discussing with all the urgency which comes from the sense of imminent catastrophe' ('John Neville Figgis, Prophet, 1866–1919', p. 332).

32. *Hopes for English Religion*, p. 200.

we are daily reminded that we do not live in the world to which T.H. Green lectured. Even the problems of faith are now fought out in fields more tragic than college bowling-greens.[33]

With apocalyptic gloom Figgis thereby reminded his congregations and audiences that the world was visibly shaking.[34]

Civilisation at the Cross Roads

Much of *Civilisation at the Cross Roads*, Figgis's most extended apologetic, serves to describe the moral breakdown and religious crisis in English society to an American audience. In Lecture One, he suggests that the 'cross roads' which had been reached by civilization was characterized by the breakdown of 'personal values and the reality of freedom'.[35] Intellectually, the modern world had lost its erstwhile moral and social consensus, and in particular freedom, the greatest achievement of western civilization, had been pushed to the margins. Similarly, the church, which existed to ensure that freedom survived, had also lost its influence. This process was expressed in the rise of mechanistic explanations of human life, as well as pantheism, which allowed for no human creativity and which buried the individual in a network of cause and effect.

This was the great loss of the modern world which no longer saw fit to treat individuals as ends rather than means.[36] And such a loss of freedom led directly to a world where higher values were cast into doubt: 'We live in an age of unparalleled anarchy both moral and intellectual. The confusion of tongues is worse than any Babel of old'.[37] Where moral consensus was lacking, the most likely end for all behaviour would rest in a 'capricious individualism'.[38] Thus, as civilization increasingly ignored freedom, so its greatest triumphs began to be

33. *The Love of God*, p. 57.

34. Alan Wilkinson (in *The Church of England and the First World War* [London: SPCK, 1978], p. 15) cites an ordinand from Mirfield (Canon H. Roland Bate) who remembers Figgis saying: 'You can hear something cracking every day'.

35. *Civilisation*, p. 9.

36. *Civilisation*, p. 19.

37. *Civilisation*, p. 34. Figgis is well aware of the critiques of moral philosophers like G.E. Moore, and the 'new realists' like Bertrand Russell (*Civilisation*, p. 41).

38. *Civilisation*, p. 59.

submerged in a 'world intoxicated with material prosperity, reckless of the life of the spirit, and callous to the misery of vast masses of its fellow-man'.[39]

In his second lecture, entitled 'Babylon or the Moral Crisis' Figgis goes into the effects of the prevailing moral anarchy in sometimes graphic detail. Inequality and greed had taken the place of any sense of treating one another from the standpoint of the higher life, which whatever its brutality, had at least provided inspiration for the middle ages.[40] In distinction to the past, in virtually all forms of modern life, money-getting had replaced mutual concern. 'To that end,' Figgis writes presciently, 'all its universities and all its education is more and more being directed'.[41] Greed and success dominated the modern world, the best individual example being King Leopold of the Belgians, who, as was evidenced in his extraordinary pillage of the Congo, according to Figgis, 'had many of the gifts of the Emperor Nero, without his artistic taste...his notions of family affection might have been learned at the court of Herod the Great'.[42] Figgis is (not surprisingly) deeply critical of the 'morbid lust of men to secure the utmost material gain at the lowest cost'[43] (which elsewhere he described as 'Americanization'),[44] as well as the sheer ugliness of modern life, descriptions of which occupy a substantial proportion of the second lecture.[45] Yet however much we might individually try to stand out against such a system, he contended, we were inevitably sucked into it. Citing his own monastic community, Figgis suggests that as soon as one ate, or as soon as one travelled, one was drawn into economic relationships founded upon injustice and greed, from which the individual simply could not be freed. Sin was thus expressed corporately: 'So long as he lives,' wrote Figgis, 'it is in him; and writhe as we may, we must bear the Nessus-shirt of modern industrialism'.[46]

Although many recognized the need for redemption from these

---

39. *Civilisation*, p. 20.
40. *Civilisation*, p. 74.
41. *Civilisation*, p. 75.
42. *Civilisation*, pp. 78-79.
43. *Civilisation*, p. 81.
44. *Religion and English Society*, p. 31. 'Americanism' had been condemned as a heresy by Leo XIII.
45. *Civilisation*, p. 102.
46. *Civilisation*, p. 85.

conditions, Figgis maintained that Western civilization in its increasingly rationalistic form was 'unable either to effect man's salvation or to satisfy his deepest needs',[47] and as evidence he cites a host of unlikely sources including Rudolf Eucken and T.H. Huxley. He also points in Durkheimian manner to an increase in stress levels and depression and the steady growth of the suicide rate, in response to something akin to anomie.[48] He concludes his analysis of the poverty of rationalism with a plea for 'something to shake men out of their complacency. In the literal sense we need seers—men who can see things as they are and burn into men the facts of life in this twentieth century'.[49] The world was indeed crying out for deliverance, for a 'revolution of the spirit'[50] which might allow for 'life', a fact borne witness to by the post-impressionists in their reaction against the sterility of photographic realism.[51]

The art critic and painter, Roger Fry, gathered together a collection of paintings in the Grafton gallery from 8 November 1910 to 15 January 1911, which he exhibited as 'Manet and the post-impressionists'. This exhibition provoked some consternation in the art world and beyond, an 'Art-Quake', or an 'assault along the whole front of art'.[52] Fry exhibited Cézanne, Van Gogh and Gaughin, as well as a few works by Matisse and Picasso. The outcry was predictable: *The Times* claimed that the exhibition 'throws away all that the long-developed skill of past artists had acquired and perpetuated'.[53] Or, as one of Britain's leading portrait painters, John Singer Sargent, said: 'I am absolutely sceptical as to their having any claim whatsoever to being works of art'.[54] The 228 images on display, with their often gross distortions and flagrant breaches of artistic convention seemed to throw into question all that the artistic community held dear. Realistic form seemed to degenerate into the childish and the naïve. A letter to the *Pall Mall*

47. *Civilisation*, p. 105.
48. *Civilisation*, pp. 92-93.
49. *Civilisation*, p. 116.
50. *Civilisation*, p. 117.
51. *Civilisation*, pp. 65-66.
52. Desmond MacCarthy, 'The Art-Quake of 1910', in Christopher Green (ed.), *Art Made Modern: Roger Fry's Vision of Art* (London: Merrell Holberton, 1999), p. 59.
53. C.J. Weld-Blundell in *The Times*, 7 November 1910, p. 12.
54. *Art News*, 16 January 1911 (cited in T.O. Lloyd, *English History 1906–1992* [Oxford: Oxford University Press, 1993], p. 27).

Gazette came to the conclusion that this exhibition was an exact analogue to the 'criminal Anarchism which accompanies Socialism like its shadow'.[55] It was nightmare art that seemed to be questioning the values of a whole generation: again as *The Times* put it: 'it begins all over again—and stops where a child would stop…it is the rejection of all that civilisation has done'. And that judgment seemed borne out by the introduction to the catalogue: 'There comes a point when the accumulation of an increasing skill in mere representation begins to destroy the expressiveness of the design'. The artist consequently 'begins to try to unload, to simplify the drawing and painting by which natural objects are evoked, in order to recover the lost expressiveness and life'.[56] The old forms of expression seemed moribund as artists sought to move to the real that lay beyond what was immediately apparent.

It is no surprise that the challenge to the assumptions of the past shocked the top-hatted exhibition-goers in 1910; but it is also no surprise that others saw the exhibition as a great liberation from the prison of photographic realism. The real was far more profound and could be expressed accurately only by means which moved away from the rational, from the normal. Art, according to Fry, appealed to the non-mechanical parts of our nature, and pointed to the mystical and vital. Similarly, the materialist culture of so-called civilization was not all that there was: instead something lay beyond which acted as a critique of the present in the name of a deeper understanding of things. Unlike many art critics, Figgis recognized this in post-impressionism: 'Here is a deliberate effort to step back into the child's view of the natural world and to thrust away the lie of the photographic artist, which, rendering every detail, obscures the whole truth and sacrifices colour and line to what is at bottom mere mechanism'.[57] Against the prosaic which had triumphed in Victorian England, Figgis's theology, under the influence of the prevalent eschatology, is marked by the clamour for the mysterious: the superficial solutions of the materialists and the rationalists are thrown into confusion by those who have eyes to see the deeper meaning of the world.

This clamour for a higher world, Figgis claims, leads directly to a stark choice

---

55. E. Wake Cook in *Pall Mall Gazette*, 10 November 1910, p. 7.

56. 'The Post-Impressionists', Roger Fry's introduction to the catalogue, cited in Green (ed.), *Art Made Modern*, p. 62.

57. *Civilisation*, p. 65.

between schemes limited to this world, or schemes which give redemption at the cost of personal existence, and the Christian scheme, which 'preaches peace to them that are far off and to them that are nigh', because it worships One who is not only the light, but is also the Life of men, and not only their life but their Saviour.[58]

In a sermon Figgis offered his congregation a similar choice: 'If you reject the claims of our Lord, and the facts bound up with them, you will ultimately be driven to that mechanical creed of all life as determined; your religion will be a materialism, which will be none the less such, that it is materialism touched with emotion'.[59] For Figgis the choice was simple: the only way to redemption was in Christ, but, as will be shown in the next section, this was not a Christ who was to be reduced by the methods of liberal rationalism. As Figgis wrote in an address:

> Whatever else the Cross of Christianity effects there is no doubt that it effects [redemption]. So far as I know on the one hand no theologian has given us a satisfactory theory of the Atonement, nor on the other has so called 'Liberalism' been able to get away from the fact of Redemption through the blood of Christ.[60]

The Eschatological Christ and Liberal Theology

It is after this bold either/or in *Civilisation at the Cross Roads* that Figgis begins to engage more explicitly with the Christian faith as a possible answer to the anarchy which he had portrayed in the first two lectures as he moves into his discussion of 'Calvary or the Challenge of the Cross'. After a brief survey of the 'vague harmony of Pantheistic' monism,[61] he looks directly at recent eschatological interpretations of the historical Jesus, connecting them explicitly with the collapse of liberal theology:

> The half-way house of German liberalism is built on sands; the storm of the apocalyptic problem is shaking it in pieces. To many, of course, this recognition makes belief harder; for they cannot delude themselves any longer into imagining they are Christians, when they are nothing of the sort.[62]

58. *Civilisation*, p. 119.
59. *Antichrist*, p. 235.
60. *The Love of God*, p. 39.
61. *Civilisation*, p. 124.
62. *Civilisation*, pp. 146-46. The anti-German polemic is also particularly strong

Pointing to the findings of Schweitzer, Burkitt and Tyrrell, Figgis emphasizes the otherness of Christ, seeing him as a figure who simply does not allow for synthesis with the thought-forms of the modern world. In a sermon in *Antichrist* Figgis similarly stresses the importance of what he calls the 'Apocalyptic school'. No 'honest treatment of the documents', he remarks, 'enables us to reduce their central figure to a merely normal, moral enthusiast'. The Apocalyptic school, 'whatever its exaggerations, presents Jesus as a strange being of wonder and power, claiming an other-worldly origin, heralding a catastrophe. And the school itself has arisen in a reaction against the unnaturalness of the materialistic Christ'.[63] Similarly, in *Civilisation*, Figgis, although devoting little space directly to the theme of eschatology, explicitly uses Schweitzer's ideas in a sustained attack on what he calls the 'unadorned sterility'[64] of liberal pictures of Jesus. He then goes on to align himself with Schweitzer,[65] who

> in a memorable phrase, has declared that if Jesus Christ came into our modern world, He would come as a stranger; that our characteristic categories hold no place for Him; that the fundamentally other-worldly claim, the apocalyptic vision of Jesus is opposed to the presuppositions of the ordinary educated man, formed as they are under the influence of naturalism.[66]

Thus, for Figgis, no synthesis between the enlightened principles of liberal education and the otherness of the figure of Christ was possible. Indeed, there could only be 'irreconcilable conflict' between 'scientific fatalism' and religion. In short, the essence of the faith, according to Figgis, was 'supernatural' and allowed for no reconciliation 'with any rationalistically designed scheme of the universe'.[67]

in *The Gospel and Human Needs*. Outlining the options available to the contemporary Christian, Figgis condemns the philosophical sort of religion which treats 'the dogmas of the faith and even its historical facts as mainly symbolic, useful for the vulgar. He would thus label himself as Christian, and accommodate by methods "made in Germany" its special doctrines with the demands of true philosophy' (*The Gospel and Human Needs*, p. 5).

63. *Antichrist*, p. 28.

64. *Civilisation*, p. 154.

65. Figgis had evidently changed his mind over Schweitzer. In a letter to Burkitt (undated but from Marnhull Rectory and therefore before 1907), he remarked: 'I don't think that *I* am convinced by Schweitzer' (CUL MS Add. 7658 B. 313).

66. *Civilisation*, p. 147.

67. *Civilisation*, pp. 147-48.

Contemporary Christianity was consequently bound to enter into conflict with the modern world, which prompted Figgis to claim in truly prophetic manner

> that Dr. Schweitzer is right; that if Jesus came once more as an individual He would come not to bring peace but a sword, and that many who for sentimental reasons cling to His name would turn and cry 'Crucify Him'. I also believe that he is doing this here and now, through His body the Church, except where she is false to her mission.[68]

Figgis goes on to suggest, however, (and here he echoes more recent criticisms) that Schweitzer is guilty of judging the saviour of the world in modern categories thereby contravening his own method. Thus having shown that Christ is not the Christ of modern Protestantism

> and descanted on His supernatural apocalyptic claim…[Schweitzer] turns away treating Him as mere man with a turn for vision. That, at any rate, is one alternative (whether or no it is adopted by Dr. Schweitzer). You may believe that the apocalyptic Jesus is nearer to the truth of history than any other, and on that very ground you may be unable to credit His claims, and are therefore driven to decline all connection with historical Christianity.

For Figgis, such a conclusion, however, did not necessarily have to be the case; and instead of resting content with Schweitzer's Christology, Figgis points to George Tyrrell, who 'has shewn how the apocalyptic theology leads straight on to a transcendent view of Jesus'.[69] Indeed, it was Tyrrell who set the whole tone for *Civilisation*, as he acknowledges in the preface:

> The title…might seem to imply that I desire to controvert the main thesis of the late Father Tyrrell's famous work [*Christianity at the Cross-Roads*]. This, however, is not the case. Too greatly am I in debt to all the writings of that arresting author and especially to his posthumous work to have any such thought.[70]

Similarly, at the beginning of the first lecture Figgis points to Tyrrell's role in demonstrating the contemporary crisis of civilization. It was, he remarked, the 'tragedy of Tyrrell's own life' that symbolized the crisis in thought of which the book was the expression.[71] Elsewhere Figgis

---

68. *Civilisation*, p. 148.
69. *Civilisation*, pp. 148-49.
70. *Civilisation*, p. ix.
71. *Civilisation*, p. 3. Figgis at this point offers a mild criticism of Tyrrell's

wrote of Tyrrell's *Christianity at the Cross-Roads* that 'whatever its defects', it 'demonstrates the transcendent and other-worldly nature of the claims of Jesus with His apocalyptic vision, and demonstrates the absurdity of those theories of German and other critics, who would relegate Him to the rank of a mere humanitarian moralist'.[72]

What was crucial for Figgis in his assimilation of eschatological thought, then, was that Christ should remain a stranger, a stranger to his own day and a stranger to ours: it is for this reason that Figgis attacks the 'reduced Christianity' of the first self-confessed 'post-modernist' J.M. Thompson[73] with particular venom.[74] Such liberal reductions, Figgis claims, fail to take seriously the historical otherness of Jesus, and they are based on a rationalism which refuses to 'remain unmoved by the accumulated weight of evidence, historic, social, personal, which points to a transcendental interpretation of these strange facts in the world's experience'.[75] This recognition of the failure of liberal Christianity leads Figgis again to present a bold assertion of the necessity of the supernatural and of the miraculous, which amounts to a stark choice between Christianity and rationalism:

over-confidence in supposing that the contemporary standpoint allowed us to judge the 'strange events which gave rise to the Christian Church' (p. 4). Figgis had no such faith in the progress of science, nor indeed in the possibility that the contemporary scientific attitude could be reconciled to the New Testament world.

72. *Antichrist*, pp. 230-31. In *The Gospel and Human Needs* (p. 46), Figgis cites a long passage from Tyrrell's *Lex Orandi* calling him a 'great living writer'.

73. See his article, 'Post-Modernism', *Hibbert Journal* 47 (July 1914), pp. 733-45. Thompson's book, *Miracles in the New Testament* (London: Edward Arnold, 1911) created a stir and led Bishop Talbot of Winchester, who was Visitor of Magdalen College, Oxford, where Thompson was Dean of Divinity, to revoke his licence. On this debate and the ensuing controversy over *Foundations* see Keith W. Clements, *Lovers of Discord: Twentieth Century Theological Controversies in England* (London: SPCK, 1988), pp. 49-106; Langford, *In Search of Foundations*, ch. 5; Stephenson, *The Rise and Decline of English Modernism*, ch. 5; Ramsey, *From Gore to Temple*, ch. 6.

74. *Civilisation*, p. 154. Figgis added an appendix to *Civilisation* explicitly discussing Thompson entitled 'King Richard the Third and the Reverend James Thompson' (pp. 235-72): the question, according to Figgis, was 'whether the law we normally see in operation, or think we do, be a part or the whole; whether there is any real freedom in the universe' (p. 271).

75. *Civilisation*, p. 156.

Christianity may be true or false, but it makes claims subversive of all the rationalist projections of life. It rests on presuppositions which cannot by any ingenuity be reconciled with any view that denies the miraculous, the unique, the individual.[76]

Christianity thus subverts the reliance on reason, and, claims Figgis, a 'very cursory perusal of the New Testament ought soon to convince even the most pronounced Liberal that, even allowing for the differences of date and expression, the experience therein recorded is something other than that contemplated by their system', which 'is far removed from the drab Philistinism of the Liberal'.[77] In short, 'one unique feature of the New Testament is the interpretation of the plainest moral precepts with the most exalted mystical ecstasy'.[78]

And this is most true for the figure of Jesus himself, our picture of whom was always 'incomplete, unchronological, unscientific, if you will; but the impression is always the same, the weird mingling of the homely and the far-off, the strange romantic tenderness for things human and little, the passion of faith; and the unbroken calm all intertwined with the power to do things, to make wonders, leaves us, as it left his earliest friends in suspense'.[79] Figgis then goes on to ask the question 'what manner of man is this?', and replies with Schweitzer in a single word: 'Stranger'. Jesus was a stranger 'to our age, He was strange to His own'. That is the message of the New Testament, and it is the message relevant for the contemporary church as it tries to preserve its central truth: in short, 'Christianity is supernatural, or it is a sham'.[80] Thus it would seem that to Figgis an eschatological interpretation of the historical Jesus was part of a broader emphasis on mystery and the supernatural as the indispensable essence of Christianity.

There is much continuity between this position developed in *Civilisation*, with its conscious dialogue with Schweitzer and Tyrrell, and Figgis's approach to the necessity of the supernatural in *The Gospel and Human Needs* and in his sermons. In a sermon preached at St Mary's Cathedral, Edinburgh, for instance, Figgis points once again to Tyrrell as crucial in re-emphasizing this need for a transcendent with

76. *Civilisation*, p. 156.
77. *Civilisation*, p. 157.
78. *Civilisation*, p. 159.
79. *Civilisation*, p. 160.
80. *Civilisation*, p. 161.

his claim that 'religion is in its nature concerned with the other world'. Figgis continued:

> Unless we believe in some power *jenseits*, with whom we can have communion, we might have a moral code but no religion. I am not intending to undervalue the need of right action here and now; or the duties of earthly citizenship, of family affection, and daily work. Only I say that the motive of Christians in doing them is different from that of men who do not look for 'that blessed hope'. The springs of our life are in the world beyond.[81]

Once again, he was deeply critical of ethicizations of the Gospel, remarking that there was 'no common ground between us and a man who could read the New Testament and then pronounce that "some of the sayings of Jesus display a relatively high moral standard" '.[82] Similarly, in a sermon entitled 'The Need of the Miraculous' preached at the University of Glasgow in 1912, Figgis discusses J.M. Robertson's contributions to the 'Jesus or Christ' debate which had taken place in the pages of the Hibbert Journal Supplement for 1909.[83]

> If we want a Christ amenable to modern notions, a sort of Athenæum Club Gospel, and a Christianity purged of everything that seems abnormal to the critical student at his coffee, our want can never be met...It is not to satisfy such that the faith and love of Christendom for generations has gone out to 'that strange Man upon the Cross'... Even apart from any single wonder, the appearance of such a Being among men is a supernatural fact, not to be reconciled with any Pantheistic dream of the Divinr in man, or rationalistic notions of continuous progress mechanically acting.[84]

Liberal Theology and Supernatural Religion

This defence of the supernatural is at the same time an attack on reductionist liberalism, and it is for this reason that Figgis hailed Burkitt's *The Failure of Liberal Christianity* as a 'most valuable' pamphlet which 'should be studied. I am not contending', he went on,

---

81. Figgis, *Antichrist*, p. 179.
82. *The Gospel and Human Needs*, p. 42 (here Figgis is citing J.M. Robertson).
83. L.P. Jacks (ed.), *Jesus or Christ?* (Hibbert Journal Supplement; London: Williams and Norgate, 1909).
84. *Antichrist*, pp. 231-32.

that the views of Professor Burkitt...are entirely satisfactory, only that they have given up the materialistic theory of the meaning of the Christian Church... I say that this movement is remarkable, and should give even the youngest academic person pause, before he surrenders at discretion to a view which in the last resort drives us to materialism, or at least to Pantheism of a mechanical type.[85]

Similarly, in an address given in 1910 he remarked that ' "liberal" Protestantism, as the more candid observers (like Professor Burkitt) are now admitting, is bankrupt'.[86]

Although Figgis remained convinced of the orthodox truths of the Christian position, he drew out, perhaps more clearly and certainly more polemically than most of his contemporaries, the failure of liberal theology with what he regarded its simplistic materialist reduction both of the New Testament and the life of Christ, as well as its anti-supernaturalist understanding of the contemporary Church. Detesting what he regarded as the 'reduced Christianity dear to the Teutonic savant',[87] which meditated on 'emasculate Immanence',[88] he thereby pointed to 'the gradual opening of men's eyes to an element strange and superhuman in the life of Jesus'.[89] And to accept this was to adopt that 'faith adumbrated in the Creeds and lived by the Church'.[90]

Like Burkitt and Tyrrell, Figgis reacted strongly against what he saw as the liberal reduction of Christianity to 'mere morality'. This he considered to be nothing more than a limitation of its supernatural claims to a purely this-worldly ethical system. Such an accommodation to the naturalistic thought-forms of the contemporary world, he felt, was bound to break up 'under the pressure of mutual criticism'. Indeed, the issue was 'daily clearer between those who accept Jesus Christ with His supernatural claim and those who, since they are unable to credit the claim, repudiate His leadership'.[91] This meant that the emphasis on

---

85. *Civilisation*, p. 291 n. 3. Earlier, in *The Gospel and Human Needs* (p. 62), Figgis had pointed to the importance of Burkitt's lecture at the Pan-Anglican Congress of 1908 where he remarked that 'It is vain to study the Bible apart from the living Church'. For Figgis, the Bible has to be understood in its historical milieu.

86. *Religion and English Society*, p. vii.

87. *Civilisation*, p. 193.

88. *The Gospel and Human Needs*, p. 41.

89. *Civilisation*, p. 203.

90. *Civilisation*, p. 222.

91. *Civilisation*, p. 146.

a supernatural Jesus threw into sharp relief the tension between religion and unbelief, and militated against any premature rationalist synthesis. Earlier, in *The Gospel and Human Needs*, Figgis had pointed out the similarities between his own world and that of the eighteenth century with its premature rationalizations of the Gospel. He asks:

> Are we not to-day in face of a movement in all essentials the same as that of the sentimental rationalism of the eighteenth century? There is the same effort to strip the Catholic faith of everything that is perplexing to the understanding, to interpret the life of the historic Church with reference to categories fashionable at the moment.[92]

Similarly in a sermon, although Figgis recognizes the need to commend Jesus to the world, nevertheless the 'danger is of mutilating him to fit its notions; and instead of transforming the world by the Church, we are in imminent risk of killing the Church by the world'.[93]

It is for this very reason that in *Civilisation at the Cross Roads* Figgis reserves some of his most hostile criticism, not for the agnostics and honest doubters, but for the liberal theologians, who, he suggests, 'in regard to the Gospel facts...take their science at second hand', telling

> us that the stories of the Virgin Birth and the Resurrection body are certainly false. Huxley, for instance, professed himself quite ready to believe it, if he had thought the evidence sufficient. It is critics like Dr. Kirsopp Lake, or philosophers like Dr. Rashdall, who say beforehand that the one or the other is plainly impossible.[94]

For Figgis, supernaturalism was a necessary factor in any interpretation of Christ and the Christian Church, and what is perhaps more important, it was a form of supernaturalism that was able to persist in the modern world without surrender, and indeed which could function as a prophetic witness against the pantheistic tendencies of the liberal reductionism of the 'New Theology' of R.J. Campbell. Such theology Figgis described as 'a recrudescence of "natural religion" in a Christianised form...certain...to exercise a powerful attraction upon the minds of the cultivated or semi-cultivated "masses", for it will never appeal to the uneducated or to the multitude'.[95]

92. *The Gospel and Human Needs*, pp. 28-29.
93. *Antichrist*, p. 25.
94. *Civilisation*, p. 51.
95. *The Gospel and Human Needs*, p. 161.

Earlier in his life Figgis had himself been prone to pantheistic tendencies, which might explain the vehemence of his reaction to Campbell. In a fascinating autobiographical aside in *The Fellowship of the Mystery*, Figgis declares the feeling of spiritual desolation which resulted from his giving up his faith in the Virgin Birth, which had led him to move increasingly to a position of 'tendencies, surmises, presuppositions rather than dogmatic statements'. However, change came and he gradually recognized that the 'notion of development that made miracles impossible was seen to be mechanical; the immanental philosophy was seen to be, if pushed to the extreme, a Pantheism identifying God and the world'.[96] In rare autobiographical moments elsewhere Figgis also points to his own inner turmoil and doubt. For him, faith was 'the angel of agony, the boon of daily and hourly conflict. In these years as God's priest I have felt the pressure of crowding doubts, and learned in bitterness that to give up agnostic views may yet leave one far from the Kingdom of God'.[97]

Against pantheism, then, revelation and miracle were vital in freeing human beings from the 'network of material forces', in breaking the 'chain of environment';[98] indeed without this emphasis on the supernatural there could be no breaking free from bondage to the cycle of cause and effect: 'For this alone assures us that we are not items in a series, cogs in a great machine; but free spirits living in society, the children of one like unto us'.[99] Indeed, Figgis points out that there is something in life that always lies deeper than anything that can be explained on the basis of our obsession with

> scientific uniformity or rational categories. The partial, relatively superficial, character of intellectual processes is revealed in a flash at the crises of life...life crashes in with 'its wonder, its beauty, and its terror'—our house of cards trembles; and we are kicked as it were from the rational to the real, from the surface to the depths.[100]

It would seem, then, that for Figgis, reality rested beyond the false security of rationalist deception.

---

96. *The Fellowship of the Mystery*, pp. 294-95.
97. *The Gospel and Human Needs*, p. 15.
98. *The Gospel and Human Needs*, pp. 22-23.
99. *The Gospel and Human Needs*, p. 26.
100. *The Gospel and Human Needs*, p. 39.

The Littleness of God

Although there had been many tendencies to rationalize the Gospel in England, they were, according to Figgis,

> at bottom alien from the English mind, whose rooted dislike of theory is based on the sense that 'reality is richer than thought'... The English vagueness which some condemn springs largely from this sense, that the springs of life are deeper than all reasoning, and are to be found in the power to act and love, in those primal instincts and unconquerable emotions which cannot be reduced to formula.[101]

In short, Figgis writes, 'Take from the Christian faith its mystery and see what is left. Is the creed when "trimmed and stripped of all that touches the skies" a beautiful or even a helpful thing?'[102] It is thus against the 'arrogance of certitude'[103] with its claims to be able to rationalize a mystery that Figgis directs his venom. He asks in *The Gospel and Human Needs*:

> Is there any here to-day who would not choose to be an ignorant peasant kneeling at the foot of the crucifix and crying, 'God be merciful to me a sinner', rather than the accomplished dilettante, who thanks God that he is critical and cultivated, not as other Christians are, or even as the parish clergy? At least we know enough to condemn the second; do we know enough to blame the first?[104]

During the War Figgis re-iterated this point: 'The great tradition, the atmosphere of Scripture, is still with the masses'.[105]

At its heart, then, a Christology true to the logic of the Cross proved that Christianity was not something comprehensible in any straight-

---

101. *The Gospel and Human Needs*, p. 47.

102. *The Gospel and Human Needs*, p. 55.

103. *The Gospel and Human Needs*, p. 49. Tucker (*John Neville Figgis*, p. 55) cites an account of a meeting of Figgis with E.W. Barnes, later bishop of Birmingham. Barnes said to Figgis: 'The trouble with you Figgis, is that you did not get to the bottom of things', to which Figgis responded, 'Barnes, there is no bottom'. Though Figgis and Barnes disagreed on most things they remained affectionate friends. According to John Barnes, Barnes regarded Figgis as the 'untidiest man he ever met' (John Barnes, *Ahead of his Age* [London: Collins, 1979], p. 44). Elsewhere Barnes wrote (in an obituary in *Challenge*, 25 April 1919) that 'throughout his life, [Figgis] read too eagerly, wrote too much, thought too hard'.

104. *The Gospel and Human Needs*, p. 53.

105. *Hopes for English Religion*, p. 25.

forward rational categories; it subverted the categories of thought and reason.[106] Thus Figgis claims that it was not so much God's omnipotence, but rather God's littleness in Christ that was so perplexing to logic: 'It is not God in His power and majesty, the pride of Deity, which was revealed in Jesus, but in deed and truth God in his humiliation, scorned, spat upon, dying, that has been the force which changed the world more than all the armies of all the emperors'.[107] In a profound set of retreat addresses published during the First World War, Figgis expanded on this theme, pointing to the importance of what he calls the doctrine of 'the *humility of God*' as the major stumbling block for so many people in the modern world. It is this doctrine, he suggests, 'which men find so hard of digestion, and yet it is involved in the very nature of love'.[108] The despisers of Christianity, according to Figgis, hated Jesus' 'ideal of gentleness'[109] and were quite unable to cope with the Christmas truth of 'God made manifest in so slight a thing'.[110] The Cross and Incarnation, where God's omnipotence was emptied out in his own Son, subverted the world's logic which could not face up to what he called the 'Christian notion of a suffering God'.[111]

The Radical Church

Figgis drew important ecclesiological implications from his emphasis on the supernatural in Christianity and the concomitant eschatological interpretation of Christ. In 1917 he remarked that 'the Church of England at the close of the nineteenth century was the most respectable institution ever known in the annals of the human race'.[112] And it was the rediscovery of the otherness of religion that in part had destroyed this state of affairs. Through its sacramental and symbolic life, the church functioned as that living supernatural power available to men and women today[113] and which carried it forward against the

---

106. On this, see also *Hopes for English Religion*, p. 23.
107. *The Gospel and Human Needs*, p. 87. Cf. p. 156.
108. *The Love of God*, p. 32.
109. *The Love of God*, p. 58.
110. *The Love of God*, p. 48.
111. *The Love of God*, p. 31.
112. *Some Defects of English Religion*, p. 40.
113. *Civilisation*, p. 183.

constraints of 'mere tradition or outward respectability'.[114] And the proof of this power rested in the blood of the martyrs of the Christian Church. Thus, in *The Fellowship of the Mystery*, Figgis remarks that Christianity

> will always be able to rise from the ashes of respectability. Should, however, Christians be so foolish as to listen to the voices of some so-called friends, and to deny the other-worldly reference, their religion would at once lose its *élan vital*; it would sink to be one of the many schemes which would be considered at a social science congress, and in all probability would not outlast a century. It is in our vision of the other world that lies the spring of vitality, and all freshness of a new activity in this.[115]

It is the power of supernatural revelation alone that allows the church to elevate itself above the level of mere respectability, and to exist for those who are scandalized by decent society. Thus Figgis wrote:

> It will not be Christ's Kingdom, but something else which will result, if you transform the Church into an institution which might be agreeable for a university extension meeting, but which has no fields where children may play, and is too respectable for the poor.[116]

Similarly, in a prophetic statement in *The Fellowship of the Mystery*, Figgis claimed that '[u]nless we can be the Church of the poor, we had far better cease to be a Church at all... More and more does it appear that no correctness of dogma, no beauty of Catholic ritual, no sentiment of devotion, no piety esoteric and aloof can secure the Church from collapse, unless she gain a "change of heart" in regard to the relations of wealth and poverty'.[117] This re-orientation away from the rich and those who wielded power in society towards those with little say would be no easy task. Many errors would be made and yet such errors were demanded:

> We may stumble on hard paths; but I cannot for the life of me understand why Christian people of this day should have such a nervous fear of error when it comes to siding with the poor—in this back-slum scrimmage we call 'civilisation'—while it was the danger of subserviency to the rich that seems to have inspired the Epistle of St James.[118]

114. *The Fellowship of the Mystery*, p. 83.
115. *The Fellowship of the Mystery*, p. 95.
116. *The Gospel and Human Needs*, pp. 33, 34.
117. *The Fellowship of the Mystery*, pp. 99-100.
118. *The Fellowship of the Mystery*, p. 103.

In a purple passage from a sermon Figgis connects the themes of the unrespectability of Christianity with liberal rationalizations of the Gospel. Religion does not exist for 'respectable people living in the suburbs of London and of University towns... It was made for bad people...it is a mockery and a lie to give this bloodless professorial abstraction the place of the living, loving Saviour who rose from the dead and gives Himself in the Eucharist'. Indeed, the most dangerous antichrist, Figgis goes on, is the

> jejune parody of the Gospel Christ, which is the creation of academic pedantry and modern comfort. This boneless Christ of the German liberals, this 'transient embarrassed phantom' living in vain and dying in disillusion, is not only incapable of producing the mighty fact of the Christian Church, or the mightier one of the converted soul, but he cannot even maintain that lofty ideal which is by some supposed to be the sole residuum of Christianity.[119]

In his vehemence and passion, Figgis certainly did not display here an attitude that was likely to endear him either to his congregation or his colleagues.

In *The Fellowship of the Mystery*, Figgis goes on, in somewhat more constructive mood, to discuss some of the tendencies in the contemporary church which he sees as signs of this fresh life and energy. Modernism, he claims, is a very real struggle to engage with the modern world without losing sight of the supernatural Gospel: against the desire 'to surrender the concrete historical character of the Gospel, the activity and transcendence of God', the Modernists have retained a 'real reverence for the heritage that is ours, together with an alertness of what is new'.[120] And this task constitutes Figgis's own understanding of the role of the modern church, which needs to be able to retain the strangeness of its message while yet attempting to proclaim it in the changed conditions of modernity. This task, he claims, 'is impossible...amid the blare in our ears of ten thousand trumpets of denial', and yet it is 'worth trying. It is only the impossible that is worth attempting'.[121] And that attempt to live out the impossible was, for Figgis, life in the shadow of Calvary with its subversive logic:

119. *Antichrist*, p. 29.
120. *The Fellowship of the Mystery*, pp. 96-97.
121. *The Fellowship of the Mystery*, p. 107.

'It is only as we are willing to suffer the Cross as a means of *realising our love of God, that there is any hope for us to attain that union which is its end*. We cannot have it at any cheaper rate'.[122] Eschatology could thus have radical theological consequences.

122. *The Love of God*, p. 33 (Figgis's emphasis).

Chapter 7

GEORGE TYRRELL:
MODERNISM, ESCHATOLOGY AND THE RELIGIOUS CRISIS

The previous chapter showed how J.N. Figgis made use of eschatology in his critical theology: in many ways it resonated with the increasingly apocalyptic world-view of the period. At several points Figgis points to his indebtedness to George Tyrrell, and although he does not regard Tyrrell's theology with unqualified approval,[1] he nevertheless distinguishes the basic method of Tyrrell's Modernism from that of the reductionism of liberal protestantism, seeing it as offering a possible (as yet unproven) way out of the modern religious crisis.[2] This chapter analyses Tyrrell's use of eschatology in his own attempts to form a solution to this crisis, concentrating in particular on his posthumously published work, *Christianity at the Cross-Roads*.

George Tyrrell, one of the most notorious and outspoken of the Roman Catholic Modernists, was born in 1861 in Dublin and educated at Trinity College. After coming under the influence of the Anglo-Catholic slum priest Fr Robert Dolling, he was received into the Roman Catholic Church in 1879, becoming a Jesuit priest in 1891. He became one of the most sought-after speakers and confessors, operating from the fashionable heart of English Jesuitry in Farm Street, London. After coming under the influence of Baron Friedrich von Hügel, he began to read the continental Modernist writers, and after a number of provocative writings, he was 'removed' to the Jesuit house at Richmond in Yorkshire. He continued to produce controversial works, however, and was eventually expelled from the Order. Finally, after writing two letters to *The Times* in response to the anti-Modernist encyclical, *Pascendi*, he was excommunicated and on his death in 1909 was refused a Catholic burial.[3]

1. *The Fellowship of the Mystery*, p. 299.
2. *The Fellowship of the Mystery*, p. 291.
3. The most important biographical sources are his own autobiography of his

Tyrrell, Loisy and Harnack

Tyrrell's posthumously published work, *Christianity at the Cross-Roads*, is a somewhat bleak and bitter book, which at the same time as presenting a drastic criticism of liberal Protestantism, also offers a thinly veiled attack on his own church. In both these characteristics, it betrays many continuities with his earlier work. Von Hügel had persuaded Tyrrell to learn German in 1899, and regularly gave him lengthy reading lists and gifts of books, and it was under this influence, together with his reading of Loisy, that Tyrrell gradually developed his criticism of the synthesis of faith and modern knowledge in Liberal Protestantism, particularly as expressed in Harnack's *Das Wesen des Christentums*.[4] Thus in his first letter to Loisy of 20 November 1902, Tyrrell commented that Loisy's *L'évangile et l'église* was the 'sole adequate refutation of Harnack', expressing particular satisfaction with the manner in which Loisy had 'assimilated and rendered helpful instead of harmful the somewhat disconcerting position of Weiss's *Predigt Jesu vom Reich [sic] Gottes*'.[5]

Weiss's book, which had been left by von Hügel after a stay with

early years and Maude Petre's classic second volume, *Autobiography and Life of George Tyrrell* (2 vols.; London: Edward Arnold, 1912); Loisy describes Tyrrell's final illness and funeral in *Tyrrell et Brémond* (Paris: Nourry, 1936), pp. 15-16, 26. See also Nicholas Sagovsky, *'On God's Side'. A Life of George Tyrrell* (Oxford: Clarendon Press, 1990); Ellen Leonard, *George Tyrrell and the Catholic Tradition* (London: Darton, Longman & Todd, 1982); David F. Wells, *The Prophetic Theology of George Tyrrell* (AAR, 22; Chico, CA: Scholars Press, 1981); on the relationship with Baron Friedrich von Hügel, see Lawrence F. Barmann, *Baron Friedrich von Hügel and the Modernist Crisis in England* (Cambridge: Cambridge University Press, 1972). There is a comprehensive bibliography in T.M. Loome, *Liberal Catholicism, Reform Catholicism, Modernism* (Tübinger Theologische Schriften; Mainz: Matthias-Grünewald Verlag, 1979).

4.   See Barmann, *Baron Friedrich von Hügel*, p. 167.

5.   Letter from George Tyrrell to Loisy, 20 Nov. 1902, cited in Sagovsky, *On God's Side*, p. 155; also in Maude Petre, *Autobiography and Life of George Tyrrell*, II, p. 394. Further extracts are included in Loisy, *Tyrrell et Brémond*, pp. 5-6 and *Mémoires*, II, p. 170. Tyrrell was, however, worried that the guardians of the faith might not be able to understand the constructive intention of the book. He wrote again to Loisy on 25 Nov. suggesting that a translation be made available as quickly as possible to ensure that success in the 'better universities' might encourage a certain circumspection in Rome (*Mémoires*, II, p. 170).

Tyrrell earlier in 1902[6] had given him 'considerable pause', touching, as he remarked to his friend Maude Petre, the 'basis of all' leaving him 'houseless and homeless in the wilderness'.[7] It was under this influence of Loisy and Weiss that Tyrrell's mature ideas gradually began to develop, as he placed increasing emphasis on the transcendent and the mysterious as a necessary factor in any understanding of Jesus. Such explicit ideas are, however, apparent in his published works from about the same period, even though there is no evidence of Weiss's influence. In his essay, 'Mysteries, A Necessity of Life' published in the Jesuit Journal, *The Month* in 1902,[8] for instance, he stressed the importance of a 'higher life' as a counter to any rationalistic reduction of religion to a purely this-worldly phenomenon.[9] The 'mystery-hunger' of the soul, he went on, was 'not to be checked, but rather deepened and fostered as an indisputable condition of subjective development'.[10] The chief influence on this position seems to have been Bernhard Duhm's work, *Das Geheimnis in der Religion*, which was also influential on the History of Religion School in Germany.[11] Following Duhm, Tyrrell views the task of theology as the science of the mystery of religion or of what he called the 'over-natural world'.[12]

> Only when we forget that the overnatural world is necessarily expressed in terms of the natural, and therefore inexactly, does theology become what Dr. Duhm thinks it must always be—the foe of mystery. Then only do its dogmas become 'Rätsel der Theologie', bristling with contradictions.[13]

6.   Sagovsky, *On God's Side*, p. 155.
7.   Tyrrell to Petre, 27 April 1902, cited in Sagovsky, *On God's Side*, p. 162. On this, see Schultenover, *George Tyrrell*, p. 263: 'Tyrrell, who was trying to walk between [liberal protestantism and orthodoxy], was suddenly left without a hold, caught the blow squarely in the middle, and was thrown for a headlong bouleversement'.
8.   G. Tyrrell, 'Mysteries, A Necessity of Life', *The Month* 461 (November 1902), pp. 449-59. This essay was republished in *Through Scylla and Charybdis* (London: Longmans, 1907), pp. 155-90. References are to the original version.
9.   'Mysteries', p. 455.
10.   'Mysteries', p. 457.
11.   *Das Geheimnis in der Religion* (Leipzig: J.C.B. Mohr, 1896). On Duhm's influence on the *Religionsgeschichtliche Schule*, and particularly on Hermann Gunkel, see Chapman, 'Religion, Ethics and the History of Religion School', p. 53.
12.   In his inaugural lecture, *Über Ziel und Methode der theologischen Wissenschaft* (Basel: Schweighauser, 1889), Duhm is deeply critical of the 'confusion of religion with theology, and the constriction of the former by the latter' (p. 7).
13.   'Mysteries', p. 459. Loisy was critical of Tyrrell precisely for his dreaming

The theme of the necessity of mystery and the supernatural, which was later to dominate Tyrrell's thought, is already evident in this essay, although as yet it is not related directly to Weiss's eschatological interpretation of Jesus.

Shortly afterwards, however, Weiss seems to have had some effect on Tyrrell's outspoken pseudonymous booklet *The Church and the Future* (originally published pseudonymously under the name of Hilaire Bourdon),[14] particularly in its emphasis on the prophetic rather than the dogmatic character of Christ. Part II of this work is entitled a 'liberal re-statement of Catholicism', and there is much that points towards the themes that would later dominate *Christianity at the Cross-Roads*, as well as Tyrrell's vitriolic attack on the Belgian Cardinal Mercier, published as *Medievalism*.[15] For instance, he remarked: 'in vain do we turn to our official guides for an answer to the perplexities raised by history and criticism. We ask for bread and they give us a stone'.[16] Similarly, against the rigid scholasticism of the Roman system, he maintained that the 'doctrinal and dogmatic system of Christianity is the understanding or the mental construction of that spiritual world to which we are related by the life of Charity'.[17] Even though Tyrrell's christological and ecclesiological ideas still had a long way to develop, the theme of the transcendence of the spiritual world is once again already stressed.

Further influence of Weiss can be detected in Tyrrell's article 'Religion and Ethics', also published in *The Month*,[18] where he endeavoured to work towards a synthesis between the ethical emphasis of Harnack's liberal Protestantism and the transcendence of Weiss's position, in a manner not wholly dissimilar from Rashdall's sermon on Loisy and

---

and mysticism. Cf. G. Tyrrell, *Medievalism* (repr.; Tunbridge Wells: Burns & Oates, 1994), p. 101.

14. Tyrrell (alias Hilaire Bourdon), *The Church and the Future (L'église et l'avenir)* (printed for private circulation only), 1903. Weiss is cited on p. 6.

15. It is interesting to note that Mercier's Lenten Pastoral referred to Christ in a sometimes Harnackian fashion. Christ 'imposed upon men the revealed word which showed them eternal life and the only way to attain it. He proclaimed a moral code for them and then the helps necessary to put its prescriptions into practice' (*Medievalism*, p. 23).

16. Bourdon, *The Church and the Future*, p. 32.

17. Bourdon, *The Church and the Future*, p. 87.

18. 'Religion and Ethics', *The Month* 464 (February 1903), pp. 130-45.

Harnack discussed in Chapter 2.[19] Tyrrell suggested that by 'pitting critic against critic, e.g. Dr. Harnack against Dr. J. Weiss, we can get a confirmation of our position'.[20] Although Tyrrell still made some concessions to Harnack's ethically reductionist reading of Jesus, he claimed that Weiss, the less '*a priori* critic', finds it

> not hard to establish from the internal evidence of the Synoptic Gospels that this...miraculous triumph of the Kingdom of God over the Kingdom of Satan was not something accidental, but was the very substance and centre of Christ's message to which all His moral and spiritual teaching was subordinated.[21]

However, although Tyrrell recognized that 'Christ's principal aim was to fix our hearts on a future life', nevertheless it was only the 'practical apprehension of God's fatherhood and man's brotherhood' which could 'prepare men for the true Kingdom of God'.[22] However, even though he retained this limited understanding of Jesus' ethics, Tyrrell was critical of Harnack for identifying these ethics of preparation for the Kingdom with the Kingdom of God itself:

> [T]hat new mode of life in which present mysteries shall give place to vision, and vague aspirations to attainment is causally continuous with that interior life we lead as Christians; not however a mere extension and deepening of it, as Dr Harnack implies, but a development and transformation such as that which changes the grub into the moth.[23]

Similarly, Tyrrell maintained that to make Jesus

> the preacher of a purely internal Kingdom of Heaven, of a merely theistic doctrine of God's fatherhood...implies a sophistical reading of the Gospel and of early Church history. A coming transformation of humanity and heaven and earth was the revealed fact in the light of which men's conduct was to be shaped and formed.[24]

What becomes apparent here is that the idea of the coming kingdom is beginning to dominate Tyrrell's thinking.

In late 1902 Tyrrell wrote about this need for a combination of Weiss and Harnack to von Hügel. What was needed above all was a

19. Rashdall, 'Harnack and Loisy', pp. 228-36.
20. 'Religion and Ethics', p. 134.
21. 'Religion and Ethics', p. 135.
22. 'Religion and Ethics', p. 135.
23. 'Religion and Ethics', p. 136.
24. 'Religion and Ethics', p. 140.

possible synthesis between Weiss and Harnack (i.e. outward-future and inward-timeless) views of the Kingdom of God. The solution is on the lines of the Mysteries article... The Future Kingdom, given us in apocalyptic clothing in the Gospel, is, I suspect, the natural *development*, not merely extension, continuation, deepening, of that inner Kingdom of love which Christ describes *in its own terms*. His emphasis is on the life of love (as opposed to legalism) as being the true preparation for the future development of the spirit into something over-human in an over-natural environment. The *nature* of that development and of the pure will-world or society of spirits—all that he leaves *mysterious* and paints in terms of current eschatological fancies; but as to the *via*, he is clear and decisive.[25]

Here Tyrrell is emphasizing the transcendence and mystery of Jesus' message as something which, at the same time, excites ethical action in a living community based on love.[26] He thereby seeks to combine Christ viewed as the teacher of the timeless kingdom with Christ understood as the founder of the community of preparation: the dominant theme, however, as is emphasized by the reference back to the earlier article, is that of mystery and transcendence.

Tyrrell gradually began to feel the gap between the Christ of the Gospels and the belief of the present, becoming acutely aware of the need to find a substantial truth which could gain contemporary expression devoid of its many often incredible accretions: the position of the historical figure of Christ seemed irrecoverable and yet there was something of timeless truth which was accessible to the Catholic church. Writing in 1905, Tyrrell remarked:

He would be a bold theologian who should affirm that such articles of belief as the Creation, or Christ's ascent into Heaven, His descent into Hell, His coming to judge the quick and the dead, and many others are held to-day in substantially the same sense as formerly. We may say that what we still hold is, and therefore always was, their substance or essential value, purged of non-essential accidents. But these accidents were once held to be essential...and those who questioned their necessity were persecuted and condemned.[27]

25. Tyrrell to von Hügel, 4 December 1902 cited in Petre, *Autobiography and Life of George Tyrrell*, II, p. 396.

26. On Tyrrell's understanding of religion and mysticism, see Daly, *Transcendence and Immanence*, ch. 7.

27. G. Tyrrell, 'The Rights and Limits of Theology', in *idem*, *Through Scylla and Charybdis*, pp. 200-41, here p. 217.

Yet in this classic statement of the Modernist position, Tyrrell is still close to Loisy: he makes little effort to link the teachings of the church with the historical figure of Christ, and in that sense there is wide scope given to the church to make its authoritative teaching, provided any such teaching was open to subsequent development.

Tyrrell, Schweitzer and Liberal Protestantism

In his last year, however, after reading Schweitzer for the first time and carefully re-reading Weiss in the early months of 1909,[28] Tyrrell came to take on board a thoroughgoing eschatological position, becoming convinced that Jesus' message itself was at its heart supernatural: and more importantly the gap between Jesus of Nazareth and the present could be bridged. The Kingdom of God could not convincingly be interpreted in a Harnackian fashion and neither could it be reduced to a scholastic system based on an alien philosophy: this meant that both the official theology of the Roman Church, together with the compromise of the liberal protestants, were equally open to critical judgment. Indeed by 1909, Tyrrell had come to feel that his 'past work has been dominated by the Liberal-Protestant Christ', a position he had come to consider 'bankrupt'.

Thus in an article in *Jesus or Christ*, a supplement to the *Hibbert Journal*, which was published shortly after his death, he wrote:

> But the great ethical and liberal Teacher of Schleiermacher and Ritschl is not less hardly pressed by criticism than the Christ of the creeds. As the gospels stand, they show us that the substance of the teaching of Jesus was partly ethical and partly eschatological. The liberal school has hitherto assumed that the latter element was accidental, occasional, negligible; that the former was principal and alone essential. Slowly but surely their methods have, in the hands of Johannes Weiss and others, inverted this judgment; have assigned the liberal and universalist elements to subsequent Pauline emendations, and have left us a Jesus whose inspiration and enthusiasm were entirely religious, mystical, and transcendent, but in no sense liberal or modern-minded.[29]

He went on to claim that the Gospel of this anti-modern Christ was

28. Tyrrell to von Hügel, 9 April 1909, cited in Sagovsky, *On God's Side*, p. 255.

29. G. Tyrrell, 'The Point at Issue', in Jacks (ed.), *Jesus or Christ?*, pp. 5-16 (15).

hope in another life against the despair of this life. Such a Jesus would have been far more in sympathy with orthodoxy than with liberalism. Hence it is that M. Loisy, accepting the basis of Criticism, has in *l'Evangile et l'Eglise* been able to supplant the construction of Dr Harnack by one of a more catholic character. Orthodoxy very naturally suspects these gifts from a hostile hand, for which a heavy bill may be presented later. But *fas est ab hoste doceri*.[30]

For Tyrrell, the transcendent Christ of the Gospels required a supernatural church which was able to maintain this transcendent voice down through the generations.

In the last months of his life Tyrrell remained very much concerned with the problem of eschatology and its resultant transcendentalism, which he understood, as he wrote to von Hügel in the Spring of 1909, as a means of combating what he increasingly came to see as the 'Sunday-school-teacher Christ' of liberal Protestantism. He went on:

If we cannot save huge chunks of transcendentalism, Christianity must go. Civilisation can do (and has done) all that the purely immanentist Christ of Matthew Arnold is credited with. The other-worldly emphasis; the doctrine of immortality was what gave Christianity its original impulse and sent martyrs to the lions. If that is accidental we only owe to Jesus in a great measure what we owe to all good men in some measure. In the sense of survival and immortality the Resurrection is our critical and central dogma.[31]

Thus, for Tyrrell, it was only the transcendence of the historical Jesus founded on eschatology that would prevent Christianity's reduction into a system of ethics.

In a letter to his friend, Alfred Fawkes,[32] written on 3 June 1909, he was even more explicit about the inadequacies of the liberal Christ. Was it not true, he wrote, that

---

30. 'The Point at Issue', p. 16.

31. Tyrrell to von Hügel, 9 April 1909, cited in Sagovsky, *On God's Side*, p. 255.

32. Alfred Fawkes (1850–1930) was, like Tyrrell, a Roman Catholic Convert, who was sympathetic to Modernism. In an unpublished pamphlet entitled *Prophet and Priest* (cited in Vidler, *A Variety of Catholic Modernists*, p. 156) he adopted a straightforwardly Harnackian position, believing, as he wrote in 1903, that Loisy was wrong. Although he maintained a lifelong correspondence and friendship with Loisy, he continued in his liberal protestant position, especially after his return to the Church of England in 1908. He was buried alongside Tyrrell in Storrington churchyard. On Fawkes, see Vidler, *A Variety of Catholic Modernists*, pp. 155-60.

there was an alien element irreconcilable with the *Jenseits*, miraculous, magical religion of *Jesus des Apocalyptikers?*... He was not primarily but only incidentally an ethical teacher... Liberal Protestantism is the development of the ethic He adopted and exemplified in common with the prophets and saints of all times; but not of his Gospel... Jesus would say that Harnack was *not far from* the Kingdom of God, but that a miss was as good as a mile... I hope I am wrong; but I feel that I have been reading the Gospel all my life through nineteenth-century glasses, and that now scales, as it were, have fallen from my eyes.[33]

This somewhat pathetic plea set the tone for Tyrrell's *tour de force* in his final great work.

Christianity at the Cross-Roads

In *Christianity at the Cross-Roads*, Tyrrell devotes his energies to attacking Liberal Protestants from what amounts to an eschatological position.[34]

They wanted to bring Jesus into the nineteenth century as the Incarnation of its ideal of Divine Righteousness, i.e. of all the highest principles and aspirations that ensure the healthy progress of civilisation... With eyes thus preoccupied they could only find the German in the Jew; a moralist in a visionary; a professor in a prophet; the nineteenth century in the first; the natural in the supernatural.[35]

With more than a hint of irony he denounces Harnack's attacks on Catholicism, echoing the anti-Germanism of Figgis:[36]

No sooner was the Light of the World kindled than it was put under a bushel. The Pearl of Great Price fell into the dustheap of Catholicism, not without the wise permission of Providence, desirous to preserve it till the day when Germany should rediscover it and separate it from its useful but deplorable accretions.[37]

At this point Tyrrell resorts to aphorism, claiming that '[t]he Christ that Harnack sees, looking back through nineteen centuries of Catholic

---

33. Cited in Petre, *Autobiography and Life of George Tyrrell*, II, pp. 399-400.
34. *Christianity at the Cross-Roads*, pp. 37-38.
35. *Christianity at the Cross-Roads*, p. 47.
36. Tyrrell pronounces that the old dismissal of German scholarship is no longer tenable because 'as a matter of fact it has reached the street and the railway bookstall' (*Christianity at the Cross-Roads*, p. 36).
37. *Christianity at the Cross-Roads*, p. 47.

darkness, is only the reflection of a Liberal Protestant face, seen at the bottom of a deep well'.[38] After giving an account of the alternative eschatological view 'unbiassed [*sic*] by the prepossessions of Liberal Protestantism', Tyrrell claims:

> Of the Jesus Who came forward openly as the Messiah in a spiritual (i.e. a moral) sense, Who preached and exemplified the righteousness of the inward Kingdom of God, Who founded the Kingdom on earth in the form of a school of imitators and Who died solely as a martyr of morality, there is not left a single shred. He did not oppose a moral world to a worldly interpretation of the Kingdom. He took the current interpretation as He found it, which was not worldly but other-worldly—spiritual, in the sense of metaphysical and transcendent, not in the immanental moral sense.[39]

Later, Tyrrell, continuing his attack on Liberal Protestantism, describes it as 'rather a system of religious ethics than a religion. It merely insists that morality is religion and adjusts our life and action to that spiritual and invisible side of the world which is an object of faith, a necessary postulate of morality'.[40] The whole tendency of Liberal Protestantism, he continued, had been to 'minimise the transcendence by establishing a sort of identity of form between this life and the other... Heaven or the Kingdom of heaven are in our midst; they are the spiritual or moral side of life'.[41] He admitted that the Jesus of Liberal Protestantism was not quite pure myth, but rather the problem was that, 'having eliminated what was principal in the Gospel, they have retained and segregated what was but secondary and subordinate—the moral element... For such, Christianity is but the morality of Christ'.[42]

Against Liberal Protestantism, Tyrrell calls for a Christian trans-cendentalism which he sees as delivered by an eschatological interpre-tation of the Gospels with its emphasis on Christ's otherness and strangeness.[43] Thus, for Tyrrell, against moralism stands apocalypticism: 'Liberal Protestant Christianity may claim Jesus, if not as the founder,

---

38. *Christianity at the Cross-Roads*, p. 49.
39. *Christianity at the Cross-Roads*, pp. 59-60.
40. *Christianity at the Cross-Roads*, p. 66.
41. *Christianity at the Cross-Roads*, p. 65.
42. *Christianity at the Cross-Roads*, p. 88.
43. For a general discussion of Tyrrell's approach to apocalyptic, see Richard Ballard, 'George Tyrrell and the Apocalyptic Vision of Christ', *Theology* 38 (1975), pp. 459-67.

yet as the Great Teacher of its morality... This religious idea of Liberal Protestantism is not especially Christian; it is not the "idea" of Jesus'.[44] The idea of the Christ of eschatology, whose 'work on earth was to prepare and hasten the Kingdom—to close the last chapter of human history',[45] which was at the heart of Jesus' message, on the other hand, is the idea of transcendence. This, according to Tyrrell, is far better preserved in Catholicism. This means, as Tyrrell put it in another aphorism, that 'the idea of the Church is the idea of Jesus'.[46]

The force of Tyrrell's criticism was recognized in a non-committal notice by the young Hewlett Johnson in *The Interpreter*,[47] and it was hardly surprising that some were highly shocked at this public (albeit posthumous) voicing of such a direct attack on Liberal Protestantism. W.R. Inge, for instance, was provoked to a position of extreme hostility. In a viciously anti-Romanist review, he attacks Tyrrell, basing his argument on what he calls the 'knowledge' afforded by liberal protestant critics: 'The attempt to kill Protestant Christianity by striking at its Lord has failed, and must fail, completely'.[48] Similarly, in his somewhat more guarded lecture on eschatology to the 1910 Cambridge Church Congress, V.H. Stanton recognized the force and importance of Tyrrell's contribution to the debate on eschatology, but felt that the higher life was not merely a life to be expected in some future time, but was also something 'we can know even here, and into which the very texture of morality enters'.[49] In turn, although the anonymous reviewer in *The Interpreter* commented more favourably that '[i]n so far as *Christianity at the Cross-Roads* is a protest against the theory of gradual, smooth and inevitable development of humanity by reason of its innate divinity, it must be considered forcible', but, he went on, 'its pessimistic outlook upon this present world and its disbelief in man are both decadent and disproportioned'.[50]

---

44. *Christianity at the Cross-Roads*, p. 89.

45. *Christianity at the Cross-Roads*, p. 51.

46. *Christianity at the Cross-Roads*, p. 90.

47. Hewlett Johnson, Review of Tyrrell *Christianity at the Cross-Roads*, *The Interpreter* 6 (1910) pp. 230-34.

48. W.R. Inge, Review of Tyrrell *Christianity at the Cross-Roads*, *Hibbert Journal* 9 (1910), pp. 434-38, here p. 438. This review in part provoked Sanday's letter to the *Guardian* of 19 August 1910 discussed in Chapter 5.

49. In *The Guardian*, 30 Sept. 1910, p. 1358; *1910 Report*, p. 64.

This last criticism seems to point to Tyrrell's real importance in the history of theology: for Tyrrell, writing in truly prophetic manner, the apocalyptic Christ challenges the assumptions of the religious solutions of the present day, with their emphasis on steady progress; the apocalyptic Christ, however much he might have been re-interpreted in terms of appropriate contemporary symbols, nevertheless remained an outsider to the modern world. The optimistic faith of late imperialism could never handle what Tyrrell called the 'incurable tragedy of human life—a tragedy that grows deeper as man rises from the hand-to-mouth simplicity of mere animal existence, extends his knowledge and control of experience and wakes ever more fully to the sense of his insatiable exigencies'.[51] In short, Tyrrell claims, liberalism simply did not have the spiritual resources to deal with the realities at the heart of human life, being 'blind to the appalling residue of human misery and to the insoluble problems that are coming up slowly like storm-clouds on the horizon'.[52] In an increasingly apocalyptic world, liberalism looked like an outmoded philosophy for happier times. In short, against the Gospel of progress, of 'social development', stands the Gospel of 'another life'.[53]

In distinction to this optimistic Gospel which proved redundant in the turmoil of the present, Tyrrell claimed that the transcendental Gospel, with its emphasis on the life of the spirit, is best embodied in a form of Catholicism, which is capable of embracing 'nearly every form of religious expression' as it strains towards 'unification and coherence'.[54] Indeed, Tyrrell goes on to claim, 'the Jesus of the first century would be in sympathy with just those elements of Catholicism that are least congenial to the modern mind...with sacraments, temples, priests and altars;...with devils and angels and all the supernaturalism of His own age and tradition'.[55]

Despite this defence of Catholicism as closest in idea to the early Church, the excommunicated Tyrrell was obviously far from a mere apologist for the contemporary Roman Catholic Church. Instead, he

---

50. Anonymous review of *Christianity at the Cross-Roads*, *The Interpreter* 6 (1910) p. 334.
   51. *Christianity and the Cross-Roads*, p. 95.
   52. *Christianity and the Cross-Roads*, p. 111.
   53. *Christianity and the Cross-Roads*, p. 116.
   54. *Christianity and the Cross-Roads*, p. 167.
   55. *Christianity and the Cross-Roads*, p. 217.

remarked, in radical fashion, that 'Modernism criticizes the very idea of dogma, of ecclesiasticism, of revelation, of faith, of heresy, of theology, of sacramentalism'.[56] In many of his writings, Tyrrell attacks what he calls the 'new-fangled dictatorial conception of the papacy— i.e. of a privileged private judgment to which all must submit'.[57] Against the system which forced submission in all details, Tyrrell commended a simple faith with few facts, preferring to allow for a wide degree of variation:

> To pretend that Christ ought to have and therefore must have provided for theological uniformity is to fly in the face of facts and to mis-apprehend the scope and meaning of the Gospel as summed up in the words: 'Repent, for the Kingdom of Heaven is at hand'. This confusion of Faith with theology, and of unity of Faith with theological uniformity, is of course one of the main supports of the individualistic interpretation of the Vatican Decrees and of the refusal to recognise the collective spirit of the whole Church as the one rule of faith.[58]

Like Figgis, Tyrrell is critical of any attempt at a harmonization of theology and philosophy, criticizing the thirteenth-century synthesis on which the modern Roman system seemed to rely for its finality. The Modernist 'denies the possibility of finality and holds that the task is unending just because the process of culture is unending... [He] is no blind worshipper of present culture. He knows it is a medley of good and evil'.[59] Tyrrell had written in a similar vein to his friend Albert Houtin a few years earlier in response to the Papal condemnation of Modernism:

> I think it important to insist that we hold the *faith* though not the theology of the Church. Of course it is not what *they* mean by faith; but it is a tenable meaning. I would never deny the divinity of Christ, or the Atonement, or the Real Presence etc. etc. partly because they symbolise real religious experiences; partly because it would enlist protestant sympathy on the side of Rome. Other symbols might do as well; but these are in possession.[60]

56. *Christianity and the Cross-Roads*, p. 10.
57. *Medievalism*, p. 47.
58. *Medievalism*, p. 57.
59. *Medievalism*, p. 135.
60. Tyrrell to Houtin, 13 Dec. 1907. Cited in Sagovsky, *On God's Side*, p. 256.

For Tyrrell, it was nothing short of nineteenth-century prejudice to wish to remove the supernatural and apocalyptic from the heart of Jesus' message: 'the fact remains that it was in the forms of apocalyptic thought that the religious "idea" of Jesus embodied itself, and exercized the most potent religious influence that the world has yet known'.[61] The eschatological picture pointed to the radical gap between the contemporary world and the first century, which could only be overcome as each age attempted a re-interpretation of 'apocalyptic symbolism into terms of its own symbolism'.[62] What was important for Tyrrell was to try to return to the underlying substance of the apocalyptic message, using what he called 'the principle of symbolism'. In this manner, he went on, 'we have no need to abolish the Apocalypse, which, as the form in which Jesus embodied His religious "idea" is classical and normative for all subsequent interpretations of the same...What each age has to do is to interpret the apocalyptic symbolism into terms of its own symbolism'.[63] And to do this '[w]e have not to compare symbol with symbol, or theology with theology, or to show that one can be deduced from the other. We have to compare life with life; feeling with feeling; action with action'.[64] The impact of the apocalyptic idea, which though shrouded in what Tyrrell called the historical envelope, was to challenge the present age with transcendent values which prevented mere recourse to the ethical constructions of the Liberal Protestants.[65] In short, 'judged by the test of life and fruitfulness, the

61. *Christianity at the Cross-Roads*, p. 102.
62. *Christianity at the Cross-Roads*, p. 103.
63. *Christianity at the Cross-Roads*, p. 103.
64. *Christianity at the Cross-Roads*, p. 104.
65. *Christianity at the Cross-Roads*, p. 145. The problems which emerged from this interpretation, however, were legion, as was observed in a letter from Burkitt to J.M. Thompson (Burkitt to Thompson, 21 May 1911 [Thompson papers; BOD MS Eng. lett. d. 182 fols. 3-4]). (Thompson's book, *Miracles in the New Testament*, which denied the possibility of miracles, had recently been censured by the Bishop of Croydon):

> It is pathetic to see how many of the clergy shut their eyes and ears to the uniformity of nature and to the difference between the world in the New Testament and that which we are obliged to figure for ourselves.

As Tyrrell says in *Christianity at the Cross-Roads*, p. 145, 'To this discrimination between substance and envelope we have been forced by the advance of human thought'. This is exactly expressed: *we have been*

symbolism of apocalyptic imagery is truer to our spiritual needs than that of Hellenic intellectualism'.[66] As the church attempted to express this idea afresh, so it asserted its faith, which was quite different from its theological and ecclesiastical formulations. As symbols became more adequate, so the transcendent church which stood beyond any liberal synthesis could begin to embrace more of humanity to become the 'true Catholicism' of which the Modernist dreams.[67]

In this way, Tyrrell claimed, authenticity would be achieved: to live the life of Christ was far more significant than to think the thoughts of the church, since the Catholic religion was not a 'theological system on paper, nor...an institution governed by a hierarchy in other than spiritual interests', but instead was a 'personal religion lived by what must always be a small minority of professed Catholics'. Religion was not so much a matter of profession, but of action. And against such a vision, the hierarchy sought to repress this living religion 'in the grip of a hawk'.[68]

Tyrrell concludes his book with a prophetic and provocative challenge:

> *forced.* The uniformity of nature is not a direct development of Christian Doctrine but an alien dogma, and it is no wonder that those who don't realise Science and History are restive at each concession to a non-Christian *Weltanschauung*. Christianity may survive: you and I believe that it will. But a good many forms and presentations of Christianity, both Catholic and Protestant, simply can't live forever in a non-geocentric universe. The real problem is whether we can manage to get the working man to take any interest in a historical point of view and a symbolic religion.
>
> Yours v. sincerely,
> F.C. Burkitt.

66. *Christianity at the Cross-Roads*, p. 209.
67. *Christianity at the Cross-Roads*, p. 281. Loisy commented on Tyrrell's *Christianity at the Cross-Roads* at length in his *Mémoires*. He felt that Tyrrell had used the historical eschatological Christ as a cypher for an idealized humanity which was 'Assertion de foi, intuition mystique' (*Mémoires*, II, p. 600). His belief that Jesus was the spirit made man was a 'Thèse indémonstrable'. According to Loisy, Tyrrell remained quite orthodox and held an 'ardent faith' until the end, but let himself down solely through his tactics and his delight in argument and polemics (*Mémoires*, II, p. 601).
68. *Christianity at the Cross-Roads*, pp. 218-19.

It is the spirit of Christ that has again and again saved the Church from the hands of her worldly oppressors within and without; for where that spirit is, there is liberty. Deliverance comes from below, from those who are bound, not from those who bind. It is easy to quench a glimmering light caught by the eyes of a few; but not the light of the noonday sun— of knowledge that has become objective and valid for all. It is through knowledge of this kind that God has inaugurated a new epoch in man's intellectual life and extended his lordship over Nature. Shall He do less for man's spiritual life when the times are ripe? and are they not ripening? Are we not hastening to an *impasse*—to one of those extremities which are God's opportunities?[69]

For Tyrrell, then, Modernism was thus no straightforward compromise with culture: it was instead an act of deliverance from the systems of the institutional church, and would surge up from below in a renewal of the church. Indeed it was to be contrasted with 'that sort of more educated and temporising ultramontanism that shrinks from an inopportune pressing of principles which the world has unfortunately outgrown; that loves to rub shoulders cautiously with science and democracy; that strives to express itself moderately and grammatically'.[70] Modernism was a form of criticism which affected the whole of Catholicism, and allowed for no half-way houses: if it is a heresy at all, wrote Tyrrell echoing the words of the Encyclical, it is 'the compendium of all heresies'.[71] This meant that at its heart, theology was called on to criticize, to avoid the 'finished and dead' system of any theology that claims to be impervious to culture.[72]

If I hold on [to the Catholic tradition] it is because I abhor runaway solutions, and spurious simplifications, whether ultramontane or schismatic, that would force a premature synthesis by leaving out all the intractable difficulties of the problem; that prefer a cheap logicality to the clash and confusion through which the immanent reason of the world works order out of warring elements of a rich and fruitful chaos.[73]

For Tyrrell, as for Figgis, a theology founded upon a Christ who proclaimed the future reign of God was subversive of all logic, and that

69. *Christianity at the Cross-Roads*, p. 282.
70. *Medievalism*, p. 140.
71. *Medievalism*, p. 140.
72. *Medievalism*, p. 144.
73. *Medievalism*, p. 168.

meant subversive of all theologies founded upon that logic. Consequently, from Tyrrell it is but a short step to the eschatological theology which came of age after the First World War, and which will be discussed briefly in the concluding Chapter.

Chapter 8

CONCLUSION: THE DOMINANCE OF ESCHATOLOGY

Through the course of this book I have sought to show that in the years before the First World War a 'crisis' theology was beginning to emerge as a protest against the hitherto dominant theologies of liberal synthesis. In their use of eschatology, Sanday, Burkitt, Figgis and Tyrrell in their different ways helped create an atmosphere in which the familiarity of the ethical Christ of liberal Protestantism was called into question: no longer was Harnack's neo-pietist solution plausible or even possible without hopelessly contorting history. The great insight of Weiss and Schweitzer was that Jesus was a child of his time; and, although they both refused to draw their discoveries to their logical conclusions, both retaining a timeless spiritual Christ who transcended history, they nevertheless helped in the often painful process of rehistoricizing theology. As Rowan Williams has suggested: '[Jesus] was important for first-century reasons, not important for timeless reasons distorted by confused first-century minds'.[1]

For Burkitt, Christ had become a radically strange first-century figure whose world view had little in common with the modern world. However, where Schweitzer himself had taken refuge in a metaphysics of will which, he felt, was able to bridge the chasm of two thousand years, Burkitt saw the only escape in a rejuvenated church proclaiming a message which, as it bore the apocalyptic message of Christ, challenged the assumptions and comforts of its own and every age, thereby ensuring that Christ remained radically strange in each generation. What became universal in the message of Christ was that in Christ one encountered the judgment of God. Following in Burkitt's direction, both Figgis and Tyrrell regarded it as the duty of the Church to pre-

1. Rowan Williams, 'Doctrinal Criticism: Some Questions', in Sarah Coakley and David Pailin (eds.), *The Making and Remaking of Christian Doctrine* (Oxford: Clarendon Press, 1993), pp. 239-64, here p. 261.

serve the picture of transcendence, mystery and otherness which they regarded as the heart of religion: no age was absolute, least of all the present, and all ages were to be brought before a higher judge. And for Figgis and Tyrrell, as prophets of the crisis in civilization and Christianity, the signs of the decay of society had already arrived. Yet both remained outside the mainstream: Figgis as an Anglo-Catholic monk of socialist tendencies from a non-conformist background was far removed from the centres of the Anglican establishment, and Tyrrell as an excommunicate convert priest was refused burial within his own communion.

Nevertheless both Figgis and Tyrrell were heralds of a style of theology which was beginning to move into the theological mainstream; their theologies were at least in part crisis theologies proclaiming a radically other Christ who judged all the systems of the world which were being thrown into confusion in the all-embracing social and political crisis of Edwardian England. The parallels with what came after the First World War cannot be underestimated; yet even before the War, the younger generation of theologians—both in England and in Germany—were beginning to pay attention to the emergent theology of eschatology.[2] For instance, in his essay, 'The Historic Christ'[3] included in the controversial collection, *Foundations* published in 1912, which represented the work of rising English scholars, B.H. Streeter (1874–1937)[4] summarized many of the themes developed initially by

---

2.   On Barth's gradual assimilation of eschatological ideas, see Bruce L. McCormack, *Karl Barth's Critical Realistic Dialectical Theology: Its Genesis and Development 1909–1936* (Oxford: Clarendon Press, 1995). Cf. Gunther Wenz, 'Zwischen den Zeiten: Einige Bemerkungen zum geschichtlichen Verständnis der theologischen Anfänge Karl Barths', *Neue Zeitschrift für Systematische Theologie* 28 (1986), pp. 284-95, esp. pp. 289-90: 'The consciousness of total crisis and the necessity of a radical new beginning determined not only theology but the whole intellectual and spiritual climate of Germany in the early nineteen twenties'.

3.   'The Historic Christ', in Streeter (ed.), *Foundations*, pp. 73-146.

4.   Streeter, a student of Sanday's, was educated at Queen's College, Oxford, becoming a Fellow in 1905 and Provost in 1933 until his death. Before the War he helped establish the widespread acceptance of the priority of Mark, as well as the 'Q' hypothesis. After the War he became more associated with the Modern Churchmen, attempting a reconciliation of science and religion in his book, *Reality: A New Correlation of Science and Religion* (London: Macmillan, 1927). On Streeter, see Peter Hinchliff, *God and History* (Oxford: Clarendon Press, 1992), ch. 10.

Schweitzer, Burkitt and Tyrrell. Indeed Streeter's essay points clearly to the acceptance of the 'Eschatological School' as a dominant theological model, as well as the role of theology in the recognition of a cultural crisis. The great importance of the 'Eschatological School', he maintained, was that Jesus became a man of his own times, who simply could not be reduced to the 'cultured respectability' of the nineteenth century; and it was recognition of this fact that allowed for the synoptic sayings to be interpreted historically without at the same time simply being explained away as pointers to some 'deeper' underlying truth.[5]

The eschatological understanding of Christ provides the basis for Streeter's own controversial interpretation, which made use (notoriously) of what he called the 'poetic' language of apocalyptic to help explain the resurrection in terms of visions 'directly caused by the Lord Himself veritably alive and personally in communion with' the disciples.[6] The student, Streeter claimed, was thus no longer confronted by the

> uninspiring choice between a Liberalism that thought it could patronise its Christ and an Orthodoxy that must needs 'defend' Him,—and neither conception to be found in the Gospels without some violence to the text. But the Christ whom this newer school reveals is a solitary arresting figure, intensely human, yet convinced of His call to an office and a mission absolutely superhuman... He came not to bring peace but division, and to 'separate them one from another as a shepherd divided the sheep from the goats'.[7]

Jesus was no longer the Christ of the liberal or idealist synthesis but was a strange figure who would destroy the '"bourgeois Christ" of Rationalistic liberalism'.[8] For Streeter, Jesus became his own forerunner, pointing to a future when he would return; and it was this message of expectation that had to be preserved in the Church.

For Streeter, it was at this point that parallels between the contemporary world and the world of the first century began to emerge. Indeed, he suggested, it was precisely because the world appeared to be dying that

---

5.   'The Historic Christ', p. 76.

6.   'The Historic Christ', p. 136. It was this language which seemed to reduce the resurrection to the level of subjective vision that provoked such a vigorous debate. On this, see Clements, *Lovers of Discord*, ch. 3 and Langford, *In Search of Foundations*.

7.   'The Historic Christ', p. 78.

8.   'The Historic Christ', p. 77.

ultimate values and eternal issues stood out before them stark and
clear... The conception of evolution...has inevitably distracted men's
attention from the fact that, in human history, at any rate, the greatest
advances are frequently *per saltum*... In each such epoch [of crisis] we
may see a partial Advent of the Christ, but is the Apocalyptic word amiss
that Anti-Christ is also then abroad?'[9]

Like Figgis and Tyrrell, Streeter perceived a crisis in theology and
began to read his own society in terms of that crisis, and that meant as
standing under the judgment of Christ.

Although, it must be admitted, Streeter did not continue to maintain
quite such a critical stance after the War, he nevertheless reflects the
deeply pessimistic mood of the times. Christ is no longer the comfort-
ing spiritual presence of eternal verities shrouded in the accidents of
history, but the 'unarmed and unlettered...village Carpenter...who
dreamed that God would redeem the world through Him, and died to
make the dream come true'.[10] The Jesus of history shattered the Christ
of faith, thereby leaving faith to search for its new foundations as it
sought a God who could not be brought to earth by any act of human
thought. And it was on these shattered foundations that theology was to
be reconstructed by the great eschatological prophets after the First
World War: Christ became the judge of all human systems. Religion
was no longer the 'soul of culture; it is its crisis'.[11] In a similar vein
Karl Barth could write:

God sends him—from the realm of the eternal, unfallen, unknown world
of the beginning and the end... He is our protest against assigning eternity
to any humanity or nature or history which we can observe. Therefore, he
is 'very God and very man'—that is, he is the document by which the
original, lost-but-recoverable union of God and man is guaranteed.[12]

9. 'The Historic Christ', pp. 119-20.
10. 'The Historic Christ', p. 144. Peter Hinchliff offers an alternative reading of
Streeter's essay in *Foundations*. Seeing it as tinged with 'the optimism of Victorian
England', and seeing such optimism shattered in the First World War, he suggests
that 'optimism, once shattered, does not encourage a new resilience' (*God and
History*, p. 246).
11. Gustav Kruger, 'The "Theology of Crisis": Remarks on a Recent Movement
in German Theology', *HTR* 19 (1926), pp. 227-58, here p. 236. Kruger is discussing
Gogarten's theology.
12. Barth, *Epistle to the Romans*, p. 277. Richard Roberts (in *A Theology on its
Way?* [Edinburgh: T. & T. Clark, 1991], p. 172) commented that 'Barth's *Römer-
brief*...presents the reader with a truly remarkable totality in which a dialectical and

To many before the First World War, however, the emerging emphasis on eschatology and apocalyptic, and the resultant critique of liberal synthesis, seemed quite misguided since it would make it quite impossible for the modern Christian to identify with Christ. Cyril Emmet, for instance, wrote:

> Schweitzer and Tyrrell compare the Christ of eschatology with the Christ of liberal, or protestant, German criticism, and pour unlimited scorn on the latter. No doubt such critics as Harnack and Bousset do give us what Dr. Sanday has called 'a reduced Christianity'. But it is a Christianity which is true as far as it goes, and it is something on which we can build. They portray for us a Christ whom we can unreservedly admire and love, even if it is a little doubtful whether logically we ought to worship Him. The Jesus of eschatology it is difficult either to admire or to love; worship Him we certainly cannot.[13]

Similarly, according to E.F. Scott, Jesus was not at root a stranger:

> Whatever may have been the limitations which were imposed on Jesus by the beliefs of His own time, He has never been 'a stranger and an enigma'. His meaning has been intelligible, like that of no other teacher, to all races and generations of men.[14]

For Emmet as for Scott, and their fellow critics of thoroughgoing eschatology, it is a very long way to Barth and the eschatological theology of the 1920s.

Yet for Burkitt, as well as for Tyrrell and Figgis, there is every chance that they would have understood Barth's *Epistle to the Romans* with its paradoxes and its infinite qualitative distinction. They too recognized an otherness in Christ and could equally well have said: 'We stumble when we suppose that we can treat of him, speak and hear of him—*without being scandalized*'.[15]

Of the major theological figures working in England after the war, it was perhaps E.C. Hoskyns (1884–1937)[16] more than anybody else who

---

eschatological supersession of the nihilistic condition is enacted an act of realisation that implies a quasi-expressionistic creation *ex nihilo*'.

13. Emmet, *The Eschatological Element*, p. 77.

14. Scott, *The Kingdom and the Messiah*, p. 253.

15. *Epistle to the Romans*, p. 280 (Barth's emphasis). See, for instance, Burkitt's speech to the Church Congress in 1910 (*1910 Report*, p. 85).

16. Hoskyns was educated at Jesus College, Cambridge, and spent a period under Harnack in Berlin. Later he became a friend of Schweitzer. From 1919 until his death he was Dean of Chapel at Corpus Christi College, Cambridge. He trans-

fought such battles for eschatology in the 1920s and 1930s: although thoroughgoing eschatology never dominated the theological scene to the extent that Barth dominated theology in the German-speaking world, so many scholars owe a debt to Hoskyns that his influence is perhaps without parallel in recent English New Testament scholarship. He wrote in 1927 in an essay on the 'Other-worldly' Kingdom of God:

> Our New Testament is almost entirely controlled by the thought of God as active and powerful, and the writers show no tendency to regard His activity as an activity within the sphere of developing history, or as the energy which gives movement and life to the physical structure of the Universe. The action of God is consequently regarded as catastrophic... The eschatological imagery was, therefore, fundamental to primitive Christianity because it adequately guarded and preserved the other-worldly character of God, of the Church, and of Christian morality.[17]

For Hoskyns, progress, development and evolution were annihilated by that eschatological preacher who died on the cross. Ethical problems are consequently

> secondary problems to a Christian. The one fundamental moral problem is what we should still possess if the whole of our world were destroyed to-morrow, and we stood naked before God. The eschatological belief crudely and ruthlessly sweeps away all our little moral busynesses, strips us naked of worldly possessions and worldly entanglements, and asks what survives the catastrophe.[18]

For Hoskyns, God was different from this world: radically unchanging and radically powerful. And that was a message which drew from the well of Loisy, Schweitzer and Tyrrell, who had brought theology to the

lated Barth's *Epistle to the Romans*. On Barth's eschatology and the alleged inadequacies of Hoskyns's translation, see Richard H. Roberts, 'Barth and the Eschatology of Weimar', in *idem, A Theology on its Way?*, p. 193.

17. E.C. Hoskyns, 'The Other-Worldly Kingdom of God in the New Testament', *Theology* 14 (1927), pp. 249-55, here pp. 253, 255. In a lecture given soon after the First World War to the Birmingham Clerical Society ('The Apocalyptic Element in the Teaching of Jesus: Its Ultimate Significance and its Abiding Function', in von Hügel, *Essays and Addresses on the Philosophy of Religion* [London: Dent, 1921], pp. 119-43), Friedrich von Hügel, while not citing Tyrrell directly, emphasized the importance of the Church in overcoming the gap between the modern world and the first century. His influence in pointing scholars to Schweitzer should not be underestimated.

18. Hoskyns, *Cambridge Sermons* (London: SPCK, 1938), p. 37.

'cross-roads'.[19] In a remarkable sermon, Hoskyns declared:

> The Lady Margaret Professor of Divinity [J.F. Bethune-Baker] recently
> defined the immediate task of Christian theology to be the re-expression
> of Christian faith in terms of evolution. I would venture to suggest that
> the task of the Christian theologian is rather to preserve the Christian doc-
> trine of God from the corrupting influence of the dogma of evolution.[20]

Against such a view, Hoskyns held God to be the God who acted
'catastrophically' in human life.[21]

If the position I have discussed throughout the course of this book is
true—that eschatology emerged some time before the First World War
as a response in part to a perceived breakdown in society—then it
might be suggested that the return of eschatology and the discovery of
the radical otherness of Jesus may not have had quite so much to do
with the First World War as has frequently been suggested. The period
before 1914 was not universally characterized by the optimism of the
past: according to Neville Talbot, for instance, the 'firm footing of
Victorian Liberalism'[22] had slipped. The adoption of an eschatological
understanding of the historical Jesus, at least by Burkitt, Figgis and
Tyrrell, is a symptom of this slippage, which manifested itself in a
prophetic critique of Edwardian pride.[23] There may no doubt have been
many other reasons as to why eschatology became such an important
feature in the Edwardian theological scene, but it seems hard to deny
that the context was well suited to such ideas. A critical context
provoked a critical theology. As Tyrrell remarked in *Christianity at the
Cross-Roads*: 'If optimism is usually associated with the youth and

19. Hoskyns, 'The Christ of the Synoptic Gospels', p. 160. See also Parsons, *Sir
Edwyn Hoskyns*, pp. 27-43.

20. Hoskyns, *Cambridge Sermons*, p. 35.

21. It would seem that Hoskyns made some rather veiled references to the
Master of his College, Will Spens. The theme of the Church was always Christ
crucified rather than some 'cosy corner' which will always have some dynamite
beneath it. Mixing his metaphors, he goes on, 'the Church always has a dagger at its
heart' (*Cambridge Sermons*, p. 91). According to C.F. Evans: 'the dagger was,
presumably, what had always threatened [the religious experience position of
Spens], namely, that in submerging Jesus within that to which he had given rise, it
lacked adequate criteria by which to assess the experience for what was true and
what false development' ('Crucifixion-Resurrection: Some Reflections on Sir
Edwyn Hoskyns as Theologian', *Epworth Review* 10 [1983], pp. 3-16, here p. 6).

22. Talbot, 'The Modern Situation', in Streeter (ed.), *Foundations*, p. 236.

23. On this point, see Perrin, *The Kingdom of God*, p. 35.

pessimism with the age of persons or peoples, it is because pessimism is the verdict of experience',[24] and, for Tyrrell and his fellow prophets, that was an experience gained in the increasingly fragmented society of pre-First World War England. The First World War merely confirmed their worst fears.

24. Tyrrell, *Christianity at the Cross-Roads*, pp. 117-18.

BIBLIOGRAPHY

Unpublished Sources

Correspondence and Papers of F.C. Burkitt, Cambridge University Library.
Correspondence and Papers of Friedrich von Hügel, St Andrew's University Library.
Correspondence and Papers of Hastings Rashdall, Bodleian Library, Oxford.
Correspondence and Papers of William Sanday, Bodleian Library, Oxford.
Correspondence and Papers of J.M. Thompson, Bodleian Library, Oxford.
Diaries of C.C.J. Webb, Bodleian Library, Oxford.

Published Sources

Allen P.S. (ed.), *Transactions of the Third International Congress for the History of Religions* (2 vols.; Oxford: Clarendon Press, 1908).

Allett, John, *New Liberalism: The Political Economy of J.A. Hobson* (Toronto: University of Toronto Press, 1981).

Anderson, Robert, *Christianised Rationalism and the Higher Criticism* (London: John F. Shaw, 1903).

Aune, D.E., 'Eschatology (Early Christian)', in D.N. Freedman (ed.), *Anchor Bible Dictionary*, II (6 vols.; New York: Doubleday, 1992), pp. 594-609.

Ballard, Richard, 'George Tyrrell and the Apocalyptic Vision of Christ', *Theology* 38 (1975), pp. 459-67.

Barbour, Robin (ed.), *The Kingdom of God and Human Society* (Edinburgh: T. & T. Clark, 1993).

Barmann, Lawrence F., *Baron Friedrich von Hügel and the Modernist Crisis in England* (Cambridge: Cambridge University Press, 1972).

Barnes, John, *Ahead of his Age* (London: Collins, 1979).

Barth, Karl, *The Epistle to the Romans* (trans. E.C. Hoskyns; London: Oxford University Press, 6th edn, 1933).

Baum, Gregory, 'Sociology and Theology', *Concilium* (NS) 1 (1974), pp. 22-31.

Bedoyère, Michael de la, *The Life of Baron von Hügel* (London: J.M. Dent, 1951).

Bethune-Baker, J.F., Review of Schweitzer, *The Quest of the Historical Jesus, JTS* 12 (1911), p. 148.

Bosworth, Edward I., Review of Weiss, *Predigt Jesu, AJT* (1901), pp. 357-58.

Bousset, Wilhelm, 'Die Religionsgeschichte und das neue Testament', *TRu* 7 (1904), pp. 265-77, 311-18, 353-65.

—*What is Religion?* (trans. F.B. Law; London: Unwin, 1907).

Brabazon, J., *Albert Schweitzer* (New York: Putnam, 1975).

Bull, Malcolm (ed.), *Apocalypse Theory and the Ends of the World* (Oxford: Basil Blackwell, 1995).

Burkitt, F.C., *Christian Beginnings* (London: University of London Press, 1924).

—'The Eschatological Idea in the Gospel', in H.B. Swete (ed.), *Essays on Some Biblical Questions of the Day by Members of the University of Cambridge* (London: Macmillan, 1909), pp. 193-214.

—*The Failure of Liberal Christianity and Some Thoughts on the Athanasian Creed* (Cambridge: Bowes and Bowes, 1910).

—'The Historical Character of the Gospel of Mark', *AJT* 15 (1911), pp. 169-93.

—*Jesus Christ: An Historical Outline* (London: Blackie and Son, 1932).

—'Johannes Weiss: In Memoriam', *HTR* 8 (1915), pp. 291-97.

—'The Apocalypses: Their Place in Jewish History', in A. Cohen *et al.*, *Judaism and the Beginnings of Christianity* (London: Routledge, 1923), pp. 49-90.

—'The Parables of the Kingdom of Heaven', *The Interpreter* 7 (1911), pp. 131-48.

—'The Parable of the Wicked Husbandmen', in P.S. Allen (ed.), *Transactions of the Third International Congress for the History of Religions*, II (Oxford: Clarendon Press, 1908), pp. 321-28.

—'Theological Liberalism', in Hubert Handley (ed.), *Anglican Liberalism, by Twelve Churchmen* (London: Williams and Norgate, 1908), pp. 18-34.

—'Twenty-five Years of Theological Study: A Lecture delivered at the University of Manchester on the occasion of the Twenty-fifth anniversary of the Faculty of Theology', *Bulletin of the John Rylands Library* 14 (1930), pp. 37-52.

Bury, J.B., *The Idea of Progress* (London: Macmillan, 1920).

Carroll, Robert P., *Wolf in the Sheepfold* (London: SPCK, 1991).

Chapman, Mark D., 'Anglo-German Theological Relations during the First World War', *Zeitschrift für neuere Theologiegeschichte* 7 (2000), pp. 109-26.

—'Concepts of the Voluntary Church in England and Germany, 1890–1920: A Study of J.N. Figgis and Ernst Troeltsch', *Zeitschrift für neuere Theologiegeschichte* 2 (1995), pp. 37-59.

—'The Kingdom of God and Ethics: From Ritschl to Liberation Theology', in Robin Barbour (ed.), *The Kingdom of God and Human Society* (Edinburgh: T. & T. Clark, 1993), pp. 140-63.

—'Rashdall, Hastings', in F.W. Bautz and T. Bautz (eds.), *Biographisch-Bibliographisches Kirchenlexikon*, VI (Herzberg: Bautz, 1994), cols. 1368-1373.

—'Religion, Ethics and the History of Religion School', *Scottish Journal of Theology* 46 (1993), pp. 43-78.

—'The Sanday, Sherrington and Troeltsch Affair: Theological Relations between England and Germany after the First World War', *Mitteilungen der Ernst Troeltsch Gesellschaft* 6 (1991), pp. 40-71.

—'The Socratic Subversion of Tradition: William Sanday and Theology, 1900–1920', *JTS* 45 (1994), pp. 94-116.

—'Tony Blair, J.N. Figgis and the State of the Future', *Studies in Christian Ethics* 13 (2000), pp. 49-66.

Chesterton, G.K., *The Works of G.K. Chesterton* (London: Wordsworth, 1995).

Chilton, Bruce, *Pure Kingdom: Jesus' Vision of God* (London: SPCK, 1996).

Church Congress, see C. Dunkley (ed.).

Churchill, Winston S., *Liberalism and the Social Problem* (London: Hodder & Stoughton, 1909).

Clements, Keith W., *Lovers of Discord: Twentieth Century Theological Controversies in England* (London: SPCK, 1988).

Coakley, Sarah, and David Pailin (eds.), *The Making and Remaking of Christian Doctrine* (Oxford: Clarendon Press, 1993).

Coates, John D., *Chesterton and the Edwardian Cultural Crisis* (Hull: Hull University Press, 1984).

Dakin, A.H., *Paul Elmer More* (Princeton: Princeton University Press, 1960).

Daly, Gabriel, O.S.A., *Transcendence and Immanence: A Study of Catholic Modernism and Integralism* (Oxford: Clarendon Press, 1980).

Dangerfield, George, *The Strange Death of Liberal England 1910–1914* (London: Macgibbon and Kee, 1966 [1935]).

David, Edward, 'The New Liberalism of C.F.G. Masterman', in K.D. Brown (ed.), *Essays in Anti-Labour History* (London: Macmillan, 1974), pp. 17-41.

Dewick, E.C., *Primitive Christian Eschatology* (Hulsean Prize Essay, 1908; Cambridge: Cambridge University Press, 1912).

Dillistone, F.W., *C.H. Dodd: Interpreter of the New Testament* (London: Hodder & Stoughton, 1977).

Dobschütz, Ernst von, 'The Eschatology of the Gospels', *The Expositor* 9 (1910), pp. 97-113; 193-209; 333-47; 398-417.

—*The Eschatology of the Gospels* (London: Hodder & Stoughton, 1910).

—'The Lord's Prayer', *HTR* 7 (1914), pp. 293-321.

—'The Most Important Motives for Behavior in The Life of the Early Christians', *AJT* 15 (1911), pp. 505-524.

—'The Significance of Early Christian Escatology', in P.S. Allen (ed.), *Transaction of the Third International Congress for the History of Religions*, II (2 vols.; Oxford: Clarendon Press, 1908), pp. 312-20.

Dodd, C.H., *The Parables of the Kingdom* (London: Nisbet, 1935).

Dolman, Robert, 'Forgotten Man of the Church of England: John Neville Figgis as Preacher', *ExpTim* 107 (1996), pp. 169-72.

Duhm, Bernhard, *Das Geheimnis in der Religion* (Leipzig: J.C.B. Mohr, 1896).

—*Über Ziel und Methode der theologischen Wissenschaft* (Basel: Schweighauser, 1889).

Dunkley, C. (ed.), *The Official Report of the Church Congress held at Cambridge* (London: George Allen, 1910).

—*Official Report of the Church Congress held at Manchester, October 1908* (London: Bemrose, 1908).

Durkheim, E., *Division of Labour in Society* (New York: Macmillan, 1933).

Elliott-Binns, L.E., 'The Apologetics of Neville Figgis', *Church Quarterly Review* 130 (1940), pp. 47-57.

Emmet, Cyril W., *The Eschatological Element in the Gospels* (Edinburgh: T. & T. Clark, 1911).

—'Is the Teaching of Jesus an Interimsethik', *The Interpreter* 8.4 (1912), pp. 423-34.

Emmet, Cyril W., and Lily Dougall, *The Lord of Thought* (London: SCM Press, 1921).

Ensor, R.C.K., *England, 1870–1914* (Oxford: Clarendon Press, 1936).

Evans, C.F., 'Crucifixion-Resurrection: Some Reflections on Sir Edwyn Hoskyns as Theologian', *Epworth Review* 10 (1983), pp. 3-16.

Fastenrath, Elmar, *'In Vitam Aeternam': Grundzüge christlicher Eschatologie in der ersten Hälfte des 20: Jahrhunderts* (Sankt Ottilien: Eos Verlag, 1982).

Figgis, J.N., *Antichrist and Other Sermons* (London: Longmans, 1913).

—*Churches in the Modern State* (London: Longmans, 1914).

—*Civilisation at the Cross Roads* (London: Longmans, 1912).

—*The Divine Right of Kings* (repr. with introduction by G.R. Elton, New York: Harper & Row, 1965 [1896]).

—*The Fellowship of the Mystery being the Bishop Paddock Lectures delivered at the General Theological Seminary, New York, during Lent 1913* (London: Longmans, 1914).

—*From Gerson to Grotius* (Cambridge: Cambridge University Press, 1907).

—*The Gospel and Human Needs* (London: Longmans, 1909).

—*Hopes for English Religion* (London: Longmans, 1919).

—*The Love of God* (London: Francis Griffiths, 1916).

—*Religion and English Society* (London: Longmans, 1910).

—*Some Defects of English Religion and Other Sermons* (London: Robert Scott, 1917).

—*The Will to Freedom or The Gospel of Nietzsche and the Gospel of Christ being the Bross Lectures delivered in Lake Forest College, Illinois* (London: Longmans, 1917).

Gardner, Percy, 'Present and Future Kingdom in the Gospels', *ExpTim* 21 (1910), pp. 535-38.

Garnett, Jane, 'Hastings Rashdall and the Renewal of Christian Social Ethics, c.1890–1920', in Jane Garnett and H.C.G. Matthew (eds.), *Revival and Religion Since 1700: Essays for John Walsh* (London: Hambledon Press, 1993), pp. 297-316.

Garnett, Jane, and H.C.G. Matthew (eds.), *Revival and Religion Since 1700: Essays for John Walsh* (London: Hambledon Press, 1993).

Garrod, H.W., 'Christ the Forerunner', in *idem, The Religion of All Good Men and Other Studies in Christian Ethics* (London: Constable, 1906).

Gayford, S.C., Review of Weiss, *Die Idee des Reiches Gottes in der Theologie*, *JTS* 4 (1903), pp. 466-68.

Glasswell, M., 'Burkitt, Francis Crawford', *TRE* 7, pp. 424-28.

Graf, F.W., 'Der >Systematiker< der >kleinen Göttinger Fakultät<. Ernst Troeltschs Promotionsthesen und ihr Göttinger Kontext', in H. Renz and F.W. Graf (eds.), *Troeltsch-Studien*, I (Gütersloh: Gerd Mohn, 1982), pp. 235-90.

Grässer, E., *Albert Schweitzer als Theologe* (Tübingen: J.C.B. Mohr, 1979).

Green, Christopher (ed.), *Art Made Modern: Roger Fry's Vision of Art* (London: Merrell Holberton, 1999).

Harnack, Adolf von, Review of Loisy, *L'évangile et l'église*, *TLZ* 30 (1904), cols. 59-60.

—*Das Wesen des Christentums* (Leipzig: J.C. Hinrichs, 1901).

—*What is Christianity?* (trans. T.B. Saunders; London: Williams and Norgate, 1904).

Harris, José, *Private Lives, Public Spirit: Britain 1870–1914* (London: Penguin Books, 1994).

Hase, Karl, *Geschichte Jesu* (Leipzig: Breitkopf und Hartel, 1876).

Headlam, A.C., *The Life and Teaching of Jesus Christ* (London: John Murray, 1923).

Heiler, F., *Der Vater des katholischen Modernismus, A. Loisy* (Munich: Erasmus, 1947).

Henson, H. Hensley, *Retrospect of an Unimportant Life* (2 vols.; London: Oxford University Press, 1942).

Hiers, Richard, *The Historical Jesus and the Kingdom of God* (Gainesville: University of Florida Press, 1973).

Hinchliff, Peter, *God and History* (Oxford: Clarendon Press, 1992).

Hirst, Paul Q., *Associative Democracy* (Cambridge: Polity Press, 1994).

180 *The Coming Crisis*

Hobson, J.A., *The Crisis of Liberalism: New Issues in Democracy* (London: P.S. King and Son, 1909).

Hoffmann-Axtheim, D., 'Loisys L'Evangile et L'Eglise: Besichtigung eines zeitgenössischen Schlachtfeldes', *ZTK* 65 (1968), pp. 291-328.

Hoskyns, E.C., *Cambridge Sermons* (London: SPCK, 1938).

—'The Christ of the Synoptic Gospels', in E.G. Selwyn (ed.), *Essays Catholic and Critical* (London: SPCK, 3rd edn, 1954 [1926]), pp. 151-78.

—'The Other-Worldly Kingdom of God in the New Testament', *Theology* 14 (1927), pp. 249-55.

Hügel, Friedrich von, 'The Apocalyptic Element in the Teaching of Jesus: Its Ultimate Significance and its Abiding Function', in *idem, Essays and Addresses on the Philosophy of Religion* (London: Dent, 1921), pp. 119-43.

Hulshof, Jan, *Wahrheit und Geschichte* (Essen: Ludgerus Verlag, 1973).

Ice, J.L., *Schweitzer: Prophet of Radical Theology* (Philadelphia: Westminster Press, 1971).

Inge, W.R., 'The Apocalyptic Element in Christ's Teaching', *The Guardian* (13 May 1910), p. 680.

—'Liberal Catholicism', in *idem, Faith and Knowledge* (Edinburgh: T. & T. Clark, 1904), pp. 279-92.

—Review of Sanday, *Christologies Ancient and Modern, JTS* 11 (1910), pp. 584-86.

—Review of Tyrrell, *Christianity at the Cross-Roads, Hibbert Journal* 9 (1910), pp. 434-38.

—'The Theology of the Fourth Gospel', in H.B. Swete (ed.), *Essays on Some Biblical Questions of the Day by Members of the University of Cambridge* (London: Macmillan, 1909), pp. 251-88.

Iremonger, F.A., *William Temple* (London: Oxford University Press, 1948).

Jacks, L.P. (ed.), *Jesus or Christ?* (Hibbert Journal Supplement; London: Williams and Norgate, 1909).

Jackson, H. Latimer, *The Eschatology of Jesus* (London: Macmillan, 1913).

Johnson, Hewlett, Review of Schweitzer, *The Quest of the Historical Jesus, The Interpreter* 6 (1910), pp. 337-47.

—Review of Tyrrell, *Christianity at the Cross-Roads, The Interpreter* 6 (1910), pp. 230-34.

Jones, Alan H., *Independence and Exegesis: The Study of Early Christianity in the Work of Alfred Loisy (1857–1940), Charles Guignebert (1857–1939) and Maurice Goguel (1880–1955)* (Beiträge zur Geschichte der biblischen Exegese, 26; Tübingen: J.C.B. Mohr, 1983).

Jülicher, Adolf, *Neue Linien in der Kritik der evangelischen Überlieferung* (Giessen: Adolf Topelmann, 1906).

Kahlert, Heinrich, *Der Held und seine Gemeinde: Untersuchungen zum Verhältnis von Stifterpersönlichkeit und Verehrergemeinschaft in der Theologie des freien Protestantismus* (Frankfurt: Peter Lang, 1984).

Koch, Klaus, *The Rediscovery of Apocalyptic* (London: SCM Press, 1972).

Köhler, Walter, *Ernst Troeltsch* (Tübingen: J.C.B. Mohr, 1941).

Kruger, Gustav, 'The "Theology of Crisis": Remarks on a Recent Movement in German Theology', *HTR* 19 (1926), pp. 227-58.

Kümmel, W.G., 'Die "konsequente Eschatologie" Albert Schweitzers im Urteil der Zeitgenossen', in *idem, Heilsgeschehen und Geschichte. Gesammelte Aufsätze* (Marburger

Theologische Studien, 3; Marburg: N.G. Elwert, 1965), pp. 328-39.

—*The New Testament: The History of the Investigation of its Problems* (London: SCM Press, 1973).

Kümmel, W.G., and C.H. Ratschow, *Albert Schweitzer als Theologe* (Marburg: N.G. Elwert, 1966).

Lacey, T.A., *Harnack and Loisy, with an Introductory Letter by the Right Honourable Viscount Halifax* (London: Longmans, 1904).

—*The Historic Christ* (London: Longmans, 1905).

—'On the Case of the Abbé Loisy', in *idem, Wayfarer's Essays* (London: Oxford University Press, 1934), pp. 141-45.

—*Shaken Beliefs: Three Lectures heard at All Saints, Margaret Street* (Oxford: Mowbray, 1922).

—'The Parousia and the Passion', *The Church Times* (16 April 1908), p. 531.

Lake, Kirsopp, 'The Shepherd of Hermas and Christian Life in Rome in the Second Century', *HTR* 4 (1911), pp. 25-46.

Lake, Kirsopp, and Foakes Jackson, *The Beginnings of Christianity* (5 vols.; London: Macmillan, 1920–).

Langford, Thomas A., *In Search of Foundations: English Theology, 1900–1920* (Nashville: Abingdon Press, 1960).

Lannert, Berthold, *Die Wiederentdeckung der neutestamentlichen Eschatologie durch Johannes Weiss* (Tübingen: Francke Verlag, 1989).

Leckie, J.H., *The World to Come and Final Destiny* (United Free Church College, Glasgow, Kerr Lectures; Edinburgh: T. & T. Clark, 1918).

Leonard, Ellen, *George Tyrrell and the Catholic Tradition* (London: Darton, Longman & Todd, 1982).

Lloyd, T.O., *English History 1906–1992* (Oxford: Oxford University Press, 1993).

Lock, Walter, 'William Sanday' (Obituary), *JTS* 22 (1921), pp. 97-104.

Loisy, A.F., *Autour d'un petit livre* (Paris: Alphonse Picard, 1903).

—*Choses passées* (Paris: Emile Nourry, 1913).

—*The Gospel and the Church* (London: Isbister, 1903).

—*L'évangile et l'église* (Bellevue: Chez L'Auteur, 1902).

—*Le quatrième évangile* (Paris: Nourry, 1903).

—*Mémoires pour servir a l'histoire religieuse de notre temps. II. 1900-1908* (3 vols.; Paris: Emile Nourry, 1931).

—*Tyrrell et Brémond* (Paris: Nourry, 1936).

Loome, T.M., *Liberal Catholicism, Reform Catholicism, Modernism* (Tübinger Theologische Schriften; Mainz: Matthias-Grünewald Verlag, 1979).

Lukes, Stephen, *Emile Durkheim* (London: Penguin Books, 1975).

Lundström, Gösta, *The Kingdom of God* (Edinburgh: Oliver and Boyd, 1963).

McCormack, Bruce L., *Karl Barth's Critical Realistic Dialectical Theology: Its Genesis and Development 1909–1936* (Oxford: Clarendon Press, 1995).

McLeod, Hugh, *Religion and Society in England, 1850–1914* (Basingstoke: Macmillan, 1996).

Major, Henry, *English Modernism: Its Origin, Methods, Aims* (Cambridge, MA: Harvard University Press, 1927).

Manning, Bernard Lord, *More Sermons of a Layman* (London: Independent Press, 1944).

Manson, William, *Christ's View of the Kingdom of God* (United Free Church College, Glasgow, Bruce Lectures; London: James Clarke, 1918).

Marsh, Clive, *Albrecht Ritschl and the Problem of the Historical Jesus* (San Francisco: Mellen Research University Press, 1992).

Marsh, Margaret, *Hastings Rashdall: Bibliography of the Published Writings* (Leysters: Modern Churchpeople's Union, 1993).

Marshall, G.N., and D. Poling, *Schweitzer* (New York: Doubleday, 1971).

Mason, A.J., *Christianity—What is it? Five Lectures on Dr Harnack's 'Wesen des Christentums'* (London: SPCK, 1902).

Masterman, C.F.G., *The Condition of England* (London: Methuen, 1909).

Matheson, P.E., *The Life of Hastings Rashdall D.D.* (London: Oxford University Press, 1928).

Mathews, Shailer, *The Messianic Hope in the New Testament* (Chicago: Chicago University Press, 1905).

Moffatt, J., *The Theology of the Gospels* (London: Gerald Duckworth, 1912).

Morgan, Robert, 'Non Angli sed Angeli: Some Anglican Reactions to German Gospel Criticism', in Stephen Sykes and Derek Holmes (eds.), *New Studies in Theology*, I (London: Gerald Duckworth, 1980), pp. 1-30.

—'Historical Criticism and Christology: England and Germany', in Stephen Sykes (ed.), *England and Germany: Studies in Theological Diplomacy* (Studien zur interkulturellen Geschichte des Christentums, 25; Frankfurt: Peter Lang, 1982), pp. 80-112.

—'From Reimarus to Sanders', in R.S. Barbour (ed.), *The Kingdom of God and Human Society* (Edinburgh: T. & T. Clark, 1993), pp. 80-139.

Mozley, J.K., *Some Tendencies in British Theology* (London: SPCK, 1951).

Neill, Stephen, *The Interpretation of the New Testament, 1861–1961* (2nd edn. rev. by Tom Wright; Oxford: Oxford University Press, 1988 [1964]).

Newsome, David, 'The Assault on Mammon: Charles Gore and John Neville Figgis', *JEH* 17 (1966), pp. 227-41.

Nicholls, David, *Deity and Domination: Images of God and the State in the Nineteenth and Twentieth Century* (London: Routledge, 1989).

—*The Pluralist State* (Basingstoke: Macmillan, 2nd rev. edn., 1994 [1975]).

Nineham, Dennis, 'Schweitzer Revisited', in *idem, Explorations in Theology*, I (London: SCM Press, 1977).

Norman, Edward, *Church and Society in England, 1770–1970* (Oxford: Clarendon Press, 1976).

Nowak, Kurt, 'Bürgerliche Bildungsreligion? Zur Stellung Adolf von Harnacks in der protestantischen Frömmigkeitsgeschichte der Moderne', *Zeitschrift für Kirchengeschichte* 99 (1988), pp. 326-53.

Nowell-Smith, S. (ed.), *Edwardian England* (London: Oxford University Press, 1964).

O'Day, Alan, *The Edwardian Age: Conflict and Stability, 1900–1914* (Basingstoke: Macmillan, 1979).

O'Neill, J.C., *The Bible's Authority* (Edinburgh: T. & T. Clark, 1991).

Parsons, Gerald, 'Social Control to Social Gospel: Victorian Christian Social Attitudes', in *idem* (ed.), *Religion in Victorian Britain*, II (Manchester: Manchester University Press, 1988), pp. 39-62.

Parsons, Richard E., *Sir Edwyn Hoskyns as Biblical Theologian* (London: Hurst, 1985).

Peabody, Francis, 'New Testament Eschatology and New Testament Ethics', in P.S. Allen (ed.), *Transactions of the Third International Congress for the History of Religions*, II (2 vols.; Oxford: Clarendon Press, 1908), pp. 305-312.

Perrin, Norman, *The Kingdom of God in the Teaching of Jesus* (London: SCM Press, 1963).

Petre, Maude, *Autobiography and Life of George Tyrrell* (2 vols.; London: Edward Arnold, 1912).

Petre, Maude (ed.), *George Tyrrell's Letters* (London: T. Fisher Unwin, 1920).

Phillips, Paul T., *A Kingdom on Earth: Anglo-American Social Christianity 1880–1940* (University Park, PA: Penn State University Press, 1996).

Pleitner, Henning, *Das Ende der liberalen Hermeneutik am Beispiel Albert Schweitzers* (Tübingen: Francke Verlag, 1992).

Powell, David, *The Edwardian Crisis: Britain 1901–1914* (Basingstoke: Macmillan, 1996).

Prestige, G.L., *The Life of Charles Gore* (London: Heinemann, 1935).

Pugh, Martin, *State and Society: British Political and Social History 1870–1992* (London: Arnold, 1994).

Raby, F.J.E., 'John Neville Figgis, Prophet, 1866–1919', *Theology* 40 (1940), pp. 325-32.

Ramsey, A. Michael, *From Gore to Temple* (London: Longmans, 1960).

Rashdall, Hastings, 'The Creeds', *Modern Churchman* 4 (1914), pp. 204-214.

—'Ethics and Eschatology', in *idem, Conscience and Christ: Six Lectures on Christian Ethics* (London: Gerald Duckworth, 1916), pp. 36-76.

—'Harnack and Loisy', in *idem, Principles and Precepts* (Oxford: Basil Blackwell, 1927), pp. 228-36.

—Review of Burkitt, *The Failure of Liberal Christianity, Modern Churchman* 1 (1911–12), pp. 23-35.

Read, Donald, 'Crisis Age or Golden Age?', in Donald Read (ed.), *Edwardian England* (London: Croom Helm, 1982), pp. 14-39.

—*Edwardian England* (London: Harrap, 1972).

Read, Donald (ed.), *Edwardian England* (London: Croom Helm, 1982).

Riches, John, *A Century of New Testament Study* (Cambridge: Lutterworth Press, 1993).

Ritschl, Albrecht, *Rechtfertigung und Versöhnung* (Bonn: A. Marcus, 4th edn, 1900).

Roberts, Richard H., *A Theology on its Way?* (Edinburgh: T. & T. Clark, 1991).

Rowland, Christopher, ' "Upon whom the Gods of the Ages have come": Apocalyptic and the Interpretation of the New Testament', in Malcolm Bull (ed.), *Apocalypse Theory and the Ends of the World* (Oxford: Basil Blackwell, 1995), pp. 38-57.

Sagovsky, Nicholas, *'On God's Side': A Life of George Tyrrell* (Oxford: Clarendon Press, 1990).

Salvatorelli, L., 'From Locke to Reitzenstein: The Historical Investigation of the Origins of Christianity', *HTR* 22 (1929), pp. 263-367.

Sanday, William, 'An Anglican View of M. Loisy', *The Pilot: A Weekly Review of Politics, Literature and Learning* (23 Jan. 1904), pp. 84-85.

—'The Bearing of Critics upon the Gospel History', *ExpTim* 20 (1908–1909), pp. 103-114; 152-62.

—'The Cambridge Biblical Essays', *JTS* 11 (1910), pp. 161-79.

—*Christologies Ancient and Modern* (Oxford: Clarendon Press, 1910).

—*Criticism of the Fourth Gospel* (Oxford: Clarendon Press, 1905).

—*Effigies Mea* (unpublished speech given at Christ Church, Oxford, 18 Oct. 1909), in Sunday papers, BOD MS Eng. Misc. d. 128 no. 380.

—*An Examination of Harnack's 'What is Christianity?'* (London: Longmans, 1901).

—*The Life of Christ in Recent Research* (Oxford: Oxford University Press, 1907).

—'A New Work on the Parables', *JTS* 1 (1900), pp. 161-80.

—*Outlines of the Life of Christ* (Edinburgh: T. & T. Clark, 2nd rev. edn., 1906 [1905]).

—'President's Address: Section VIII: The Christian Religion', in P.S. Allen (ed.), *Transactions of the Third International Congress for the History of Religions*, II (2 vols.; Oxford: Clarendon Press, 1908), pp. 263-82.

—Review of *Contentio Veritas*, *JTS* 4 (1902), pp. 1-16.

—*The Sacred Sites of the Gospels* (Oxford: Clarendon Press, 1903).

—'Theological Reconstruction at Cambridge', *JTS* 7 (1906), pp. 161-85.

Schultenover, David G., S.J., *George Tyrrell: In Search of Catholicism* (Shepherdstown: Patmos Press, 1981).

Schweitzer, Albert, *The Quest of the Historical Jesus: A Critical Study of its Progress from Reimarus to Wrede* (trans. W. Montgomery; London: A. & C. Black, 1910).

—*The Mystery of the Kingdom of God* (trans. Walter Lowrie of *Das Abendmahl im Zusammenhang mit dem Leben Jesu* (Tübingen: J.C.B. Mohr [Paul Siebeck], 1901); London: A. & C. Black, 1914).

—*My Life and Thought* (London: Allen and Unwin, 1933).

—*Von Reimarus zu Wrede. Eine Geschichte der Leben-Jesu-Forschung* (Tübingen: J.C.B. Mohr (Paul Siebeck), 1906; 2nd edn. published as *Geschichte der Leben-Jesu-Forschung*, 1913).

Scott, E.F., *The Kingdom and the Messiah* (Edinburgh: T. & T. Clark, 1910).

Selwyn, E.G., 'The Outlook for English Theology', *Theology* 40 (1940), pp. 6-14.

Selwyn, E.G. (ed.), *Essays Catholic and Critical* (London: SPCK, 3rd edn, 1954 [1926]).

Smend, Friedrich, *Adolf von Harnack. Verzeichnis seiner Schriften* (Leipzig: J.C. Hinrichs, 1927).

Souter, A., 'William Sanday: Bibliography', *JTS* 22 (1921), pp. 193-205.

Stephenson, Alan, *The Rise and Decline of English Modernism* (London: SPCK, 1984).

Streeter, B.H., 'The Historic Christ', in B.H Streeter (ed.), *Foundations: A Statement of Christian Belief in Terms of Modern Thought: by Seven Oxford Men* (London: Macmillan, 1912), pp. 73-146.

—*Reality: A New Correlation of Science and Religion* (London: Macmillan, 1927).

Streeter, B.H. (ed.), *Foundations: A Statement of Christian Belief in Terms of Modern Thought: by Seven Oxford Men* (London: Macmillan, 1912).

—*Studies in the Synoptic Problem* (Oxford: Clarendon Press, 1911).

Swete, H.B. (ed.), *Essays on Some Biblical Questions of the Day by Members of the University of Cambridge* (London: Macmillan, 1909).

Sykes, Stephen W., and Derek Holmes (eds.), *New Studies in Theology*, I (London: Gerald Duckworth, 1980).

Sykes, Stephen W. (ed.), *England and Germany: Studies in Theological Diplomacy* (Studien zur interkulturellen Geschichte des Christentums, 25; Frankfurt: Peter Lang, 1982).

Talbot, Neville S., 'The Modern Situation', in B.H Streeter (ed.), *Foundations: A Statement of Christian Belief in Terms of Modern Thought: by Seven Oxford Men* (London: Macmillan, 1912), pp. 1-24.

Thomson, David, *England in the Twentieth Century* (Harmondsworth: Penguin Books, 1965).

Thompson, J.M., *Miracles in the New Testament* (London: Edward Arnold, 1911).

—'Post-Modernism', *Hibbert Journal* 47 (July 1914), pp. 733-45.

Thompson, Paul, *The Edwardians* (London: Routledge, 2nd edn, 1992).

Troeltsch, Ernst, 'Das Wesen des modernen Geistes (1907)', in Ernst Troeltsch, *Aufsätze zur Geistesgeschichte und Religionssoziologie* (ed. Hans Baron; Tübingen: J.C.B. Mohr, 1925), pp. 297-338.

—*The Social Teaching of the Christian Churches* (London: Unwin, 1931).

Tucker, Maurice G., *John Neville Figgis: A Study* (London: SPCK, 1950).

Turner, C.H., 'William Sanday', *DNB* (1912–1921), pp. 482-85.

—'William Sanday', *MC* 10 (1920), pp. 407-413.

Turner, J.M., 'J.N. Figgis: Anglican Prophet', *Theology* 78 (1975), pp. 538-44.

Turrani, Francesco, *The Condemnation of Alfred Loisy and the Historical Method* (Uomini e Dottrine, 24; Rome: Edizioni di Storia e Letteratura, 1979).

Tyrrell, George, (alias Hilaire Bourdon), *The Church and the Future (L'église et l'avenir)* (printed for private circulation only, 1903).

—*Christianity at the Cross-Roads* (London: Longmans, 1910).

—*Medievalism* (repr.; Tunbridge Wells: Burns & Oates, 1994).

—'Mysteries, A Necessity of Life', *The Month* 461 (November 1902), pp. 449-59.

—'The Point at Issue', *Jesus or Christ?* (Hibbert Journal Supplement; London: Williams and Norgate, 1909), pp. 5-16.

—'Religion and Ethics', *The Month* 464 (February 1903), pp. 130-45.

—*Through Scylla and Charybdis* (London: Longmans, 1907).

Vidler, Alec, *The Modernist Movement in the Roman Catholic Church: Its Origins and Outcome* (Cambridge: Cambridge University Press, 1934).

—*Twentieth Century Defenders of the Faith* (London: SCM Press, 1965).

—*A Variety of Catholic Modernists* (Cambridge: Cambridge University Press, 1970).

Warschauer, J., 'Liberal Theology in Great Britain', *AJT* 16 (1912) pp. 333-58.

Weaver, Walter P., *The Historical Jesus in the Twentieth Century 1900–1950* (Harrisburg: Trinity Press International, 1999).

Weber, Max, *Economy and Society* (3 vols.; New York: Bedminster Press, 1968).

Wegener, R., *Albrecht Ritschls Idee des Reiches Gottes* (Leipzig: Deichert, 1897).

Weiler, Peter, *The New Liberalism: Liberal Social Theory in Great Britain, 1889–1914* (New York: Garland, 1982).

Weiss, Johannes, *Die Idee des Reiches Gottes* (Giessen: J. Ricker'sche Buchhandlung, 1901).

—*Die Predigt Jesu vom Reiche Gottes* (Göttingen: Vandenhoeck & Ruprecht, 2nd rev. edn, 1900 [1892]).

—*Jesus' Proclamation of the Kingdom of God* (trans. Richard H. Hiers and D.L. Holland; intro. Richard H. Hiers; Philadelphia: Fortress Press, 1971).

Wellhausen, J., *Einleitung in die drei ersten Evangelien* (Berlin: Reimer, 1905).

Wells, David F., *The Prophetic Theology of George Tyrrell* (AAR, 22; Chico, CA: Scholars Press, 1981).

Wenz, Gunther, 'Zwischen den Zeiten: Einige Bemerkungen zum geschichtlichen Verständnis der theologischen Anfänge Karl Barths', *Neue Zeitschrift für Systematische Theologie* 28 (1986), pp. 284-95.

Wernle, Paul, Review of Sanday, *Life of Christ*, *TLZ* 34 (1909), cols. 98-101.

—Review of Schweitzer, *Von Reimarus zu Schweitzer*, *TLZ* 31 (1906), cols. 516-19.

Wilkinson, Alan, *The Church of England and the First World War* (London: SPCK, 1978).

—*The Community of the Resurrection: A Centenary History* (London: SCM Press, 1992).

Williams, Raymond, *Culture and Society, 1780–1950* (Harmondsworth: Penguin Books, 1963).

—*Marxism and Literature* (Oxford: Oxford University Press, 1977).

Williams, Rowan, 'Doctrinal Criticism: Some Questions', in Sarah Coakley and David Pailin (eds.), *The Making and Remaking of Christian Doctrine* (Oxford: Clarendon Press, 1993), pp. 239-64.

Woolf, Virginia, *The Hogarth Essays* (London: Hogarth Press, 1924).

Zahn-Harnack, Agnes von, *Adolf von Harnack* (Berlin: W. de Gruyter, 1951).

Zahrnt, Heinz, *The Question of God* (London: Collins, 1969).

INDEX OF AUTHORS

JOURNAL FOR THE STUDY OF THE NEW TESTAMENT
SUPPLEMENT SERIES